A Division of
O'RAGHAILLIGH INC.
P.O. Box 128
Brigantine Island, N.J. 08203
(609) 266-6500

A BLIND BARGAIN

Reconstructed by

Philip J. Riley

Ackerman Archives Series Volume Two
Atlantic City, New Jersey

Pictures, Filmscript and titles from the film A BLIND BARGAIN used with the permission of and by special arrangement with MGM/UA Entertainment Co. and Turner Entertainment

The film A BLIND BARGAIN © 1922 by Goldwyn Production Co. Distributed by Goldwyn Cosmopolitan. Renewed Loews Inc. 1950

Special art and matte work © 1988 by PB & J Productions

Foreward by Robert Bloch © 1988

Library of Congress No.: 88-90745

Main Entry under title:
A BLIND BARGAIN (Motion Picture)

  Includes the original script: The Octave of Claudius/by Hawks, J.G.
  Includes index:
  1. A Blind Bargain (Motion Picture) I. Riley, Philip J., 1948-
  II. Hawks, J.G. III Chaney, Lon (Actor) 1883-1930
  IV. Barry Pain (The Octave of Claudius) 1864-1928, V. Bloch Robert (Author) VI. Miller, Patsy Ruth (Motion Pictures) 1904-

  ISBN: 0-929127-00-5

Manufactured in the United States of America

Typesetting and Mechanicals by:
PerfecType, inc.
Atlantic City, N.J.

Printed by Arcata/Halliday Lithograph
West Hanover, Mass.

A Blind Bargain was originally dedicated to my wife Marisa, but due to the untimely death of our friend Carlos Clarens, we would like to share the dedication:

If there ever had been an official ambassador to the world from Hollywood—not the city but the magic of its film culture—it would have been Carlos. He will be sadly missed. (Even if the title reflects some of the misadventures he got me into from time to time.)

Carlos Clarens
1931-1987
"Hollywood—you're always driving to a city, but you never seem to get there."

The author wishes to thank the following individuals and institutions for their generous assistance:

MGM/UA Entertainment Co. and Herbert Nusbaum. Legal Department, without whom this project would never have been possible.

The late James Earie, former head of the
Research Library
Ben Presser, Legal files
Norman Kaplan, Still Department
Dore Freeman, Still Department
Wes Meyers, Film Library
Bob Peacock, MGM Lab
Tony Villone, Art Department
The late Buddy Gillespie, Art Department
Florence Warner, Script Department
Alan Gavoni, Still Department
Susie Battle, MGM Library Copy Department
Betty and Keith, MGM Copy Department

without their trust and support the rare material in this volume would be lost to the world—and still buried in the vaults.

Also many thanks to:

David S. Horsley A.S.C.
Patsy Chaney
Chris Hartnett
Andrew Lee, Universal Research Department
Jerome P. Goldstein
Don Mayerson

Special Acknowledgments
Mr. James Pepper of Santa Barbara, one of the country's top specialists on English and American rare books, for his friendship and for locating many hard-to-find research material.

For Jerome J. Cohen of Miami, a patron of the arts.

Eric Kramer, Fantasy Archives of New York City for his care and tireless quest to preserve and protect Science Fiction and Fantasy books for us collectors and for future generations.

Dr. William Cumiford, curator of the History Division of the Los Angeles County Museum of Natural History and David Debs for their allowing me to photograph the Chaney Make-up Box, but mostly for their strict security and protection of the Chaney Artifacts and other historial items.

To Dian Spitler of the Atlantic City Free Public Library, reference library and information department.

One of the happiest events during this project was Kevin Brownlow's introduction of Wallace Worsley Jr. I noticed the name at a screening of E.T. when the credits were rolling and wondered if he was a relation to Wallace Sr. That's not as dumb as it sounds for I met Peter Lorre Jr. and he was no relation to Peter Lorre—you can't tell about Hollywood these days. The quality of the material that Mr. Worsley has preserved has given us all the best possible representation of this lost film.

Diana Brown for negotiating new rights with Turner Entertainment so that these books would be financially possible.

To Kevin Brownlow, perhaps the greatest name in silent film preservation for all time. I say that because when he is finished with his work there will be nothing left in the future for the rest of us to work on. He provided stills, reviews and other valuable research material.

To Dan Woodruff and Robert Cushman of the Academy of Motion Picture Arts and Sciences Library for their care and preservation of the original nitrate negatives of MGM's past.

To Gary Dorst for saving my rare copy of "The Octave of Claudius".

To Elias Savada, Motion Picture Information Services & A.F.I.

The author gratefully acknowledges permission to reprint excerpts from the following:

From "The Hazardous Properties of Nitrate Film", reproduced with permission of Eastman Kodak Company. Patent Library.

From "Can Old Age Be Deferred"—Interview with Dr. Serge Voronoff, "Scientific American" October 1925.

From "Human Grafting" The Brilliant and Successful Experiments of Serge Voronoff by May Tevis, "Scientific American Monthly", April 1920.

From "Something about the Camera" and "What is Characterization" originally published in "The Truth About Hollywood", Hollywood Publishers 1924.

Quotes from the Ruth Waterbury article "The True Life Story of Lon Chaney" with permission of "Photoplay" Magazine.

From "Variety Weekly", December 6, 1922, with permission of "Variety".

Photographs:
O'Raghailligh files and:
The Bison Archives, Marc Wanamaker
National Film Archive, London
Phototique, Carlos Clarens, Howard Mandelbaum
John Kobal Collection,
The Museum of Modern Art, Mary Corliss
David A. Gibson, Photo Equipment Museum, Eastman Kodak
The Ackerman Archives
The Stan Caidin Collection
The Steven Joschberger Collection
The Michael Blake Collection
Culver Archives, NYC
The University of Wyoming, from the
Patsy Ruth Miller Collection
Wallace Worsley, Jr.
Viktor Privato, Gosfilmofond, Moscow
Richard Bojarski
Clarence Bull
The Academy of Motion Picture Arts and Sciences collection
The Michael Hawks Collection
Eddie Brandts Saturday Matinee
The late Henri Langlois of the Cinemateque Francaise
Mitchell Tromboli
David Sheperd

More thanks to:

Cary Black, Ron Barlow, Misc: Man Rare Movie Posters and the Chaney family

Matthew Miller Studio

Lab work by:
Cre-Art PhotoLab, Hollywood
Atlantic Photo Center, Atlantic City, N.J.

Cover Art by:
Marisa Donato-Riley

Cover Photograph by Alexander Anton, Studio 53 Pleasantville, N.J.

Special Photography by Matt Miller, New York City

Medical Advisors
Tome Naciemento M.D.
Francis W. Previti M.D. F.A.C.S.

What can I say about Patsy Ruth Miller—The original cover girl. She was as beautiful in 1923 as she is today. Thank you Patsy for sharing the excerpts from the forthcoming autobiography—MY HOLLYWOOD When Both of Us Were Young.

So much has been written about Forrest J Ackerman that I thought it best to end up this volume with a few words about his lifework and the future of his collection.

And thanks to Jon Mirsalis for his to preserve in film preservation.

I have to say to Robert Bloch, and I claim no rights to the story as it was related to me by PerfecType, inc. of Atlantic City, N.J., whose revival of old world crafts and combined with modern computer technology made this book mechanically and artistically the best!

It's a hot August day and Lon Chaney is busy perfecting his bell ringing technique when he gets word that the director will not allow him to jump from gargoyle to gargoyle 60 feet above the ground for the beginning of the Hunchback of Notre Dame. Lon gripes and cusses as was his usual habit in these situations, but his protest went unheeded until an edict from Irving Thalberg himself backed up Mr. Worsley.

Reluctantly Lon agreed to show the two stunt men how to do the stunts, but first they have to show their metal by ringing one of the two ton bells set up on the set about 25 feet above the ground stage.

Up on the wooded stairway the three went until they reached the top of stage 23. First Lon jumps up and uses his weight to pull the bell rope. The giant clapper slowly begins to move and after 3 passes it strikes the bell and a deftening toll rings out over the Universal lot. The first stunt man thinks this is nothing. He steps up to the bell rope and gives it a yank and dislocates his shoulder. He is quickly dismissed by Lon. Nervous and sweating at the failure of his comrade the second stunt man steps up to the bell rope. Lon crosses his arms and smiles as if to say "Okay yah sap. Ya think what I do is easy?" The stunt man responds to the challenge. He concentrates. He studies the bell. He notes the distance of the bell to the large window near the platform. He estimates the weight of the clapper. From 15 feet back he gets down in a runners starting position and with all the force he has he lunges at the bell, jumps 15 feet into the air, lets his weight carry the rope down and the clapper slams into the bell which again resounds over the Universal lot. He is about to let go, however, when the force of the downward thrust carries through and pulls him back with such force that he loses his balance. In a split second, when he reaches the top of the rope he reaches out, so as not to fall and grabs the clapper as it speeds to the other side of the bell at a hundred miles per hour. Instead of a loud toll there is a sickening thud, the bell carries upward and as it carries back the stuntman is thrown from the bell and out the window to the ground below next to the second stage.

Lon throws his hands up and rushes down the interior staircase. He flies out to the street where a crowd has formed around the unconscious stuntman. A studio policeman sees Lon's concerned look and says "Is he a friend of your's Lon? Do you know him? Lon brings his hand to his chin, looks at the policeman and says, "I don't know his name, but his face rings a bell."

Your turn Bob.

INTRODUCTION

by Robert Bloch

In 1928, the year which marked the end of the silent film era, many male stars flickered in fame upon the American screen. Charlie Chaplin was at the height of his career, competing in comedy with Harold Lloyd and Buster Keaton. Tom Mix and dashing Douglas Fairbanks were the heroes of small boys everywhere, though many of their parents preferred the serious performances of Emil Jannings or John Barrymore. Women swooned over matinee idols Ramon Novarro and John Gilbert.

But the annual box-office poll tells the story. In the final year of the entire silent film era the most popular actor was—Lon Chaney.

Studio publicists called him "The Man of a Thousand Faces." And what faces they were—those countenances he created from a simple makeup box without the aid of modern technology and special effects! Even today, in retrospective showings of the films which were preserved or still-photos from those seemingly lost forever, those faces hold a haunting power. The bulging eyes and saw-toothed grin of the vampire in "London After Midnight", the malevolent menace of the oriental villains in "Outside The Law" and "Bits Of Life", the ugliness of "Quasimodo", the death's-head of Erik—these and a score of others constitute an unforgettable gallery of grotesques.

Chaney's bodily shapes were equally memorable, a combination of masterful mime and artful physical restraint which enabled him to portray characters who were crippled, paralyzed, hunchbacked, armless or legless.

Above all, however, his sheer versatility as an actor dominates every role, with or without disguise. Chaney was equally adept playing criminals or detectives, clowns or scholars. The only constant in his characterizations was their diversity—a tough Marine sergeant, a gentle Chinese laundryman, a blind pirate, an elderly railroad engineer, a French-Canadian fur trapper, a Russian peasant.

Perhaps the most impressive aspect of Chaney's artistry was his ability to rise above the mawkish melodrama of the films in which he appeared. One need only consider some of the cliches which, with slight variations, were repeated again and again.

Like W.C. Fields, Chaney often found himself doting upon a daughter—in "The Tower Of Lies"," Where East Is East", "Mr. Wu", "The Road To Mandalay", "Flesh And Blood", and the climatic moments in "West of Zanzibar".

Parental affection was not the sole emotion he had to contend with. As Quasimodo, Erik, Sergeant O'Hara, Alonzo the Armless and the clowns, Tito and "He", Chaney suffered the pangs of unrequited love.

He was also the victim—and at times the perpetrator—of identity crises. "The Frog" in "The Miracle Man" is a pseudo-paralytic, while Phroso, aka "Deadlegs" in "West Of Zanzibar" has actually lost the use of his lower limbs.

The legs of Blizzard, in "The Penalty", have been amputated below the knees. Surgery cannot restore them, but it does remove a brain tumor and transforms him from a sadistic villain to a caring human being. "The Unknown" presents a hunted murderer who disguises himself as an armless knife-thrower; then, in response to preposterous plot-demands, he actually has his arms amputated. In both "The Blackbird" and "Flesh and Blood" he poses as a kindly but fake cripple on crutches; in "The Shock" his handicap is real. His vampire in "London After Midnight" is actually Burke of Scotland Yard.

Again and again familiar changes are rung in familiar fashion—the Bad Man pretending to be Good, the Good Man gone Bad, the Bad Man redeeming himself by turning Good. Scores of actors played similar parts throughout the silent era, but Lon Chaney made such stereotypes believable, despite the absurd plots in which they figured—or disfigured.

Somehow he managed to make audiences overlook the lunatic devices of "The Unholy Three" in which a sideshow strong man and a midget disguised as a baby join forces with ventriloquist Chaney who masquerades as an old lady and runs a pet-shop as the cover for robbery and burglary schemes. If this seems a little hard to swallow, consider the fact that this modest little pet shop contains a cage housing a vicious, full-grown gorilla!

But Chaney, in both the silent version and the remake—his only talking-picture role—made it work.

In "West of Zanzibar" he plays a music-hall magician whose wife is stolen by Lionel Barrymore, a scoundrel who tumbles Chaney in a fall which leaves his legs permanently paralyzed. Just why Chaney takes his wheelchair to darkest Africa and becomes an ivory-trader who impresses the natives with his magic tricks is never made clear. Even less likely, Lionel Barrymore shows up twenty years later; he too seems to have become a trader and just happens to reach Chaney's residence for a less-than-joyous reunion.

Credibility is equally strained in "London After Midnight" when Chaney's very proper Scotland Yard detective solves a five-year-old homicide by pulling off a complicated vampire hoax as part of a complicated plan employing hypnosis to identify and trap the murderer. Perhaps the detective had his reasons.

But what was the point of the spurious vampire amusing himself by scaring poor housemaid Polly Moran out of her wits?

Unquestionably the worst example of the idiot plot is Chaney's most successful film, "The Phantom Of The Opera". Because Erik is his best-remembered role, it might be helpful to examine its excesses in greater detail. Herewith, some bad examples.

The new managers of the Paris Opera see the mysterious Phantom—the "Opera ghost"—seated in Box Five during a performance. They flee, but when summoning courage to look again, discover he has disappeared. Since they soon learn that he is human, he couldn't have vanished into thin air; there must be a secret exit in Box Five itself. But no one ever tries to find it.

Our heroine, Christine, is a singer talented enough to replace the "diva" in a performance of "Faust". But she doesn't seem to have any friends or family, no home, no manager, not even a voice-coach. Instead she learns to sing by listening to the "Spirit of Music" who speaks to her as an unseen presence when she's alone in her dressing room. One wonders how she can rehearse without musical accompaniment—and without question of who or what her mysterious mentor may be?

Hero and lover Raoul overhears one of her conversations with the "Spirit" after leaving her dressing-room. He makes no attempt to go back in and discover who she could be talking with.

The Phantom drops the huge Opera House chandelier on the audience during a performance, bringing injury, death and panic.far as we know, there's no police action or investigation, the Opera House isn't searched, and a few days later we find a crowded house attending another gala without apparent fear. Getting that chandelier back up or replacing it with a new one doesn't seem to have been any problem either.

Christine is instructed by the "Spirit of Music" to reach him by walking through a secret panel behind her dressing-room mirror. We never learn if he constructed that panel and if so, how and when. Nor does Christine reveal the panel's existence, even after her terrifying experience with the "Spirit"—during which she learns that he is actually the Phantom.

His lair is "five cellars below" the Opera House, reached through a labyrinth of tunnels. Wearing a mask, he conducts Christine partway by placing her on a horse—which then disappears without explanation. Where would it be stabled, and why?

The rest of the trip is by gondola, across a subterranean lake. Again, no explanation; did the Phantom build the vessel, and if so, how?

In the lair Christine finds a luxuriously-furnished bedchamber, complete with wardrobe and lavish toilette accesories bearing her initials. Where did the Phantom get the money for such costly items, how did he shop for them, how were they installed—along with the organ he plays? And how did he manage to construct the lair which houses them? We never get the answers.

After Christine rips off her abductor's mask and reveals him as the hideous Phantom she is allowed to return to the Opera on condition she keep silent. We don't learn her means of getting back, but once arrived she uses the same dressing-room, seemingly unconcerned about its secret access to the catacombs below. When she breaks her promise and warns Raoul about the Phantom she gives no details. Somehow the Phantom appears at the Opera Ball, masquerading as the Red Death; we don't know where he got his elaborate costume or how he managed to precede the lovers to the rooftop where he eavesdrops on Christine's disclosures without being observed.

When an Opera stagehand is found hanged in a backstage passageway, his murder isn't reported to the authorities. Instead a mysterious "Persian" seen slinking around in the background, informs police he has been "studying this Phantom for months" and produces a brief item from their own files about a criminal lunatic named Erik who escaped from Devil's Island. "This is your Phantom," he announces—without offering any evidence to support his claim. But the police don't follow through to help solve the mystery.

Yet when Christine is again kidnapped—this time from an onstage performance—by the angry Phantom, the location of his secret lair suddenly seems to have become public property. The hanged man's brother leads a huge backstage crew of workers to a hidden passageway. Meanwhile the "Persian" tells Raoul that he is actually "Ledoux of the Secret Police." He too knows about the opening behind the dressing-room mirror and volunteers to seek out Christine—without weapons or a police escort.

Raoul's brother also seems to know about the lair; he goes in search of Raoul and somehow arrives ahead of him, only to be drowned in the sunken lake by the Phantom, who swims underwater, using a reed as a primitive snorkel-device.

While the Phantom is away on his murderous mission captive Christine makes no effort to escape. Returning, the Phantom throws a cloak over his dripping garments to play the organ—and a dramatic scene—soaking wet.

As Raoul and his companion venture underground, a strange apparition with a lantern glides past, warning them to turn back. They ask no questions, and we never see him again. Who is he?

Falling into an old torture-chamber with mirrored walls and a device for producing intense heat, the two men's whereabouts is made known to the Phantom. He threatens to kill them unless Christine becomes his bride. The two discover a trapdoor in the chamber floor and drop into a cellar filled with kegs of gunpow-

der. The Phantom shows Christine a chest containing a metal scorpion and a metal grasshopper. If she agrees to wed she can save her lover's life by turning the scorpion. If she turns the grasshopper, the gunpowder will blow the opera to pieces. Just how the Phantom constructed this device we never learn.

The Phantom set as conceived by Art Director Ben Carre. (Below) The scene as it appeared in the 1925 Universal film.

The Phantom sets as they appear today.

I have dwelt at such length upon this film because a print of "A Blind Bargain" is unavailable for viewing. But I have reason to suspect, from the evidence of the script, that what one sees in "The Phantom Of The Opera" also holds true for this "lost" film.

Of course these discrepancies exist mostly in the 1929 reedited and shortened "sound" version which is often mistaken for the original 1925 release print and ALL of these unanswered questions are satisfied in the 1911 novel. The point made is to show Chaney's power as a character actor and to suspend over plot and technical short comings.

Again, the story-line seems contrived and a bit preposterous. But it does contain the essential ingredient which makes Chaney's films memorable—his virtuoso performance. Or performances; this time in dual roles.

Dr. Lamb is our trite-but-true figure, the Good Man turned Bad. As such he serves as the prototype of hundreds of other "mad scientists" in later offerings throughout the three decades following this primitive pioneering effort in the "genre".

The Hunchback (as the ape-man is called in the scenario) is the victim of deformity whose ugliness masks instincts for Good. It is interesting to speculate whether this characterization might have served as the basis of Chaney's concept of Quasimodo when "The Hunchback of Notre Dame" was filmed a year later. In both parts he exercised his talent for mime and makeup—the still-photos of Dr. Lamb's apelike creation convey both pathos and menace. One can sense the former in a scrutiny of Chaney's eyes, and imagine the latter as it might be evoked by simian shambling when this contorted creature is roused to angered vengeance upon the scientist.

Christine turns the scorpion and the water of the underground lake pours into the cellar where Raoul and his companion are trapped; the Phantom rescues them by opening another trap-door in the cellar ceiling directly below his lair. They emerge unconscious.

The lowered water-level allows the revenge-bent mob of stagehands to wade across the lake to the Phantom's hideaway. Though the massive door is closed, they have no trouble breaking in. The Phantom drags swooning Christine off through another secret passage in his bedroom which Raoul discovers immediately upon regaining consciousness.

He, the "Persian" and the stagehands go after the Phantom. And despite its location five levels below the Opera House, the passage apparently leads directly to the street where a carriage awaits. The Phantom shoves Christine inside, knocks the coachman from the box, and drives off.

Raoul, the "Persian" and the mob pursue on foot along a street which contains no other pedestrians or vehicles. Christine recovers consciousness and jumps out of the speeding carriage. When the Phantom tries to halt, it overturns. Before he can get to Christine the avenging horde arrives, apparently traveling almost as fast on foot. Raoul and Christine are reunited as the mob beats the Phantom to death and throws his body into the Seine.

The illogic, inconsistencies and absurdity of the story are matched only by only thankless roles offered to the supporting cast. The heroine is a credulous ninny and the hero is a stick-figure. The film is a compilation of grimaces and gesticulation, sudden swoons and even more sudden recoveries.

That it remains a horror classic is due solely to Chaney's performance. His pantomime is superb; the melodramatic over-reactions of other characters are perfectly in-character for his portrayal. Even when his features are concealed by a mask his eyes and body "act" with appropriate emotion. On first viewing one is apt to concentrate on the horror of his unmasked face; a second time affords an opportunity to see how, when masked, he communicates characterization through the use of his hands and fingers.

From what little I have been able to gather, "A Blind Bargain" was a commercial and critical failure when released. Given the absurdity of the story-line, this is understandable.

Again we may find that a comparison is helpful. While "The Phantom Of The Opera" lacked logic, audiences were diverted from its lapses by the lavishness of its impressive sets, the spectacular operatic sequences, the crowd-scenes and the dazzling display of the masquerade ball. Both the ball and the opera excerpts benefited from the then-novel use of the early Technicolor process, and a special musical score was written expressly for the film.

In contrast, "A Blind Bargain" offers little to distract attention from its simplistic story. Much of the film is played against mundane settings, and apparently the use of tinted stock and a few shots that were hand-colored could not transform commonplace costumes and backgrounds to a degree which would disguise their commonplace content. Evidently producer Goldwyn and director Worsley were aware of this problem, which they hoped to overcome by introducing "A Fashionably Charity Ball" with "girls dancing in bubbles"—but it seems to be a case of too little and too late. The scene is extraneous to the main thrust of the story, and any genuine visual impact is relegated to the confrontation with Dr. Lamb's captive creatures in the underground chamber.

Unfortunately it's not enough to redeem the ridiculous actions and reactions of the characters playing supposedly normal roles, and the burden of the film—as in so many other instances—rests solely upon Chaney's shoulders; a burden neither he nor the audience could bear.

In retrospect, "A Blind Bargain" ranks as an early failure. Its importance lies in the way Chaney's dual role embodies many of the elements responsible for his later success.

Such successful films, hampered by equally primitive premises, became popular because audiences had learned to ignore the plots and devote their attention to Chaney's unique performances.

In so doing they were seldom disappointed. No actor in motion pictures ever exceeded his range of characterization or gave so much of himself in perfecting each portrayal. Behind the "Thousand Faces" was just one man with a superb talent.

Unless the Fates are kind, it's unlikely that any of us will be offered a glimpse of "A Blind Bargain" in filmic form. But thanks to the efforts of Philip J. Riley, what is assembled in the pages which follow has captured and conveyed the essence of Lon Chaney. For this we owe him our great gratitude. Blind as we may be to the film our eyes may never see, he has certainly bestowed us a bargain.

"PSYCHO"
An Alfred Hitchcock Production   A Paramount Release

A scene cut from the Film where the Phantom plays "The Resurection of Lazarus" in the graveyard of Perros.

FINDING A FEW MORE FACES. . .

by Jon C. Mirsalis

Lost films are a fact of life among film enthusiasts, historians, and archivists alike. Hardly any actor or director who worked prior to 1930 can claim that all of his or her work is extant and in many cases, major portions of careers are lost. Greta Garbo's admirers bemoan the fact that her silent feature THE DIVINE WOMAN is apparently lost. Likewise, students of the Oscars cannot study Emil Jannings' award-winning performance in THE WAY OF ALL FLESH. Ernst Lubitsch's THE PATRIOT, F.W. Murnau's THE FOUR DEVILS, and Josef von Sternberg's THE CASE OF LENA SMITH have all met similar fates, victims of either neglect, carelessness, or nitrate decomposition. Even a few of D.W. Griffith's 457 Biograph Shorts cannot be found in any film archive.

THE CASE OF LENA SMITH, Paramount 1929

But pity the poor Lon Chaney buff. The films of "The Man of 1,000 Faces" have not fared well over the years. Of Chaney's over 150 billed appearances, a mere 29 of his films exist in a more-or-less complete form. Another six exist minus a few reels, fragments of three or more are extant. Period. That leaves over 110 of his films that are completely missing.

Why are so many of Chaney's films missing when other artists are so well represented? The major enemy is the instability of nitrate film stock. Prior to the adoption of triacetate "safety" film in the late 40's, nearly all theatrical films were printed on nitrocellulose or "nitrate" film stock. Nitrate is a highly flammable and unstable film base which gradually deteriorates, resulting in a mottling of the image on the film, and ultimately leads to the formation of a highly explosive (and obviously unprojectable) mass of jelly. Studios were reluctant to pay storage charges for this highly dangerous film stock once a film had completed its theatrical run and many prints were junked. Even when prints or negatives were stored, the nitrate stock deteriorated with time, eventually resulting in cans of goo where a print once sat on a shelf.

Another reason for the relative dearth of Chaney films is related to the policies of the individual studios he worked for. While MGM (more than any other studio except for Disney) has been preservation-minded for many years, other studios were a good deal less far-sighted. Few studios saw any potential future market for silent films, and hundreds of films were sent off for silver salvage or decomposed out of neglect. Fox let hundreds of their nitrate prints rot in the vaults and many Paramount silents suffered a similar fate. But Universal was the king of the silent film neglect. Faced with increasing storage costs and no possible market for old film material, nearly the entire pre-1928 output of the studio (i.e., any film without a soundtrack) was destroyed for a few dollars in salvaged silver per reel. Hence, of Chaney's roughly 110 early films for Universal (excluding the much later OUTSIDE THE LAW, HUNCHBACK OF NOTRE DAME, THE SHOCK, THE TRAP, and THE PHANTOM OF THE OPERA), only eight exist in any form, and only four are complete.

The PATRIOT with Emil Jannings, Paramount 1929

FATHER AND THE BOYS, with Lon Chaney, 1915 Universal/Broadway

So what does exist? Not surprisingly, Chaney's two most famous roles, THE HUNCHBACK OF NOTRE DAME (1923) and THE PHANTOM OF THE OPERA (1925), both Universal Super Jewel releases, are readily available, but even these are not entirely complete. Some footage is probably missing from HUNCHBACK, but the lack of a 1923 cutting continuity (a listing of every scene/title in a film that is used by editors to assemble the negative from the various pieces of film) makes it impossible to determine what, if anything, is missing. One famous still shows Chaney kneeling next to a chest, but the scene does not appear in the film. I had always assumed that this was merely a publicity still until I saw an actual clip of the sequence in part of a 1930's documentary on silent films. Universal Show-At-Home 16mm prints exist in the hands of collectors, but even these prints, though made up in the 20's and 30's presumably from original printing materials, have running times less than that of the original release.

Several sequences of PHANTOM were originally shot in the early two-color Technicolor process, but only the famous Bal Masque sequence remains. One striking scene with Chaney on the rooftop in black and white, with his cloak hand-painted in bright crimson exists only in b/w. Studying PHANTOM OF THE OPERA is even more confusing due to the availability of several different versions. The film was reissued in 1929 with an added soundtrack that included redubbed dialogue sequences and an eerie prologue spoken by a man holding a lantern in the catacombs. All of the opera footage was restaged for this re-release, although no new Chaney footage was added. The soundtrack from this release is lost (perhaps fortunately!), but this version, containing the now mute man-with-a-lantern opening, is the most frequently shown print of the classic. The original and the reissue prints have probably been recut and combined over the years, making it nearly impossible to judge exactly what was released in 1925. The issue is further confused by the fact that current prints of the 1925 version have the ending from Rupert Julian's MERRY GO-ROUND spliced on at the end!

Much of Chaney's career would have been a complete mystery had he not gone under contract with MGM in 1924. Of Chaney's 18 films for MGM, the majority have been preserved and beautiful 35mm prints are available. HE WHO GETS SLAPPED, THE MONSTER, THE UNHOLY THREE (both the 1925 and 1930 versions), THE BLACKBIRD, TELL IT TO THE MARINES, MR. WU, THE UNKNOWN, MOCKERY, WEST OF ZANZIBAR, and WHERE EAST IS EAST all exist in essentially complete versions, although some of these are more recent additions to MGM's collection. The only known 35mm print of THE UNKNOWN resided at the Cinematheque Francaise for many years. When archivist Henri Langois was asked to ship the print to the U.S. so that a preservation negative could be made, it literally took years to find it amongst all the cans of unidentified titles marked "UNKNOWN."

WHILE THE CITY SLEEPS also resides in the MGM vaults, but reel six is missing. Likewise LAUGH, CLOWN, LAUGH is missing reel four, as well as the alternate happy ending. In addition to their own films, MGM acquired many of the early silent titles from Metro Pictures, Goldwyn Pictures, and Metro-Goldwyn Pictures. Included in this groups are the Goldwyn releases THE PENALTY, ACE OF HEARTS and VOICES OF THE CITY. . . but sadly not A BLIND BARGAIN.

Even MGM has lost several titles. LONDON AFTER MIDNIGHT is the best publicized deficiency in their collection (and the subject of Philip Riley's last "restoration" book), but THE BIG CITY, THE TOWER OF LIES, and THUNDER are also on the studio's lost film list. Even Tod Browning's THE ROAD TO MANDALAY existed in the studio vaults in only fragmentary form until recently. I had heard of a few 9.5mm French prints of the elusive title available in Europe, and through a U.S. collector obtained a print. Pathescope released many licensed silent features and shorts throughout Europe in the 20's in the 9.5mm format. This particular gauge had nearly the same aperture size as a 16mm print due to the full-frame picture made possible by putting a sprocket hole in the middle of the frame line. When I first screened the print, it turned out to be a 35-minute abridgement of the original 7-reel version, but the continuity held up well. Unfortunately, a literal translation of the French titles back into English took all of the rather florid original language out of the movie. In one sequence, Chinaman Sojin backs down in a knife-fight with Chaney. In the French version, Chaney mutters "Lache," which translates to "Coward." The original title from the cutting continuity, "You ain't got the guts you yellow scum," has a bit more punch to it!

THE SCARLET CAR, Universal 1915

THE BIG CITY, MGM 1929

RIDDLE GAWNE with William S. Hart, Paramount Artcraft

For the restoration of ROAD TO MANDALAY, I had a 16mm negative optically printed from the 9.5mm print and new inter-titles, taken from the original MGM cutting continuity, were typeset and photographed. A few bridging titles were added to improve the coherence of the abridgement and I cut the final negative together for the version that now resides in the MGM vaults.

Assorted other Chaney titles can be found in U.S. and foreign film archives. The American Film Institute collection at the Library of Congress holds the first two reels of the 3-reel A MOTHER'S ATONEMENT (1915, Universal/Rex) and essentially complete prints of THE SCARLET CAR (1917, Universal/Bluebird), VICTORY (1919, Paramount), and SHADOWS (1922, Preferred Pictures). The National Film Archive in London has DOLLY'S SCOOP (1916, Universal/Rex). The International Museum of Photography at George Eastman House in Rochester, New York has a nitrate print of THE FALSE FACES (1919, Paramount/Ince), and a safety print is in the MGM vaults.

Some of Chaney's films exist through the most peculiar of circumstances. THE LIGHT IN THE DARK (1922, Hope Hampton Productions) was released by Associated First National but does not exist in a complete print. A Rhode Island film distributor specializing in religious subjects acquired the film in the mid-20's and re-edited it to a 3-reel short, retitled THE LIGHT OF FAITH, which emphasized a subplot involving the Holy Grail. Thankfully, state law required that films for schools and churches (the major market for the distributor) be printed on the nonflammable safety stock. As an added bonus to being on safety stock, the print was multitinted, a common practice in the 20's but rarely seen in current prints of silent features. The films from this distributor were eventually acquired by the Rhode Island Historical Society who donated them to the American Film Institute.

Other Chaney titles can be found in the hands of private collectors. A British collector acquired a nitrate print of the one-reel BY THE SUN'S RAYS (1914, Universal/Nestor) and released prints in the Super-8mm collector gauge. Other collectors own fragments of the 1920 Pathe serial DAREDEVIL JACK and reel one of the 1920 C.R. Macauley Photoplays release, THE GIFT SUPREME. THE TRAP (1922, Universal/Jewel) and FLESH AND BLOOD (1922, Irving Cummings) were both available as home library prints in the 20's and a few prints have survived and been copied. THE SHOCK and NOMADS OF THE NORTH were re-released in a 16mm format by Blackhawk Films, an Iowa-based company specializing in home collector's prints. Ironically, one of Chaney's earliest appearances survives in private collections: Lois Weber's 1913 Universal/Rex release, SUSPENSE, which has an unbilled Chaney on screen for about 6 seconds.

THUNDER, MGM 1929

THE KAISER, THE BEAST OF BERLIN, 1918 Universal

13

FOR CASH, Universal 1915

THE MIRACLE MAN, Paramount Famous Lasky Players 1919

So many of Chaney's key performances are missing, especially those done in his early years at Universal, that it is nearly impossible to study the development of his screen persona. If we could locate some lost films from which to judge Chaney's career, what would the list include? Certainly his first billed appearnace, POOR JAKE'S DEMISE (1913, Universal/Imp), as well as his first makeup role, THE SEA URCHIN (1913 Universal/Powers). One of his early comedy roles such as AN ELEPHANT ON HIS HANDS (1913, Universal/Nector) would certainly be a curiosity, as would any of the films Chaney directed, including THE STOOL PIGEON, FOR CASH, THE OYSTER DREDGER, and others, all 1915 Universal/Victor releases. FATHER AND THE BOYS (1915 Universal/Broadway) and HELL MORGAN'S GIRL (1917, Universal/Bluebird) were pivotal films in Chaney's career and probably led to his establishment as a true star at Universal. THE KAISER, THE BEAST OF BERLIN (1918, Universal/Renowned) was a major success at the time and is on the American Film Institute's "Ten Most Wanted" list of lost films.

Of the films Chaney made after he left Universal, the survival rate is much better, but there are still many major films that are unavailable, including RIDDLE GAWNE (1918, Paramount/ Artcraft), where he appeared with William S. Hart, TREASURE ISLAND (1920, Paramount/Artcraft) which may be of greater interest for the the stylish direction of Maurice Tourneur than for Chaney's appearance, and THE NEXT CORNER (1924, Paramount), which would probably be a real curiosity with Chaney very much out of character playing a fiery latin seducer. Likewise, ALL THE BROTHERS WERE VALIANT (1923, Metro) should be a fascinating straight role for Chaney as a courageous brother of a whaling family. One of the most important lost films is Chaney's star-making role in THE MIRACLE MAN, although a brief clip does exist as part of a "Movie Milestones" series that Paramount issued in the 30's. These shorts contained clips from big Paramount hits of the silent era including BEAU GESTE and THE COVERED WAGON and the brief MIRACLE MAN sequence where crippled Chaney is "healed" by the fake preacher.

ALL THE BROTHERS WERE VALIENT, Paramount 1919

The most encouraging piece of news is the fact that lost films are still being found around the world, bringing hope that similar finds will continue. One of the major finds of the last decade was the 1922 OLIVER TWIST, an Associated First National release. Not only was the film of interest for Chaney's fascinating portrayal of Fagin, but young Jackie Coogan appeared as Oliver shortly after his success in Chaplin's THE KID. The film was found in Yugoslavia, with no intertitles. With assistance from Jackie Coogan (over 50 years after the filming!), appropriate intertitles were created by Blackhawk Films and the film was released to the home collecting market.

A Minnesota film collector received a call in the 1970's from a farmer that he had "some old cans of films in the barn that the kids like to play with," so he made a trip to investigate. Buried under all the chicken feathers was a nitrate print of Tod Browning's OUTSIDE THE LAW which he donated to the American Film Institute for preservation. The nitrate print was in excellent condition except for a few short scenes with extensive decomposition. Based on the principle that "when it rains it pours," a rare Universal Show-At-Home 16mm print was donated to the archive a few years later!

Perhaps the most bizarre film find in the history of film preservation occurred within the last decade in the Canadian Yukon. In 1978, when an excavaton for a new recreation center was begun in Dawson City, a bulldozer came up with a shovelful of reels of nitrate films, and the titles were stored at the local library until 1929 when the flammable nitrate was used as a landfill in a condemned swimming pool. Stored for 50 years under the permafrost of the Yukon, the films turned out to be extremely well preserved, although sadly, many reels that had survived the years unscathed were damaged in thawing and show water marking on the edges. Included in the amazing treasure trove were films by Pearl White, Harold Lloyd, Douglas Fairbanks. . . and Lon Chaney. Chaney made three films for Red Feather/Universal productions in 1916 and two of these were found amongst the frozen reels. The five-reel melodrama THE PLACE BEYOND THE WINDS was missing reel 1 but was otherwise complete. Reels 1 and 4 were missing from IF MY COUNTRY SHOULD CALL, also originally a five-reeler, but enough was there to follow the story and catch a glimpse of Chaney in a small role. These films are now housed at the Library of Congress.

The most recent Chaney find is proof that films can literally turn up anywhere. When a Georgia family decided to rebuild their front porch in 1983, three metal cans were found under the steps. The contents turned out to be a nearly perfect, partially tinted copy of THE OUBLIETTE (1914), the first installment of

a then-lavish 101 Bison/Universal release with Murdoch MacQuarrie and Pauline Bush. Chaney appears only briefly in the second reel as the villain and is quickly dispatched by the hero. Using funds donated by the Society for Cinephiles, the film was promptly preserved by the American Film Institute.

Given the precarious condition of nitrate film, few finds of this nature can be expected for many more years into the future. Many archivists promote the slogan "Nitrate Can't Wait" which underscores the need to aggressively seek out old prints before they decompose.

But the search goes on. 1921-22 were busy years for Chaney and it was a key time in his career because it was his last stint as a character actor before THE HUNCHBACK OF NOTRE DAME would catapult him to fame and MGM. In addition to several films made at Goldwyn, this period was marked by a number of independent productions for minor companies like Preferred Pictures and Irving Cummings Productions. From the beginning of 1920 through THE HUNCHBACK OF NOTRE DAME in 1923, Chaney appeared in 21 features and was the "star" of about half of these. Amazingly, 12 of these 21 exist, in addition to fragments of a few others. It is ironic that so many mediocre films from this period do exist, yet A BLIND BARGAIN, arguably one the most interesting films of Chaney's career, remains lost (or, as optimistic archivists might say, "misplaced"). Much of the availability of these other titles may be due to the fact that independent producers were much more lax about print control than the major studios. In addition, these films were generally kept in distribution longer and often sold to other distributors. It is not too surprising to find an Irving Cummings Production in someone's attic, but original release prints from MGM and Paramount rarely show up in private hands.

Still, even studios do not always know what is in their vaults and one can hope for a startling discovery. As an example, prints of THE ANIMAL KINGDOM (1932) and HUMORESQUE (1920) were found in the Warner Brothers vaults recently, which proves that "lost" films can still show up exactly where they are supposed to be! An interesting point to note is that neither of these two films were made by Warners, but they were remade by the studio, and prints and negatives apparently came in the package when the studio bought the remake rights. If only Warner Brothers had remade A BLIND BARGAIN as a talkie. . . we might have a print to look at today.

Jon Mirsalis is a researcher and film collector living near San Francisco. He is currently writing a book on the films of Lon Chaney, Sr.

THE FOUR DEVILS by F.W. Murnau
1929 (Sound)

THE WAY OF ALL FLESH, Emil Jannings

NOTES ON THE RECONSTRUCTION OF THE FILM

A BLIND BARGAIN, Goldwyn Production No. 165 is a lost film. It was previewed on November 22, 1922, pulled back and released nationally on December 10, 1922. It was directed by Wallace Worsley and starred Lon Chaney.

It was the most difficult film to date for reconstruction in this series of lost film books. I could not follow the same format as LONDON AFTER MIDNIGHT since the material available for research was limited; the Goldwyn files having been moved several times over the past sixty years. In fact, they were practically taken right out from under my hands as Turner Entertainment Company, the new owners of MGM's library of films, was taking possession of the files and moving them off the lot to make room for the new lot owners, Lorimar Telepictures.

It was not considered as important a film as THE DIVINE WOMAN, MGM 1927, starring Greta Garbo, the title of the next book in this series. Nor would it cause the excitement of a re-surfaced Murnau or Leni film. It might not receive the acclaim that Kevin Brownlow's masterful reconstruction of Abel Gances NAPOLEON. So!, As John Kobal asked me from his London archives, why a book solely to this obscure film?

I picked A BLIND BARGAIN as my next project because, of all the films of Lon Chaney, this was the only one that could actually be considered a horror film, in the accepted meaning of the term. Also it was important in retracing the social consciousness of the 20's. This was a time of growth for the United States. World War I had ended a few years earlier. Modern medicine had advanced rapidly due to the need to heal our soldiers and return them to their families.

Most of the personnel involved in the making of the film were to become major forces in the film world. But most of all, I wanted to see the film and this is the only way possible today.

Research on these lost films began in 1973 while I was working as assistant to Forrest J. Ackerman in his Museum of Fantasy and Science Fiction or the Ackerman Archives. At first, my concentration was on the films of Chaney, but soon I became aware of other lost films. Upon finding a copy of Gary Carey's book LOST FILMS, published by the Museum of Modern Art in 1970 I expanded my work to all the films made at MGM which were considered lost. (see appendix B)

*Although covered already by Jon Mirsalis I have added additional information.

In the 70's MGM was still a very active studio with in-house productions. In my breaks from the vaults I would walk down to the stages and watch Martin Scorsese directing Robert DeNiro and Liza Minelli NEW YORK, NEW YORK, Michael York filming LOGAN'S RUN, directed by Michael Anderson, THAT'S ENTERTAINMENT, Gene Kelly and Fred Astaire dancing or I would buzz around the backlots with Frederico DeLaurentis as he checked up on the technical crews making KING KONG, often to be caught by the directors who didn't know my face and I'd have to duck out the first available exit. This usually resulted in me finding myself in a forgotten room filled with munchkin costumes or rare stills, matte paintings or even film cans. Some things were still there in 1986, where at the instigation of Richard P. May, Special Projects Manager, we checked a shipment of the early MGM sound discs that were being packed to be deposited in the U.C.L.A. Archives for film and television and discovered a complete set of discs from THE ROGUE SONG. (The ROGUE SONG MGM 1930, is the only sound film on which I have begun reconstruction work for a future publication. It was Laurel and Hardy's only color film and instead of titles it will include, with cooperation of Turner Entertainment, a cassette of the sound track safely stored by the university). But in 1973 the MGM Grand was preparing to open in Las Vegas and the backlots were being sold off to real estate developers. Most of the "unnecessary material" and duplicate files were either sent to museums or bulldozed over to make room at the remaining Culver City lots. There was very little concern for saving film history except for the experts and archivists. Most of the business end of the film industry was not aware of the deterioration that could occur in improperly or unsupervised storage of old nitrate films. They were thought to be safely stored away in their cans. Had not Richard Dayton, Don Hagans and Pete Comandini of YCM Labs of Burbank, Richard May of MGM, Peter Williamson, Eli Savada, Dan Woodruff, Robert Gitt, Kevin Brownlow and others not given all they had there probably would be fifty percent of the original classics, B films, serials and shots surviving today. Likewise had john Kobal, Carlos Clarens, Forrest J Ackerman, Marc Wanamaker, Robert Cushman of the Academy and Mary Corliss of MOMA along with a few major collectors who wish to remain nameless, not cared as much as they did there would be even less surviving in Still Photograph form. Even the old photographs could be sold for their silver content.

Figure 2

Top: Nitrate film in which the image has disappeared and in which the emulsion has become sticky along the edges as a result of decomposition.

Center: Nitrate film in which the image has disappeared and in which the emulsion has become sticky near the center of the roll as a result of decomposition.

Lower left: Nitrate film with a hard "froth" on the side of the roll as a result of severe decomposition.

Lower right: Nitrate film, part of which has decomposed to the stage that only a fine brown powder remains.

The subject of the first book in this series, LONDON AFTER MIDNIGHT MGM 1927, had been lost due to accident along with THE DIVINE WOMAN which had been stored a few feet away. In 1965 a fire in one of the underground filmvaults at MGM destroyed the last known prints and negatives. There was a short memo in THE DIVINE WOMAN file stating that a print was sent to the EASTMAN HOUSE in Rodchester N.Y. in 1954. Hopefully they never sent it back. But up until 1983 their records show that it had been returned. A print of THE BIG CITY MGM 1928, starring Lon Chaney, had been shipped to Australia in the early sixties and 2 years ago a short 8MM excerpt of A BLIND BARGAIN was reported to be in the hands of a private collector, also in Australia.

The reason for these losses is best explained in a booklet provided to the Motion Picture Industry published by Eastman Kodak company in 1951.

"Concern is felt in many quarters that with the time approaching when most motion picture films will be on safety support, but with substantial quantities of nitrate film still in use or in storage, safety precautions may be relaxed too soon or a mistake in identity may be made and a disastrous fire could result.

This booklet is offered to the motion picture industry in the hope that it will aid in the promotion and maintenance of safety in the handling and storage of nitrate and safety motion picture film.

THE DIVINE WOMAN, 1928

The information contained herein should be of particular value during this interim period when the conversion from nitrate to safety base materials is taking place.

The hazardous properties of nitrate film have been described frequently and in detail in the past and are given only briefly here. The most dangerous aspect of nitrate film are its ease of ignition, its very high rate of combustion, and the fact that the gases given off are extremely poisonous and, under some conditions, explosive.

Nitrate film decomposes readily when heated above room temperature, even below the ignition range. The decomposition is both exothermic and autocatalytic, and once it starts it goes faster and faster. The quantity of heat produced is such that, if not dissipated, it may rapidly raise the film temperature to the ignition point. Even local heating at one point can raise the temperature of the film to a dangerous level, thus initiating decomposition in the entire mass. Cellulose nitrate also contains enough oxygen within the molecule so that decomposition or combustion proceeds rapidly even in a limited air supply, and a nitrate film fire cannot be extinguished by smothering."

TOWER OF LIES, 1925

This was not the case with A BLIND BARGAIN. In 1931 it was destroyed along with THE MAGICIAN,* MGM 1926 (Rex Ingram's study of Somerset Maugham's novel inspired by Aleister Crowley.) It was a timely film that didn't fair well after 1925, except in France which had it's own version of the film. A novelization of the script with stills of the film was published also in France in 1924 and was very successful although, because of the pulp format, very few copies survive today. It also dealt with a then-unpopular subject. Because of the cuts ordered in the release print the continuity suffered and lastly it fell victim to the rapid takeover of Goldwyn Productions by MGM. The only person that I knew who actually saw 2 reels of the film in France or Brussles about 22 years ago was my friend, the late Carlos Clarens, to whom I owe many thanks for providing the elusive stills (along with Wallace Worsley Jr.) which enabled me to reconstruct the ending of the film and for his classic reference book on the subject AN ILLUSTRATED HISTORY OF THE HORROR FILM, Putnam 1967.

```
        D.O.DECKER                    MR.PAUL COHEN
                                      December 9th 1931.

        This is a partial check-up of the list for destruction
of negatives.

        The following negatives may be destroyed as we own all
silent rights:-

            BLIND BARGAIN
            THE ARAB
            THE WIND
            AFTER MIDNIGHT
            ALIAS JIMMY VALENTINE
            ALTARS OF DESIRE
            ANNA CHRISTIE
            BABY CYCLONE
            BECKY
            MAGICIAN
            FAIR CO-ED

        As to the following, either we have no right to destroy
the negatives, or there is some doubt:-

        GREAT DIVIDE  - Sold to Warner Bros. June 18,1930,-all
                        right, title and interest, including positives
                        and negatives

        BABY MINE     - Have rights until September 15,1939, then
                        reverts to a royalty contract again. Nothing
                        said about negatives.

        BARDELYS THE
        MAGNIFICENT   - Rights granted only to April 1,1936, with
                        optional periods of 4 years each. At final
                        termination... contract... own all
                        all negatives and positives and render state-
                        ment or proof thereof to owner.

        BATTLING
        BUTLER        - This is owned by Buster Keaton Productions
                        Inc.

                        D.O.DECKER
```

*Magician survived

Story by Marie Corelli
Scenario by Luther Reed

Marion Davies
in
"THE YOUNG DIANA"
Created by Cosmopolitan Productions

Directed by Albert Capellani and Robert G. Vignola
Presented by Famous Players-Lasky Corporation

In the 20's the executives who ran the business of movie making and a large percentage of the public did not look at films as we do today. The business man saw rooms filled with old film cans as an unnecessary expense after the films made their tour of the theaters. The public saw magic. It wasn't a case of going to a movie just for something to do on Saturday night. It was an event. A favorite star's newest picture was anticipated with delight. Films became part of their lives. The spectacle of heavenly miracles as depicted by C.B. DeMille became the accepted truth of religious ideas. Hollywood's version of the old west replaced the actual happenings.

Films held their magic because they were only seen once, maybe twice if you were lucky enough to catch a re-release print a few years later. Today we see films maybe 4 times a year on television, 4 times a week on cable TV and now with video tape we can watch it every night until we can't stand to look at it anymore. But there was magic back in the early days. You saw a film once and carried it in your mind for years. You went over the plot, mentally watching the film trying to remember your favorite scene wishing you could have saved the heroine or warned the hero of the danger right around the corner. Soon you could even make up your own colors for the suits of your favorite western star or imagine the muted greens and blues of the dark, creepy vaults of a mad doctor. The black and white format was very close to our dream images which allows your imagination to release the artist in us all. Soon the film became yours. You became the hero or monster or heroine. It was a magic that came from within, but it was a magic that could be destroyed with repetitive viewing much the same as wearing your best suit everyday for a month or eating your favorite dessert three times a day. UNLESS! Unless you love movies and then the magic never leaves or more important that the actors, directors, producers and technicians loved making the films, thus creating the magic that we shared. This was rare in the twenties and even rarer today.

Lon Chaney has always been a favorite of mine. I have considered writing a biography based on many interviews and file cabinets of information on the man and his art, but a lot of the most interesting information was told to me in confidence and couldn't be repeated to anyone let alone put into print. What I would be left with would be: he loved photography and fishing. He had a box seat at the fights. He hated interviews. Died with a two million dollar estate. Liked to cook; gave generously to out-of-work actors and to charities; Was distantly related to the Kennedys of Boston; Liked mechanical and mathematical puzzles. Was a musician and dancer. Had a great singing voice and he was liked by almost everyone that I interviewed. He was the greatest character actor in the history of film. The darker sides of his personal life are best left in the shadows. The fact that he was so secretive about his personal life is the cause for all the myths to be told and retold by his fans even today. Like the one about him having a miserable childhood. Here, in his own words, as related to Ruth Waterbury, a well known and credible reporter of the early Hollywood days:

"It isn't true that I had an unpleasant childhood," he said. "I was a pretty good football player and played a fair game of baseball. I had a lot of friends, too. For some reason people want to sympathize with me, having gotten the idea that I was an unhappy kid. That's the bunk, I don't think any childhood is really unhappy, for youth has boundless optimism and an infinite capacity for achieving happiness under any circumstances."

"It's the same way today. A lot of fools seem to assume that I'm lonely, because I don't go to parties in Hollywood, because I don't show up at openings, and make personal appearances, and, perhaps, because the roles I play seem a little out of scope of other actors. But that's bunk too. My wife and I have a very close circle of friends, and we have great times. Just because I would rather pack my kit and duck up into the mountains and fish or hunt than attend one of the grand movie openings is no sign that I'm a morose sort of cuss. I'm not."

As he is quoted as saying, "Between pictures there is no Lon Chaney."

Fortunately one of our top film preservationists, Jon Mirsalis is working on a book about the films of Chaney and makeup artist Michael Blake of Hollywood has just about completed what will be the definitive life story of Chaney, so for the moment I am relieved of duty. However, I feel that the short biography published for his obituary in the Los Angeles Times on August 27, 1930 is worth sharing.

A Newcomb shot from WHERE EAST IS EAST, MGM 1928. Chaney and LupeVelez are on the elephant. Director Tod Browning is on the right walking toward camera. The Newcomb shot is named after Warren Newcomb. It is a method of combining the actual sets with a matte painting to complete the scene. In this still the sets end on the first floor of the buildings. The skyline is the painting.

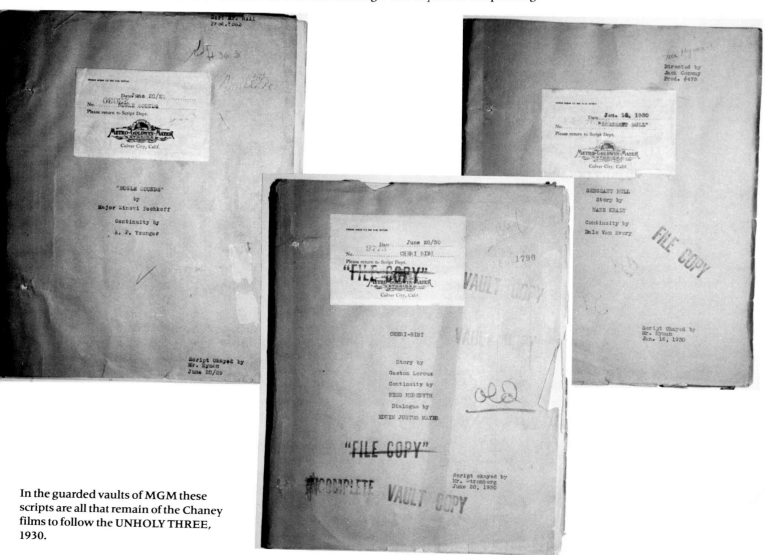

In the guarded vaults of MGM these scripts are all that remain of the Chaney films to follow the UNHOLY THREE, 1930.

The Weather

FORECAST FOR LOS ANGELES AND SOUTHERN CALIFORNIA: Fair today and tomorrow with continued warm weather. Maximum and minimum temperatures for yesterday: 87—68.

Los Angeles Times

In Two Parts — 36 Pages

PART II — LOCAL SHEET — 18 PAGES

CITY NEWS—EDITORIAL—SOCIETY

Vol. XLIX. WEDNESDAY MORNING, AUGUST 27, 1930. C

YOUNG COUPLE SLAIN ON BEACH

Los Angeles Co-ed and Her Fiance Victims

Mutilated Bodies Discovered at Ensenada

Man Seen with Pair Hunted in Border Hills

Their bodies each mutilated by nearly a dozen knife wounds, Lois Marion Kentle, 21-year-old Los Angeles co-ed sorority leader, and her fiance, Francis Conlon, Monrovia paint-store manager and former Pasadena High School football player, were found dead on Ensenada Beach, Lower California, yesterday morning.

Police of Lower California, Federal border guards and San Diego county officers had spread a net over the border hill district last night in an effort to capture an unidentified man who was seen with the young couple a few hours before they were murdered.

Undersheriff Sexson of San Diego county, declared last night his men are working on the theory that the mysterious second man was an acquaintance of Conlon and the girl.

NATIVE THEORY SCOUTED

Mexican police scouted the belief that a native may have done the knifing on the lonely beach and escaped into the back country of Lower California.

Any one of the wounds on the bodies would have proved fatal, examination showed. The bodies were en route to San Diego last night, where a more complete autopsy will be conducted today.

The couple were found sprawled on the sand twenty feet from the tent they had pitched on the beach half a mile from the center of Ensenada. The port captain discovered them early yesterday morning.

MANY WOUNDS

Examination of the bodies by Mexican health officials indicated Conlon and his fiancee were killed about 10 p.m. Monday.

Miss Kentle had been stabbed seven times and Conlon eleven, the report stated. The knife was not located.

Clutched in the girl's hand was a copy of the book, "The End of the Honeymoon."

Conlon, 23 years of age, and Miss Kentle planned to be married next month, it was declared by relatives at the girl's apartment where she resided with her mother and brother at 1246 North Berendo street.

TELEGRAM RECEIVED

It was learned in Pasadena that Conlon last Saturday received a telegram from San Diego, signed "John." The message read, "Everything is all right. Meet me."

Conlon's aunt, Miss Margaret Moran, 1100 Mar Vista street, Pasadena, declared last night that the telegram came from John De Wilde, who operates an avocado ranch at Vista, a short distance from San Diego. De Wilde's father, according to Miss Moran, is a wealthy hotel operator and recently constructed a hotel at Vista.

Young De Wilde, located last night at his father's hotel, admitted sending the telegram to Conlon in answer to the latter's request that De Wilde and his wife accompany the local couple to Tia Juana.

FOUR GO TO TIA JUANA

Conlon and Miss Kentle arrived at the hotel in Vista last Saturday and stayed there Saturday night, according to De Wilde and Deputy Sheriff O. C. Macumber.

Sunday, De Wilde stated, he, his wife, Conlon and Miss Kentle went to Tia Juana and started back to Vista in the afternoon.

At a gasoline station about four miles from Tia Juana on the Coast Highway, Conlon and Miss Kentle separated from the De Wildes, telling them they were going to Mt. Lowe for a camping trip, De Wilde recounted. In order to reach Ensenada they would have had to retrace their route and cross the border back into Mexico. De Wilde saw them for the last time at 3:45 p.m. and returned with his wife to Vista, he said.

S. B. Reachi, personal representative of Gov. Tapia of Lower California, in charge of the Mexican investigation, declared last night that De Wilde's story does not check with records of the Mexican immigration office. The records, Reachi said, show that Conlon's car was registered at the border at 9 a.m. Sunday morning by the girl, who signed as Francis and Lois Conlon. At 3 p.m., Reachi declared, informants told him the slain couple had pitched their tent at Ensenada.

COUPE MISSING

Relatives of the girl stated last night that they had been informed Conlon's coupe could not be found.

(Continued on Page 2, Column 1)

SAN GABRIEL DAM REPORT DUE IN WEEK

Board of Engineers will Resume Session with End of Vacation

A definite report on the survey of the abandoned San Gabriel dam site to determine whether contractors were overpaid for their excavations is expected to be made by the committee of specially appointed engineers to the county grand jury when it resumes its sessions next week after a six-week vacation, it was announced at the District Attorney's office yesterday.

The inquiry was precipitated a month ago when private engineers charged the contractors had collected for the excavation of 250,000 cubic yards of earth and rock that never was removed, costing the county an overcharge of $750,000.

County Engineer Eaton, however, replied that the charges are erroneous and based upon a hasty survey which cannot compare in accuracy with the one made by a group of county engineers who spent several months in the field. When the matter was placed before the grand jury Eaton demanded appointment of a committee of unbiased experts to survey the dam site to determine definitely the truth or falsity of the charges.

According to Percy Hammon, deputy District Attorney in charge of grand jury matters, the grand jury also is expected to consider a reindictment of E. K. Fleming, Charles Glanz and M. G. Phillips, members of the firm of E. K. Fleming & Co., who recently were charged with operating a bucket shop and with grand theft. The original indictment was thrown out of court under a demurrer and referred back to the grand jury for further action.

MEMBER OF BANK BOARD SUCCUMBS

Calvin Seeley of Citizens' National Directorate Dies of Heart Attack

Calvin Seeley, 60 years of age, director in the Citizens' National Trust and Savings Bank, died of a heart attack yesterday at his home, 256 South Camden Drive, Beverly Hills.

A native of Oswego county, New York, Mr. Seeley had been a resident of Los Angeles forty-five years and participated in Southern California's growth in many directions. For twenty-three years he was a district manager for the telephone company. Later he was treasurer of the Fairchild, Gilmore and Wilton Paving Company. Several years ago he retired, retaining only his directorate in the bank.

He was a member of the California, the Los Angeles Country, and other clubs.

He leaves his widow, Mrs. Charlotte Seeley and a daughter, Mrs. Donald McGaffey.

Funeral services will be conducted at Pierce Brothers Mortuary, 10 a.m. tomorrow. Burial will be in Forest Lawn Cemetery, Memorial Park.

Miss Del Rio Has Relapse in Poisoning

Stricken almost two weeks ago with an attack of ptomaine poisoning induced by a dinner of tainted fish, Dolores Del Rio, motion-picture actress, yesterday was ordered to bed by her physician after she had suffered a relapse while attending a rehearsal.

DOLORES DEL RIO

Queries at her Beverly Hills home yesterday were answered with the statement that Miss Del Rio had been weakened by the poison attack and the strain of starting work had been too much for her.

Miss Del Rio and Cedric Gibbons, art director, were married in a colorful ceremony during the Fiesta at Santa Barbara on the 6th inst., and the dinner which brought on her illness was held at the end of the short honeymoon.

MAN OF THOUSAND FACES TAKES BUT ONE TO GRAVE

Versatile Actor will Play Final Role in Drama of Death Tomorrow

"Laugh Clown, Laugh"
"The Hypnotist"
"Mr. Wu"
Lon Chaney
"Tell It To The Marines"
"The Unknown"
"The Road to Mandalay"

Lon Chaney And Some of the Characters He Made Live

LON CHANEY, beloved of millions throughout the world for his immortal portrayals on the motion-picture screen, will be borne to his lasting resting place tomorrow.

While his legions of friends and admirers within and without his chosen profession pause a moment to contemplate their loss, the body of the great charactor actor, who died in St. Vincent's Hospital at 12:55 a.m. yesterday, will be entombed in Forest Lawn Memorial Park, Glendale, where the body of his father lies in another crypt.

The entombment, which will write the closing chapter to one of the most colorful careers in the history of American amusement, will follow brief services to be conducted at 2 p.m. in the Cunningham & O'Connor chapel, 1031 South Grand avenue.

PALLBEARERS LISTED

The active pallbearers will be John Jeske, Clinton Lyle, R. L. Hinkley, Phil Epstein, William Dunphy and Claude I. Parker, and the honorary pallbearers, Louis B. Mayer, Nicholas Schenck, Irving G. Thalberg, Gen. Smedley D. Butler, Milton M. Cohen, Dr. John C. Webster, Hunt Stromberg, Paul Bern, Chester Vanderlip, M. E. Greenwood, Dr. Hugo A. Kiefer, Tod Browning, Harry Carey, Lionel Barrymore, Ramon Navarro, William Haines, Lawrence Tibbett, Harry Rapf, Cliff Edwards, Dr. E. L. Commons, Jack Conway, George Hill, Henry Sharp, Fred Niblo, Edgar Selwyn, Benny Rubin, Fritz Tidden, Wallace Beery, Jack Benny, Sammy Lee, Pete Smith, Dr. Zeiler, James Dugan, Wallace Chewning, W. H. Hendry, H. Roy, Tom Gubbins, M. H. Newman, C. A. Locan, Jack Feinberg, Sam Feinberg, Merritt Gerstad and M. K. Wilson.

The mausoleum in which Mr. Chaney will sleep his last sleep in the shadow of the cross atop Forest Lawn is located in the section known as Dahlia Terrace. It comprises six crypts and was purchased by the actor on the death of his father, Frank H. Chaney, in April, 1927.

SHOCK TO FRIENDS

Mr. Chaney's death came as a distinct shock to all who had watched and waited with bated breath as he waged a valiant fight for life since last Saturday, when three blood transfusions were resorted to in an effort to repel anemia resulting from an acute attack of lobar pneumonia. At intervals on Monday bulletins issued by his physicians stated he had rallied and appeared to be on the road to recovery.

Shortly after midnight, however,

(Continued on Page 5, Column 1)

LAS TUNAS BRUSH FIRE DEFEATED

Large Force of Men Sent to Scene of Blaze Gets it in Control After Fight

A heavy brush fire on the heights overlooking Las Tunas Canyon, not far from the mountain home of Richard Dix, motion-picture actor, was brought under control late yesterday by a force of men jointly detailed by Deputy Fire Warden Weinert and the Bel-Air Company.

The fire was reported at 2:30 p.m. by Constable McNabb of Malibu Township. It was feared the flames might work their way toward Fernwood, and decisive steps were taken to check the danger. Soon after fire fighters left Fernwood station for the scene of the fire a truck load of additional fighters was sent out by the Bel-Air Company.

City Insurance Plan Favored

A recommendation that the city continue to carry its own automobile accident liability insurance has been made to the City Council by the Finance Committee. The experience of the past year shows this policy to be cheaper than the purchase of insurance.

This action was required by the adoption of an act by the Legislature in 1929 declaring that municipalities are liable for accidents in which city vehicles and city drivers are at fault.

BACLANOVA, FILM STAR, BEARS SON

Nine-Pound Baby Born to Russian Actress, Wife of Nicolas Soussanin

Another film actress has achieved motherhood, it was learned yesterday with the announcement that Olga Baclanova, exotic Russian star, in private life the wife of Nicolas Soussanin, actor, has given birth to a nine-pound boy. The event took place last Friday at Cedars of Lebanon Hospital, with Dr. Nahum Kavinoky in attendance. Dr. Kavinoky last night reported both mother and child are doing well and will be allowed to leave the hospital early next week.

OLGA BACLANOVA

Miss Baclanova came to Hollywood several years ago from Russia and scored an instant success in American-made films, being identified almost wholly with fiery, temperamental roles. On her arrival here she renewed a friendship of long standing with Soussanin, also a native of Russia, and the pair were married secretly in March, 1929. The actress formerly was the wife of Vladimir Zoppi, a Moscow attorney, whom she divorced.

BATTLE FLEET WETS ANCHORS

Maryland First to Reach Berth at San Pedro

Overhauling of Machinery on Early Program

Aircraft Carriers to Return Later in Week

San Pedro roadstead resumed the colorful role of Man-o'-War Row yesterday as the battleship divisions began straggling in from San Francisco during the afternoon; heralding the battle fleet's return from the summer vacation on Puget Sound. By midnight eight dreadnaughts had joined their sister, the Mississippi, and ships of the fleet train already in port.

First to anchor was the Maryland, temporary flagship of Vice-Admiral Richard H. Leigh, commanding the battleship divisions. She arrived at 4 p.m., followed at 5 o'clock by the Tennessee; at 6 p.m. by the Nevada, and at 6:30 by the Idaho. The fleet flagship California, carrying the four-starred pennant of Admiral Frank H. Schofield returned at midnight, accompanied by the Oklahoma, New York and the United States Fleet flagship Texas, carrying Admiral William V. Pratt and his staff. The New Mexico, flagship of Battleship Division Four, turned north yesterday noon and is proceeding direct to the Puget Sound navy yard for annual overhaul.

SHIPS UNDER REPAIR

The squadron flagship West Virginia, undergoing overhaul at Puget Sound, will not rejoin the fleet until October 1, while her division sister, the Colorado, undergoing repairs at the Brooklyn navy yard, will not return to the Pacific until next spring. The aircraft carriers Saratoga, Lexington and Langley, delayed at San Francisco, will come south late this week.

The fleet will remain at anchor during the next fortnight, undergoing machinery overhaul following the arduous twenty-four-hour full-power and smoke-prevention tests which the battleships ran off en route from San Francisco, and for leave and athletic competition. On September 8 the dreadnaughts will begin their fall gunnery training with practice runs for short range battle practice, which the ships will fire during the week of September 22.

TRAINING PLANNED

The last week of September will be another "at-anchor" period and in October the squadron will again go to the drill grounds for anti-aircraft, night battle and long-range battle practices and preliminary training for these exercises.

Operating plans provide for a two-months' training cruise to Panama next spring, the fleet departing San Pedro on February 7.

Large Crowds Due at Bowl as Vacations End

With the annual summer season ending Saturday night, Glenn M. Tindall, business manager of the Hollywood Bowl, expects more than 45,000 people to hear the last four concerts, the first of which was presented last night.

Henry Eichheim, Santa Barbara conductor-composer, is featured tomorrow night, and will conduct the musicians in playing his own composition "Burma."

Alfred Wallenstein, Los Angeles 'cellist, who has been featured by conductors all over America, appears Friday evening. Enrique Arbos, noted Spanish conductor, will direct the three remaining programs.

Salvation Army Officers Meet Today at Camp

Salvation Army officers will meet at the Redondo Fresh Air camp today for the second annual encampment of the staff of the Los Angeles and South Coast division. Brig. James C. Bell, officer commanding the division, will be in charge. The sessions will continue tomorrow and Friday.

Capt. Frank Mann, in charge of the citadel corps of Los Angeles, will be the opening speaker.

Brig. and Mrs. Bell, the former division head, the latter commander of the fresh air camp, will each have a place on the program.

The Lancer

by Harry Carr

SANTA MARIA:

Old Juan Dana is the greatest "find" I have ever made.

He knew Fremont and saw [illegible] marching across the hills to [illegible] conquest of California.

He knew Jack Powers, the [illegible] bloodthirsty and villainous of the California bandits.

And he also knew Tiburcio [illegible] quez and the jovial and hu[illegible] freebooter, Solomon Pico, [illegible] killed gringos wherever he [illegible] them; made a necklace of [illegible] ears and draped the [illegible] around his horse's shoulders.

THE OLD CASA

Old Juan is the son of [illegible] liam Goodman Dana, one [illegible] old-timers in Santa Maria [illegible] The first Dana was a [illegible] the Dana who wrote "Two [illegible] Before the Mast." He was [illegible] and came to California [illegible] sailing ship ab[illegible] 1821. After [illegible] ing in Santa Barbara for [illegible] he finally settled on a great [illegible] in this valley. He had [illegible] credible number of childr[illegible] one of the sons was Juan.

Juan now is 92—with a [illegible] clearer than mine, and I [illegible] pretty good one.

He lives in a lovely old [illegible] a grove of great trees. It [illegible] Spanish and half New [illegible] with the winding stairwa[illegible] New England houses and [illegible] formal fireplaces but the [illegible] patios of the hacendado [illegible]

WENT TO SEE FREM[illegible]

When he was a [illegible] of 8 years of age, a [illegible] troops in blue uniforms [illegible] into the valley. It was [illegible] army marching down fr[illegible] Juan Bautista to the co[illegible] Santa Barbara and Los [illegible]

Fremont sent over to [illegible] ther's ranch to buy some [illegible] meat. A vaquero went [illegible] quest to show the [illegible] butcher them. Boy[illegible] Juan jumped on a cattle [illegible] rode along with the vaquero[illegible]

YELLOW CURLS

He found Fremont ca[illegible] one end of the ranch. Ju[illegible] he remembers the wea[illegible] and the wagons. He also [illegible] bers that Fremont had a [illegible] of Indians with him.

At that time, Juan [illegible] hair in a long mane and [illegible] yellow. Fremont saw [illegible] shouted to his other [illegible] "Here is a regular Yank[illegible] no Mexican about him." The [illegible] officers gathered around as [illegible] mont lifted the blond cu[illegible] them to see.

DESPERADOES

In the 'fifties, the Santa Maria Valley was a terrible place. Desperadoes driven out of San Francisco by the Vigilantes had drifted down here. Scum deserting from the ships; Mexican bandits waging war against the gringos. Sheriffs warned travelers to ride only in the daytime and then to ride as fast as they could.

The most notorious bandits were Solomon Pico and Jack Powers.

EARS FOR SOUVENIRS

Pico, like Joaquin Murrieta, had declared war against the gringos because of outrages to his women folk. He killed all he met and draped their ears on his horse. Solomon Pico Mountain marks the place where he watched for the dust of travelers.

Powers was a handsome young society blade of Santa Barbara. Welcomed at all the functions, no

(Continued on Page 2, Column 2)

POOR PA

BY CLAUDE CALLAN

JUDGE VISITS OIL ARENA

Jurist Falk Seeks Data on Venice Situation in Stone's Suit for Ban on Drilling

[illegible] knowledge of the Venice oil-field situation was sought [illegible] by Superior Judge Falk in a visit to the beach, now the [illegible] of an injunction suit instituted by Lewis S. Stone, actor. Judge [illegible] presiding at the hearing, to be resumed today, at which Stone [illegible] permanent injunction restraining the city or its playgrounds' de[illegible] from leasing Venice beach tidelands for oil drilling.

'MA' JUST LOVES NEW NOSE AND THINKS IT LOOKS NICE

Additional fuel was fed to the McPherson-Kennedy feud yesterday when assistants at Angelus Temple made public two affidavits regarding the cause of the nose operation of Mrs. Minnie (Ma) Kennedy.

Both statements sworn to by officers of the temple assert that the mother of Aimee Semple McPherson, evangelist, was not struck in a fist fight with her daughter which resulted in a broken nose, but that the recent operation was necessitated by two things—"a fall in her youth which affected her nasal passages" and a face rejuvenation.

Last night the cause of the trouble, Mrs. Kennedy's nose, was revealed for the first time minus metal braces and stitches. The operation was declared complete and physicians said she could leave the Brentwood Sanatorium, where she has been recovering from the facial-nasal operation, any time she cares to. She refuses to discuss the offi-

DESTROYERS WILL BE SUNK

Decommissioned Units will be Used as Targets in Gunnery and Aircraft Practice Off Coast

Plans for aircraft bombing of actual destroyers and for use of a third decommissioned destroyer for battleship target practice were announced yesterday by the Navy Department. These spectacular bombing exercises, to be held off the Southern California coast this fall, will be entirely independent of previously announced plans for sinking the battleship Utah by high-altitude aircraft bombing.

Battle Fleet planes will hurl thirty [illegible] batteries of battleships. The ma[illegible] chine-gun attacks on the Stoddert

AUNT HET

BY ROBERT QUILLEN

CHANEY'S RITES FOR TOMORROW

Beloved Character Actor to be Paid Final Tribute

Death Proves Great Shock to Legions of Friends

Body will be Entombed in Forest Lawn Crypt

(Continued from First Page)

he was seized with a hemorrhage of the throat. He sank speedily into a coma and breathed his last before the arrival of his physicians. At his bedside when he died were his wife and Creighton Chaney, a son by a former marriage. The physicians later announced the direct cause of death was carcinoma of the bronchus.

MANY LAUD HIM

They called Lon Chaney "the man of a thousand faces," a phrase coined from the wide variety of the roles he had assumed on the screen. And they were unanimous yesterday in voting him an unassailable niche in the hall of the screen's immortals.

"It is with deep regret that we learned of his passing," said "Uncle Carl" Laemmle, president of Universal Pictures, under whose banner the actor made his first bid for fame on the silver sheet. "At Universal City we saw him make a humble start and then reach the heights of a brilliant career in the two roles he best loved. He has passed from the 'set' but he is one of screendom's real immortals, and we always will cherish the memory of his days with us."

QUALITIES PRAISED

From his associates at Metro-Goldwyn-Mayer studios, where he was under contract at the time of his death, came eulogies by the score, couched in words sprung from deep and lasting love of the departed artist.

"His life will stand as an inspiration to all who aspire to achievement," Louis B. Mayer said. "He was kindly, sympathetic, understanding—a friend of the friendless, blessed with a humanness seldom encountered in this modern day."

Irving Thalberg called him "a great artist whose passing leaves a void none can fill;" and his words were echoed in the expressions of all others at the studio, from the lowliest to the mightiest.

MOURNING EVERYWHERE

A pall of sorrow enveloped the realm of motion pictures yesterday; and every "lot" was in mourning for its friend. Lon Chaney died in the very prime of his life and at the zenith of his extraordinary career. He was a few months more than 47 years of age. Born on April Fool's Day (April 1) 1883, he started out in life as a mime; and by an odd twist of fate achieved one of the greatest successes of his career as a buffoon, namely, the heart-broken funny man in "Laugh, Clown, Laugh."

Friends in Colorado Springs, his birthplace, yesterday were quoted as always having attributed Lon Chaney's supreme artistry as a pantomimist to the fact that his parents were deaf mutes. They recalled that as a boy he found it necessary to combine facial expression with sign language in order to convey impressions to his father and mother. This, they contended, undoubtedly laid the foundation for the remarkable performances that were to follow in later life.

VARIED VENTURES

Mr. Chaney's first venture in the theater was as a property boy in a Colorado Springs theater. When he was 17, he made his first public appearance as an actor, he and his brother playing an engagement as a comedy team. A year later he participated in a full-length play, produced for benefit of the stage hands' union. Between performances he helped install seats in a motion-picture theater, where thousands later hailed him for his striking portrayal of the grotesque role of Quasimodo in "The Hunchback of Notre Dame."

Fired with ambition, Mr. Chaney and his brother, George, took their benefit play on the road, but its existence was short-lived, and Lon ultimately landed broke in Chicago. He took a fling at musical comedy without notable success, then came West, appearing with the Hartmann Opera Company in San Francisco and later with Kolb and Dill. In the Bay City he married Hazel Hastings, a member of the theatrical troupe, and she was his wife for twenty-two years.

STARTS AS "EXTRA"

It was back in 1912 that Mr. Chaney came to Hollywood and began his motion-picture career. He started as an extra in westerns produced at Universal City, and not long afterward was assigned to direct J. Warren Kerrigan. He guided the latter star through seven productions, then returned to acting, achieving screen credit for the first time in "Hell Morgan's Girl," an outstanding picture of its era, in which Dorothy Phillips was the star.

In 1919 Mr. Chaney was chosen by the late George Loane Tucker to play "The Frog" in "The Miracle Man," and the performance he gave catapulted him overnight from obscurity to world-wide fame. He was regarded as occupying a unique position for his proven ability to distort his body in simulation of a hopeless cripple and to make up his face to resemble the most unearthly creatures imaginable as prescribed by the scenario writers. In short, he became an institution.

OTHER SUCCESSES

After "The Miracle Man" came "Outside the Law," "The Trap," "The Hunchback of Notre Dame," "The Shock" and "The Phantom of the Opera," in succession for Universal; and then "Treasure Island," "The Penalty," "Flesh and Blood," "Oliver Twist," "He Who Gets Slapped," "Tower of Lies," "The Monster," "The Unholy Three," "The Blackbird," "The Road to Mandalay," "Tell it to the Marines," "Mr. Wu," "The Unknown," "Mockery," "Laugh, Clown, Laugh," "While the City Sleeps," "West of Zanzibar," "Thunder" and "Where East is East."

With the advent of talking pictures, Mr. Chaney became one of the few "holdouts," maintaining a tenacious loyalty to the silent screen for many months and declining to speak into the microphone. He finally was persuaded to give his voice to the screen, however, and his debut in the audible form of films was made recently in one of his greatest silent successes, "The Unholy Three." Completing his performance he went to New York for treatment of the throat affliction which was to cause his death; and there contracted lobar pneumonia, which sapped his strength and rendered him a victim of anemia. It was to combat this malady that he entered St. Vincent's Hospital last week.

HE LIVED SIMPLY

Mr. Chaney's private life was one of considerable mystery. He shunned personal exhibitions, premiere showings, and interviews, telling intimates they were anathema to him, and although he reputedly possessed a fortune he lived simply, foregoing pomp and servants. He was a prodigious reader and loved especially to pore over tomes on mathematical subjects. The chapter on screen make-up in the Encyclopedia Britannica was a contribution from his pen.

On the set he was gruff and acquired the name among those who did not know him well of being "hard-boiled;" yet once he scaled a precipitous roof to replace a baby bird in its nest. He is known to have contributed generously to numerous charities, though he never made publicity capital of his donations; and not one among his intimates but knew that his sympathies always were with the underdog in a struggle.

Besides his widow, brother and son, Mr. Chaney leaves an infant grandson. The son, Creighton, is in the water-heater business and lives at 735 North Laurel avenue.

OKLAHOMA CITY REMEMBERS ACTOR, TOO

OKLAHOMA CITY, Aug. 26. (AP)—Lon Chaney, character actor, who died in Los Angeles today, formerly was a clerk in a furniture store here.

V. C. Light, Oklahoma City real estate broker, recalled he was teamed with Chaney in his first home talent production in 1907 and related their exploits together the following two years.

Chaney in 1907 worked as head of the rug department of the Street & Harper Furniture Company here.

Light said he was driving an express wagon and he and Chaney played the principal parts in "La Mascot," a light comic opera produced by home talent.

Charles Holmes, now dead, then operator of a local opera company, witnessed the show and employed both Chaney and Light, Chaney for the comedian roles.

When the season ended Chaney and Light were employed by a musical comedy company for three months, touring the Southwest. When the company split up, Chaney and his wife returned here where he and Light became connected with a small-time vaudeville circuit. Their act was a blackface sketch with Chaney playing the part of a hunchback.

Chaney's study of character interpretations began with long walks before breakfast. Meeting beggars and passers-by in all walks of life, he talked with them, studied them, then returned to the theater to make up as nearly like them as possible.

AUDIENCE PAYS TRIBUTE AT THEATER

ROCK SPRINGS (Wyo.) Aug. 26. (AP)—Fifteen hundred theater-goers of many nationalities tonight paid tribute to Lon Chaney, who died today, at the showing of his latest picture here. As the picture flashed on the screen the spectators rose and stood silently for five minutes.

The tribute was repeated at each succeeding performance.

This town, a mining center, has forty-seven nationalities, speaking fifty-one languages or dialects.

NEW HEALTH PROGRAM MAPPED

Y.W.C.A. Announces Broader Schedule

Lots of Fun

Clementine Van Doran, Mary Fitzpatrick and Alma Hanson, poised to plunge into swimming pool.

A BROADER health program than ever before is announced by the Young Women's Christian Association, 941 South Figueroa street, to start Monday, September 8, next.

The schedule includes almost every conceivable form of exercise and recreational activity, swimming, limbering and stretching exercises, basketball, baseball, tennis, golf, tap-dancing, ballroom and rhythmic dancing, horseback riding, athletic tournaments, hiking parties and splash parties.

Miss Ella Stevens, director of the health-education department, will be in charge, assisted by Alma Hansen, Pearl Ross and Betty Beam.

Registration for the classes will open Thursday.

KEATON'S CASE GOES ON TODAY

Defense Alienists will be Placed on Stand

Counsel Expect to Take Up Remainder of Week

Defendant Continues Asleep During Testimony

Defense alienists who will testify that Frank D. Keaton, slayer of Motley Flint, is insane are expected to take the witness stand today in the sanity hearing in Superior Judge Schauer's court. Most of last week testimony of friends and neighbors, all of whom asserted that Keaton was subject to fits and strange moods, went into the record.

According to Defense Counsel Paul D'Orr and Thomas Reynolds, all of this week will be required to complete the defense testimony while Dep. Dist.-Attys. Burgess and Russell probably will take at least a week to present the prosecution's side.

Keaton, in his seat at the end of the counsel table, has paid no attention to anything going on in the courtroom. Most of the time he has been asleep.

Direct testimony already in the record shows that Keaton walked into Superior Judge Collier's courtroom on July 14 and shot down and killed Flint, retired banker, as he left the witness stand where he had been giving testimony in a civil action. Keaton made no effort to escape following the shooting. According to police the slayer had been brooding over stock market losses which he blamed on Flint and other bankers.

CHANGES IN AIR SERVICE ANNOUNCED

T.A.T.-Maddux Lines will Go on New Schedule to Aid Traveling Public

Several important changes in schedules are announced by T.A.T.-Maddux Air Lines, all improvements being designed to facilitate commercial activities throughout the Southwest. The new time readjustments now are in effect, according to a statement made yesterday by H. W. Beck, traffic manager.

Business men in Northern California cities now may breakfast at home, devote more than three hours to business in Los Angeles and return home the same evening. This plane departs from Alameda at 9:20 a.m. and arrives at Glendale at 12:50 p.m. Returning, it departs from Glendale at 5:05 p.m. and arrives in Alameda at 8:35 p.m.

Los Angeles business men visiting northern cities may have almost three hours in San Francisco. Angelenos will fly from Glendale at 9:30 a.m., this plane arriving in Alameda at 1 p.m. Returning, it will leave Alameda at 4:55 p.m. and arrive in Glendale at 8:25 p.m.

Those of the San Diego area may leave home, give eight hours to business in Los Angeles and get back home the same evening. They will use the plane leaving Agua Caliente at 7:45 a.m. and arrive in Glendale at 9:15 a.m. Returning the plane leaves Glendale at 5:15 p.m. and arrives in Agua Caliente at 6:45 p.m.

Southbound Angelenos may leave home, give six hours to business in San Diego and return here all in one day. They will leave Glendale at 10 a.m., arriving in San Diego at 11:10 a.m. and Agua Caliente at 11:30 a.m. Returning, the plane leaves Agua Caliente at 5 p.m. and San Diego at 5:25 p.m., arriving in Glendale at 6:35 p.m.

Passengers from Agua Caliente or San Diego northbound or eastbound beyond Los Angeles can make direct connections in Glendale where they arrive at 9:15 a.m. Both the northbound coastal and the eastbound transcontinental routes depart at 9:30 a.m.

Transcontinental passengers from the East arriving at 4:55 p.m. can make connections with the northbound plane leaving at 5:05 p.m. and the southbound plane leaving at 5:15 p.m.

To most people today, Chaney is remembered as the first horror actor, leading the way for Boris Karloff, Bela Lugosi and his son Creighton Chaney, known as Lon Chaney Jr. Not many realize that his portrayal of detectives and gangsters led the way for Bogart, Cagney and Robinson. He was so great a star at the time of his death, that the public accepted his version of characterizations as the mold and rarely would accept another actor's work if he broke it. Often the amount of research that Chaney put into his character brought reality to the portrayals.

Whenever he had no real-life studies on which to base his make-up he would turn to the descriptions of the authors in the original novels. The Phantom was a madman born with a hideous face. The Hunchback, likewise was deformed from birth. In most of his earlier and later films he played straight roles. In each case his goal was always the perfection of his art.

To see a studio print of his silent films, with proper accompaniment makes one wonder why the art form of the silent film didn't continue. Most of us only have the chance to see scratchy off-speed 16MM prints or video tapes of the same prints.

With the perfection of acting comes the control of the emotions, something that each of us knows deep-down-inside equals freedom of spirit. Fear is an emotion and most of Chaney's films dealt with this emotion. Fear of abandonment, fear of poverty, fear of death or just fear of life itself. Those who were children at the time of the original release of the films remember being frightened out of their wits by the Phantom or the L.A.M. Those who, were adults back them remember films like ROAD TO MANDALAY or THE UNKNOWN for their psychological terrors. Lon Chaney will always be associated with fear. However, from all those who knew him, from his family and from all my research I tend to theorize that his motivation was just the opposite. He wanted to show that there was really nothing on this planet which we should fear!

No matter what happens to us, take a look at what is happening to this guy on the screen and your fears aren't so bad after all, or:

So you're worried about a little acne, or that your nose is too big and people won't accept you. Well take a look at THIS FACE! He pretty much simplified life with one of the last lines in his only talking film THE UNHOLY THREE, MGM, 1930, "You know the old gag. That's all there is to life. Just a little laugh, a little tear."

Once you isolate fear and recognize it as a thing you are on your way home.

About the closest I've ever come to understanding fear came from my family on two occasions. The first was on the day my wife and I met. We both had jobs as "monsters" at a summer amusement pier called The Castle. I was a hunchback and she, something that looked like the corpse of a 50's prom queen. I was stationed at the very top of this five-story structure and when the customers, who paid their $2.50 to be scared senseless, reached this point they were greeted by what we called the Rat Professor. It was his job to attack the subconscious of the people by telling them tales of horror about rats. Usually at the end of the day it had deteriorated into puns such as ratiation, eraticate or the worst of all rat-on.

Once the customers were spooked enough they were turned over to me. I would lead them out onto the parapet so that the sun would cause their pupils to contract and then lead them into a pitch black corridor with several turns. When the last one had entered I would slam the door, throwing them into total darkness. Never once did it fail to bring a chorus of blood-freezing screams.

Now, I knew that around the first turn, inside the room, were one-foot sections of garden hose with springs inside. On the

Patsy Ruth Miller and cover artist Marisa Donato at Miss Miller's New England estate, 1987.

floor were randomly-placed pieces of foam rubber, for the effect of stepping on rats. I had the routine down to a science and knew exactly when the first person in the group would make the turn into the rat maze bringing on the second wave of screams.

On this day I had a realization about fear. The only difference between me and the customers was that I knew what was in the room and therefore it didn't scare me. The elements of fear were darkness and the unknown. I was feeling very cosmic when I slammed the door and there my future wife was glaring at me with dead eyes and an evil grin; seaweed in her matted hair, gown flowing in the ocean breeze and holding rotted hands out toward my neck. My hair stood up, my eyes rolled and I wet my Hunchback suit within two seconds!

I learned something new about fear. The unexpected! Being a new member of the cast I had not been informed that by late in the summer actors turned on each other out of boredom to see who could survive the season. Her laughter at my situation was so contagious that it broke my catelepsy and I laughed with her. Then I threw her over the side. Not really. When we laughed together we had fallen in love even though we had no idea what each other looked liked until later in the evening when we took off our costumes and make-up.

The second insight to fear came 5 years later when my first born and I were watching John Landis' AN AMERICAN WEREWOLF IN LONDON, while the little one, Katie slept in her diaper, curled up on the floor in front of the TV. I told Jessica that the movie was scary, but with the opening scences where the two guys are happily walking through the English moors with Creedence Clearwater singing "Bad Moon Rising", she saw nothing to be afraid of and insisted on watching. A few moments later, when the two guys were thrown out of the Inn and the werewolf was circling them and howling she cleared the ten feet from the couch to my chair in one second! Saying in a quivering voice, OK it's scary—Change it. . . NOW!

So I switch to Seven Little Foys and about five minutes later she asked me to switch back to the werewolf. Again I tell her that it might scare her but she insists and I switch it just at the second where David Naughton, the werewolf, flashes open his eyes in his hospital bed. His eyes are glowing yellow and he has large fangs. Jess was up my back with her arms around my head and her face buried in my hair before I could move. Back to Bob Hope for a while and then she asked me to turn back again. She just loved being scared. Like all of us, we are attracted to the negative side of life. The fears, the repulsive, the unknown, the evil, we all want to light up the darkness and the only way we can is to walk into the middle of it and strike a match.

Maybe that's what Lon Chaney did that makes his films still popular today. Even though 58 years have passed since he died there has never been anyone to replace him. No one that captured his formula for success in movie acting.

I made two trips to MGM in 1986. The first was in the spring to finish this book and the second to complete three other lost films. The second trip was made at the urging of my friends at the studio for by November the MGM lot would be turned over to the new owners.

We arrived on the closing day October 23 , 1986 and for the rest of my life I will hold the feeling of that day. Within an hour after the plane had landed we drove to Santa Monica and checked into our favorite hotel, the Miramar, and I was then on my way to MGM. I immediately rushed into the Thalberg building where I was told that Herbert Nusbaum of the legal department and the sponsor of my projects was waiting for me at the farewell party.

The gathering was in Irving Thalberg's old office and from the window I watched the moving vans lining up on Washington Boulevard. From this window you could also see the main gates. The gates where Greta Garbo, Lon Chaney, Joan Crawford, Clark Cable, Lillian Gish, Judy Garland, Robert Taylor and hundreds of the greatest stars and actors arrived each morning to punch the timeclock and report to work.

Writers, F. Scott Fitzgerald, William Faulkner, James Mehin and Anita Loos drove up from their parties in Malibu or Beverly Hills to have about 15 cups of coffee and prepare for a hopefully inspiring day in their 8 x 8 writers' rooms. The greatest directors' in the art of film making from Charles Brabin and Rex Ingram to Martin Scorsese and George Cukor fought battles with the corporate powers to keep art ahead of the dollar or at least equal in importance. All of these things were going through my head as I prepared for the last week that I would ever have to preserve these lost films in book form.

It wasn't a real party. There were no reporters, no media coverage. None of the old stars came out that day to say good-bye. It was just Herb and I toasting Leo the lion trademark and wishing Mr. Kerkorian success in the new MGM offices as the sun was setting.

Outside, in the hallways the workmen were busy removing one-sheets of all the great MGM films. Files were being shifted from hall to hall awaiting their new home either at the corporate headquarters in Beverly Hills or the new building next door where construction was nearly completed by Turner Construction (no connection to Turner Entertainment.)

There I was in Thalberg's office, the center of the greatest film producer in MGM's history watching the scaffolding go up to remove the MGM sign on the water tower and I could feel the emotion of all the wonderful memories, as if all the old actors, directors, artists, technicians, bankers and executives who stood in that room and discussed, argued or fought about how their films were to be made, were using my eyes to look at the studio for the last time.

Moving day at MGM after 62 years in Culver City.

But I came away from that last week of research with something much greater than feelings. It was a knowledge that MGM was, is, and shall be much, much more that the Culver City lots. I have tried to capture, in this series what it was like to be there and I think I have succeeded. In the year 2023 I plan to be at the 100th anniversary of MGM. Hopefully by that time someone would have found the subjects of my books and we can all see how well I did.

One last word and then on with the show.

There has been a lot of negative press on the colorization of the films made in the black and white format by Turner Entertainment and Hal Roach Studios. For the record. I am probably the only film historian in the world that is in favor of colorization. In researching these books I had to keep an objective eye on the work as it progressed so I didn't become a captive of my own love for film history. I've had the chance to see the 20's as they actually existed. The point that I'm making is: most people are once again resisiting change and thus denying themselves a possible improvement on current situation. The greatest stars and producers of the 20's thought sound films to be a novelty that would soon wear off. Chaney, Chaplin, Garbo and others resisted as long as they could and the critics brutilized the sound format. Many people had a big investment in silents and it would be expensive to wire the old houses. A few years went by and it was accepted, but not until technology made a few improvements and the sound quality became satisfactory. Technicolor films had the same troubles. In the earlier days, around the time of A BLIND BARGAIN the process involved pasting two strips of film together. One with the reds and the other with the greens or blues. This made it much thicker than normal black and white silents and often caused the home-town projectionist to panic when it split in two or knocked the film out of focus. However, by 1927 Technicolor had finally developed a way of printing both dyes on one side of the film. In a rush to combine sound and color they were flooded with orders and could not keep up with the pace. Often

producers and directors with little artistic background would bathe their sets and costumes with the most obnoxious and garish colors, again with the thoughts of money in the foreground. The results of these two factors caused Technicolor's future to look bleak. Especially in 1930 when the depression was in full force. The critics viewed the hastily prepared prints along with the mismatched color direction and condemned color with a vengeance! Within a few years the industry began to listen to the executvies at Technicolor and the result has been 57 years of enjoyment to billions of film-goers. Along came Television in the early 50's but there was only black and white reception available at first. The new generation of corporate heads looked into their storage vaults and found that the early technicolor prints took up three times the space of black and white prints (and negatives) so there was no rush to restore and repair the color prints for sale to television. Thus almost causing the loss of these early films in their original format.

Now we come to the 60's and 70's. Eastman offered a new approach to color photography and the old 3-strip technicolor became history. It has taken 20 years to see the result of this change. Once again, not understanding the care that the Eastman prints require has resulted in loss.

If you haven't noticed they have been showing the orange and blue versions of KING OF KINGS and IT'S A MAD, MAD, MAD, MAD WORLD on television lately.

No one really knows the life of a video tape. But I would guess at about 8 years before the inherent make-up of the tape loses it's magnetism. But who cares! The original has been preserved and you can buy another tape. I look forward to seeing a few silents colorized, maybe THE PHANTOM OF THE OPERA (which had several two-tone technicolor sequences), the early Universal horror films, the Abbott and Costello films, the early Fred Astaire films and Marx brothers Paramount features. Many of these films would have been in color had budget permitted and that statement is not an opinion for I have interviewed the directors of the films that I have mentioned.

Maybe with the success of home video and laser discs, art will join with the bank and it will become financially feasable to secure our present day films for future generations. The success of Ted Turner's and Hal Roach's colorization has turned out to be a blessing for the black and white classics. In order to colorize a film the original negatives are carefully and lovingly restored giving years of new life to an art form that would have faded in the not too distant future.

Philip J. Riley
July 4, 1987

Herbert Nusbaum preparing for the move to his new corporate office.

Ben Presser, head of Legal Files Department.

YOU HAVE TO ACT THE PART

by Patsy Ruth Miller

I did not appear in A BLIND BARGAIN but I can recount my memories of the picture I made with Lon Chaney and Wallace Worsley, THE HUNCHBACK OF NOTRE DAME, that same year. I don't remember when THE HUNCHBACK was released: we started shooting on it in December, 1922, and I worked on it until the end of June, 1923.

It was an epic, the only one I was ever in. It was known as an epic from its inception, but even better known as one of the first actual Million Dollar Movies. Today, a budget of a million dollars is hardly enough to make a two minute commercial, but in 1922, when the picture went into production, a million dollars was just what it sounds like. Those dollars were real, honest-to-goodness 100 cent dollars, and they were all spent on actual production, not on taxes, or labor disputes or politics. Of course salaries were included in the cost of production, but I assure you that no one, not even Lon Chaney, received enough to make a dent in the million. My salary certainly didn't account for much of that sum, but on the other hand, what I received was mine, all mine. No deductions. Cigarettes were 15 cents a pack, two for a quarter. Gasoline was eight cents a gallon. You could get a good meal in a good restaurant for two or three dollars, and tips were five percent for really good service.

I knew that I was lucky to get the part of Esmeralda, the Gypsy girl, but I didnt' dream that it was going to be the picture by which I was remembered. Sometimes I've been a bit annoyed by being introduced as Esmeralda. It's always: You remember "The Hunchback" don't you? She played the Gypsy girl in it. Then, if the recipient of this world shaking news is under sixty, the response is generally, Oh, really? I thought it was Maureen O'Hara!

My memories of "The Hunchback" are good ones; the friendliness of everyone, the grips, the propmen, the camaramen, as well as the other members of the cast. And I remember Lon Chaney as being a very gentle and kind man.

He was completely dedicated to his art and approached it in a workmanlike manner. He watched every detail, not only of his own performance, but of the picture as a whole. He actually shared the direction of scenes with Wallace Worsley, and I couldn't help learning a great deal from him.

I had already been in eleven pictures, all in a matter of three years! But no one had coached me, or explained anything about acting. I had done western—well, I did learn how to ride a

Worsley, Chaney and Kerry preparing a scene in THE HUNCHBACK where Quasimodo buys Esmerelda clothes, while she is protected by the sanctuary of the Church—missing from most prints today.

horse— and I had played comedy and tragedy and silly parts that took no ability, but it was all done by my own instincts; I lacked technique. I depended too much on my own emotion in dramatic scenes. I remember being terribly excited after filming a scene for "The Hunchback" because I had cried real tears. But Lon explained that crying real tears didn't make an actress good; it was making the audience cry that mattered, and that you didn't do if you emoted all over the set. He didn't believe that an actor should "lose himself" in the part; he should always be aware of what he was doing. There's a fine difference.

Norman Kerry, who played Phoebus in a curled wig and ornate costume, and who was completely irreverent, also gave me some advice. His was, "Don't look at the camera and try not to giggle in the love scenes." He added, "And don't forget to pick up your check every week."

Norman really wasn't really an actor at heart. He was just a fun-loving, handsome guy who made a living by "making faces in front of a camera," as he described acting. He took nothing, least of all himself, seriously. Much to the aggravation of Mr. Chaney who took his art quite serious. However once or twice Lon's sense of humor an occurance which always took one by surprise, did indear him to me.

During the shooting of one of my close-ups, he stood off-camera, ostensibly to inspire me. As I raised my gaze, looking at Norman with wide-eyed innocence, he said in a girlish falsetto, "Oh, Mr. Kerry, are my eyes too big for pictures?" It broke everyone up, and the scene had to be taken over.

He did that sort of thing constantly throughout the shooting of "The Hunchback". But when it came to Norman's clowning, I don't think Lon ever quite understood it.

I also remember Ernest Torrence, who played Clopin, King of the Beggars, in a violent, blustering manner. Actually he was a most charming, Scottish gentleman with a delightful, dry humor, as unlike his screen character as it is possible to be. I remember very little about the director, Wallace Worsley. Novice though I was, I was aware that he was not a very forceful man, and it seemed to me that Lon did as much directing of the personal scenes as Mr. Worsley. Although the responsibility of such a big budget picture and it's hundred of daily problems probably must have been a very big burden, the crowd scenes were handled by use of a then—innovative technique—an electic Loud Speaker system! Even in those scenes, Lon seemed to have a hand, and often a suggestion.

I also remember a young man just over from Europe, Alsace Lorraine, it might have been. I'm not sure now. Anyway, he and his brother, Robert, were nephews of Uncle Carl Laemmle, who was head of Universal. Willy was the other brother, and their last name was Wyler. Willy was put to work as sort of second assistant to the assistant director, and seemed to take to it with great enthusiam. I don't remember what Robert did, but he was the one I'd have bet on; he was taller than Willy, and quite goodlooking, although not blond and blue-eyed, which was my preference. No one could have called Willy goodlooking, but he was very pleasant. I enjoyed chatting with him between scenes, in my fractured French, and I was impressed by how quickly he seemed to catch on to everything, the camera work, the set-ups, and all that.

Willy became completely Americanized; he changed his name from Willy to William, and became one of our finest directors.

Another memory returns to me, a little lecture from Lon one day. He was not in his terrible make-up, so he was free to chat, which was almost impossible when he was wearing that painful Hunchback outfit. He led up to the subject gradually, saying how pleased he was with my performance, going on to tell me that he was sure I would have a successful career, and he finally got to the point by saying, "It's all very well to be generous, but don't let people make a sucker out of you."

As was often the case, I didn't know what he was talking about. As was equally often the case, he looked at me with that "Are you for real?" look. Then he patiently explained that I was becoming known as a soft touch. Before I could protest that no one had been touching me, soft or otherwise, he gave a deep sigh and said, "What I'm trying to tell you is, don't fall for all those hard luck stories you've been getting from some of the extras, Meg and Skeets, for instance."

Then I knew what he was talking about; how he knew I had lent them money I didn't know. Maybe he was just familiar with Meg and Skeets and their tactics. He ended his little lecture by saying, "You'll probably make a lot of money in this business, but just remember—you worked for it. So don't be a sucker."

I think it was very sweet of him to be concerned about me and my financial welfare. And I was careful from then on not to let him see me talking to any of the extras.

After six months of happy work, despite the daily drive from Beverly Hills to the Valley, the picture finally came to an end, and it was time to say goodbye to the cast, the crew, and Lon. Most of us would never see each other again; friendships are formed on the set, but they usually don't carry over into "civi-

Facsimile of the original script of THE HUNCHBACK with Director Worsley's hand written notes. (Courtesy Wallace Worsley Jr.)

lian" life. We might meet at parties—occasionally some of us worked together in other movies—but for the most part we went our own ways, in our own circle of friends. Romances also occasionally blossom, but seldom lasting ones.

Norman had given me a good hearty kiss, and said, "Let's work together again some day when you're grown up." Mr. Worsley had politely said it was a pleasure to work with me, and I had replied that it was a pleasure to work with him. Then it was time to tell Lon goodbye.

He was in the projection room looking at the rushes. I knocked on the door. He opened with a look of annoyance, which changed into a smile when he saw me. Telling the projectionist to hold it, he came out into the hall, saying, "Well, you're leaving, eh? When I thanked him for being so tolerant and so helpful, he smiled again, that rare, very sweet smile, and said that I looked fine in the rushes, and that he wished me the best of luck, but even as he was speaking, I had the feeling that he was no longer with me.

The scene described in the script to left.

Permit me to tell about something that happened fifty years later. Some time in the Seventies, when my husband and I were in Edinburgh, we decided to fly to Glasglow to visit his Aunt Joan. We called her to say we'd be there on Sunday, and she said that she and Uncle George would meet us at the airport.

We arrived as scheduled, but there was no one at the airport to greet us. Worried that there might have been an accident, or that one of them was ill, my husband rushed to a phone. Her number rang and rang until it was answered by an apologetic Aunt Joan.

"Do forgive me, dear boy," she said. "We've been watching an old movie on the telly, and I'm afraid we completely forgot about you and Pat. It's "The Hunchback of Notre Dame". . . it's still on as a matter of fact. . . do forgive us."

My husband said it didn't matter, to go back and watch the movie, we'd take a taxi, which we did. It's about a twenty minute drive to Bearsden, the suburb in which they lived, and by the time we got there the TV show was over. I couldn't resist asking Aunt Joan whether seeing me on the screen hadn't reminded her that we would be at the airport.

"Not a bit of it, dear," she said. "In my mind I never connected the two of you at all."

That's about the way it was that summer day in 1923, at the Universal Studio, when I felt Lon Chaney drifting away from me.

I, Patsy Ruth Miller, was already gone, over and done with. She, Esmeralda, was just beginning to live, and in his mind he no longer connected the two of us at all.

Wallace Worsley, Patsy Ruth Miller and Lon Chaney reviewing the script of THE HUNCHBACK OF NOTRE DAME.

The Court of Miracles from THE HUNCHBACK as it exists today on the UNIVERSAL backlot. Notre Dame having burnt down about 20 years ago leaves only these surviving sets. The archway below was also used in THE GHOST OF FRANKENSTEIN where Lon Chaney Jr. saved the little girl trying to catch her balloon. (Sets can be seen as part of the Universal Studio's Tour).

DIRECTOR WORSLEY (to the right of camera) and crew.

Lon Chaney and Grouverner Morris, author of THE PENALTY on the Goldwyn lot.

Samuel Goldwyn 1881-1974.

PRODUCTION BACKGROUND

The Goldwyn Production Company and Studio had only Samuel Goldwyn's name in 1922. He would once again regain sovereign rule with his own company, now known as Samuel Goldwyn Productions, two years later. But by 1922 he was replaced as studio head by F.J. Godsol who then merged the company with Marcus Loew of Metro and Louis B. Mayer on April 26, 1924 to become Metro-Goldwyn-Mayer.

Goldwyn had become partners a few years earlier with William Randolph Hearst forming the Goldwyn-Cosmopolitan Distributing Corporation. This too only lasted until the end of 1923 when Hearst became part of the MGM merger as an independent production company operating on the Culver City lot.

Many great talents were under contract to Goldwyn: Art Director Cedric Gibbons, who created the designs for A BLIND BARGAIN; Directors Eric Von Stroheim, King Vidor, Marshall Neilan, Charles Brabin and Victor Seastrom; Actors Conrad Nagel, Blanche Sweet, John Gilbert, Eleanor Boardman, William Haines and Marion Davies. Also the Lion trademark had been Goldwyn's.

The Culver lot in 1922.
(Courtesy Marc Wanamaker-Bison Archives)

Raymond McKee with the original glass stage in the background.

The Goldwyn lot was originally built in 1915 by Thomas Ince. It exists today as Lorimar Telepictures and with the exception of the Thalberg building, built in the 1930's, it is basically the same. (The expansions to Backlots 2 through 5 by Mayer had dwindled back to the original Lot One by 1978) The six glass stages had been replaced years before by the giant enclosed sound stages, but the lab, library, construction, wardrobe and a few other buildings exist today as they had in 1915.

Goldwyn was always one to recognize the importance of the written word in moving making. He sought out and signed the best writers of the day for his films. Motion pictures were reguarded by him as part of the writing trade. Although he didn't have Chaney under exclusive contract at this time he had ordered story ideas to be purchased for future Chaney vehicles. Two years earlier another lost film THE MIRACLE MAN, Paramount 1919, had made Chaney an even bigger star. So in 1920 Chaney was signed by Goldwyn to make THE PENALTY, written by Gouverneur Morris and directed by Wallace Worsley. In 1921 he made another Morris story entitled THE ACE OF HEARTS and had a small part in FOR THOSE WE LOVE with Betty Compson. Early in 1922 he starred in THE NIGHT ROSE, again with Worsley as director and on September 13, 1922 they began filming A BLIND BARGAIN.

The word around Hollywood was, if you want a sure success, find a story in which Chaney could create another characterization. Chaney took as many pictures as his schedule could handle. Not because he needed the money for by this time he could command $1000.00 per week or about $30,000.00 by today's standards, but because it gave him a chance to work. Acting was his work. A BLIND BARGAIN was his eighth film in 1922 (THE TRAP, VOICES OF THE CITY, FLESH AND BLOOD, THE LIGHT IN THE DARK, SHADOWS, OLIVER TWIST, QUINCY ADAMS SAWYER had preceeded).

Out of his imagination came the famous thousand faces. His make-up box was a simple fisherman's tackle box covered in leather the legend "Lon F. Chaney, Hollywood California" stamped in gold next to the handle. It is finally, properly displayed at the Museum of Natural History in Los Angeles, California, where Hazel Chaney had donated it around 1932 along with many of his costumes. Some are still in good shape; such as: his marine suit from TELL IT TO THE MARINES, the wig and hunchback materials from THE HUNCHBACK OF NOTRE DAME, the dress and wig from the sound UNHOLY THREE and the LONDON AFTER MIDNIGHT dentures and top hat (at the Ackerman Archives).

Some original buildings remain today at Lorimar.

A few of the props from MR. WU were in the possession of Lon Chaney Jr.'s first wife and his smaller make-up kit, used for on-location shooting is also on display at the Ackerman Archives along with a suit worn in THE BIG CITY, a stage costume from Sad Pasha and his personal fishing gear, kept for many years by his son until given to me for safe keeping. His Red Death costume from the PHANTOM OF THE OPERA was last seen in Atlantic City on a wax figure, in the now closed Toussauds wax museum. The boat bed in which Christine slept before she unmasked the Phantom is in the possession of a collector in the San Fernando Valley and a New York Ventriloquist is using the dummy from THE UNHOLY TREE in his act today. Unfortunately we could not save many of the props and costumes and original art work which was stored by the Chaney family but destroyed in a storm which hit the San Diego area in the early 70's.

In creating the visual portion of his make-up characterizations Chaney remained true to the written word and respected the author's original descriptions. Scenes from the 1911 Gaston Leroux novel THE PHANTOM OF THE OPERA literally jumped from the page to the screen. Illustrations from the 1913 Gouverneur Morris novel, THE PENALTY were matched for the film. Quasimodo as described by Victor Hugo:

"It was, in truth, a countenance of miraculous ugliness which at this moment shone forth from the circular aperature. After all the faces, pentagonal, hexagonal, and heteroclite, that had followed each other at this window, without realizing the idea of the grotesque which the crowd had set up in their frantic imaginations, it required nothing short of the sublimely monstrous grimace which had just dazzled the multitude to obtain their suffrages. Master Coppenole himself applauded; and Clopin Trouillefou who had been a candidate—and God knows what intensity of ugliness his features could attain!—confessed himself conquered. We shall do the same; we shall not attempt to give the reader any idea of that tetrahedron nose, of that horseshow mouth, of that little left eye stubbed up with an eyebrow of carroty bristles, while the right was completely overwhelmed and buried by an enormous wen; of those irregular teeth, jagged here and there like the battlements of a fortress; of that horny lip, over which one of those teeth protruded, like the tusk of an elephant; of that forked chin; and above all of the expression, that mixture of spite, wonder and melancholy, spread over these exquisite features. Imagine such an object if you can.

The lucky Pope of Fools was brought out in triumph, and it was not till then that surprise and admiration were at their height; what had been mistaken for a grimace was his natural visage; indeed it might be said that his whole person was but one grimace. His prodigious head was covered with red bristles; between his shoulders rose an enormous hump, which was counterbalanced by a protuberance in front; his thighs and legs were so strangely put together that they touched at no one point but the knees, and seen in front resembled two sickles joined at the handles; his feet were immense, his hands monstrous; but, with all this deformity there was a formidable air of strength, agility and courage, constituting a singular exception to the eternal rule which ordains that force, as well as beauty, shall result from harmony. He looked like a giant who had been broken in pieces and ill-soldered together."

Yes, Chaney respected the written word. But what did all the greasepaint, appliances and props mean without the inner workings of this great actor. It is best described in his own words. In 1928 he wrote the preface to a book written by the Director of make-up at MGM, Cecil Holland

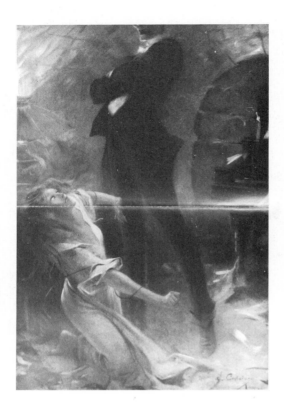

Above illustration by Andre Castaigne, from the 1911 Bobbs-Merrill 1st American Edition novel by Gaston Leroux. Below, the same scene from the 1925 film.

Above illustration by Andre Castaigne, from the 1911 Bobbs-Merrill 1st American Edition novel by Gaston Leroux. Below, the same scene from the 1925 film.

PREFACE

Undoubtedly the greatest single gift to the civilization of mankind is the printed word and, as a corollary, the most useful tool in the world is the test-book. It is the chisel by which the worker can carve out a structure of knowledge, by which he can inspect the experiences of others, go through these same experiences himself, and, with the knowledge gleaned during another man's span of life and activity, advance one step further on the road of progress.

This is as true of the stage and screen as of any other profession, but the student of stage and screen has had few such tools to work with. A practical compendium on makeup therefore fills a very important niche in the existing testbooks of the play. Cecil Holland has given the student such a textbook.

Mr. Holland approached the problem from the standpoint of an actor, for it was as an actor that he learned the art. In fact, his textbook is really a mirror of a lifetime of experience of an actor on the stage and screen; the problems he discusses and solves are the problems he met and solved by experiment in his own calling, and are the problems that the student actor is most likely to meet himself.

With these problems solved, the student of the technique of screen or stage will be equipped to strike out on his own—to advance further through adapting his knowledge to new experiences as they come up. As I said, the textbook is a tool, and, like any other tool, its usefulness depends on the way that is is used. One may create a masterpiece with a tool, another a slovenly piece of workmanship.

Therefore the student must bear in mind that no textbook can completely educate him in any art— but it can help him adapt his own mind to problems that arise and thus help him make himself an artist. When a student has learned all there is in a textbook he has advanced just as far as the man before him—and from then on he must move forward as an original searcher. Thus everything progresses—engineers of today are moving forward beyond the heritage of knowledge left them by Faraday, Steinmetz, and Marconi; physicians beyond the experiences of Lister, Metchnikoff and Pasteur to new discoveries—and so must the actor of tomorrow tread across the experiences of those of us who worked today—to achieve a more advanced knowledge in the dim tomorrow.

Cecil Holland's book can help the student do this. It is crammed with practical hints on the modus operandi of makeup, and describes carefully the study of the face necessary to make a given disguise convincing. Mr. Holland is an expert in the reproduction of cuts, scars, and other forms of illusion. I have long watched his work in the studios with interest; the different disguises he worked out for Mary Pickford, Claire Windsor and others. Of course, makeup is a hobby with me, hence perhaps I was more interested than anyone in Holland's work.

He created the office of staff makeup expert at a studio, and is acting in this capacity at the Metro-Goldwin-Mayer plant, where it was found that such a functionary could save much trouble and time dealing with such problems as special disguises for principals—or wholesale disguises for extras, such as the crowds in "Ben Hur," etc. Holland knows both angles. He can dispense illusion wholesale or retail.

I trust that his attempt to dispense knowledge of this rather abstruse art fulfills his aim—which is to help the actors of the world solve a few problems. If this book can help the actor in at least one important emergency, I know that the actor will feel that Mr. Holland's effort was well worth while—and so will Mr. Holland.

And, if I may be permitted just a word of advice to the student who may peruse this book—remember that this textbook is a tool—and how you use it depends on yourself. Careful study of its facts, and careful application of them to original problems is your stepping stone to possible fame—at any rate to the joy of knowing, in your own heart, that you are, as an actor, a competent workman.

In 1924 he wrote a short piece in a book edited by Laurence A. Hughes published by Hollywood Publishers entitled THE TRUTH ABOUT THE MOVIES. The article called "What is Characterization."

WHAT IS CHARACTERIZATION

Some people are especially born for characterization. You feel the call of it and you answer the call. It is your dramatic destiny. In the character and emotions of those personages of bygone times, you experience a change, an interest and yet you realize that, fundamentally speaking, emotion is always the same. But the passions and emotions of bygone peoples and characters were, it seems to me, much more intense than ours of this modern era. Therefore, one releases himself from comparatively infantile passions and emotions when one depicts the tremendous loves and hates, sufferings and triumphs of those who made fictional or dramatic or real history in the eras when the world was in the making.

First you read of them, then you visualize them to the best of your ability, then you characterize their customs and throw off modernity and go back, and convey to the public an immortal emotion which has grown and enthralled a world under the pen of a supreme master of emotion. You have taken a heavy responsibility for there was a fascination, reality, tremendous, volcanic qualities in those character which taxes your strength, your mind and your soul.

It takes a man or a women who, emotionally, is very strong to undertake these tasks and, once undertaken, the days pass into weeks and still you live and breath and suffer the emotions which may lead to happiness and which may lead to those sombre, gruesome shades which also form a part of Life.

Characterization is not easy. With so little of real authenticity to go on, it becomes more difficult, for strange to say, an audience will sense the authenticity of a character which you are portraying and sense it intuitively. But characterization has its rewards in work well done, sincerly done and you bring back, in reality, those characters which generations have loved.

LON CHANEY

Chaney rarely spoke about his make-up secrets after his stardom with THE HUNCHBACK in 1923. During the filming of A BLIND BARGAIN he allowed photographs to be taken not only of his make-up box but the actual application. Some preparing for the apeman and others just of different characterizations.

On the following pages you will see the make-up box, in detail, as it exists today at the MUSEUM OF NATURAL HISTORY in Los Angeles and with it, special appliances and items, grouped with the photographs of the films in which they were used.

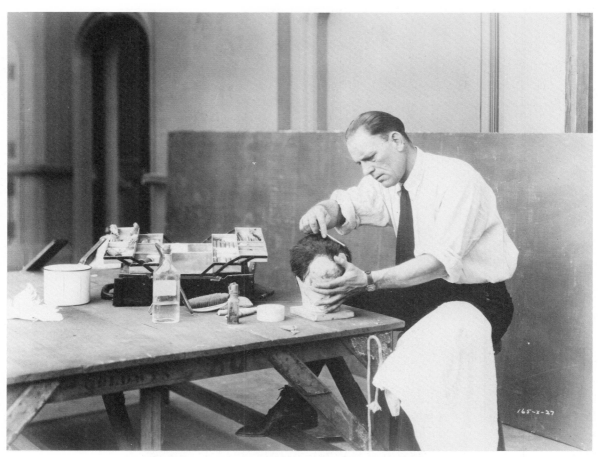

Making up as the hunchback for A BLIND BARGAIN.

An Oriental characterization.

LON CHANEY'S MAKEUP KIT

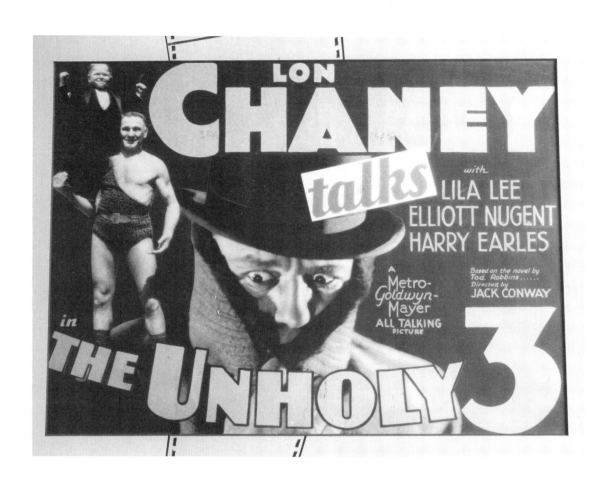

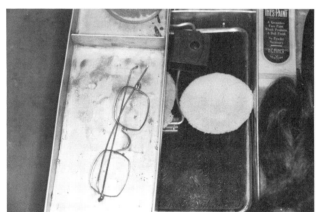

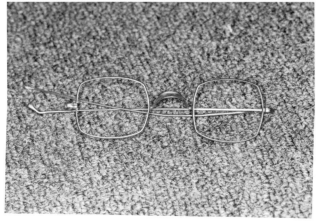

(Top) Illustrations from THE PENALTY by Grouvenor Morris published in 1913 by Charles Scribner's Sons. Illustrated by artist Howard Chandler Christy.

(Middle) A scene from the 1920 Goldwyn film.

(Bottom) The display at the Los Angeles Museum of Natural History.

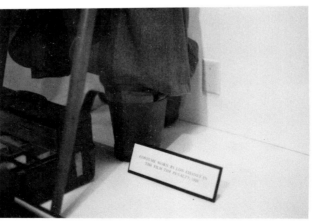

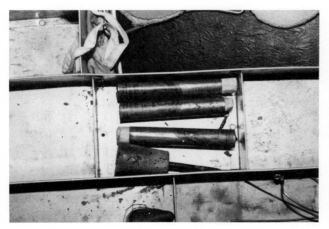

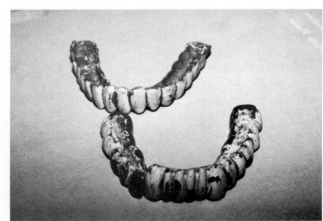

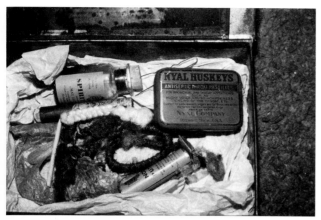

A sad reminder for Lon Chaney fans.

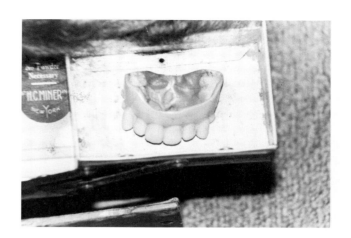

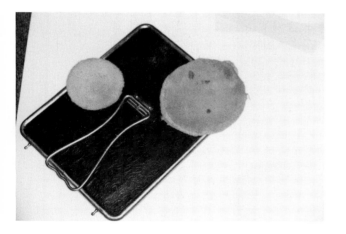

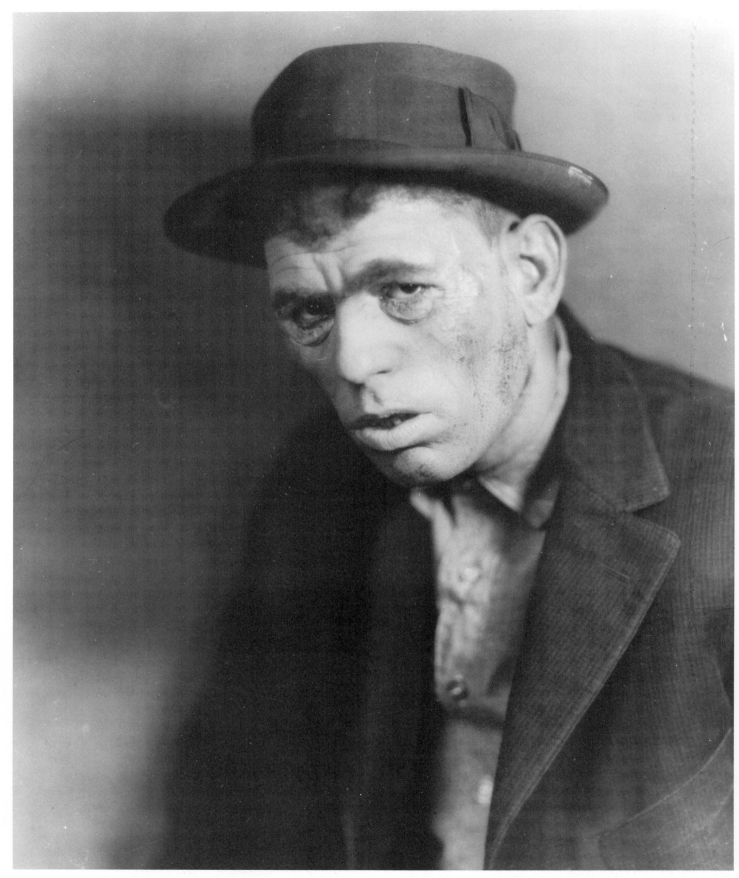

The most amazing discovery in the researching of this film. There was a flashback planned where Chaney appeared at the house as a beggar. He agreed to the same experiment and the result was him turning into the ape-like hunchback of the film. This still is apparently a transitional make-up on the way to ape. (courtesy Michael Blake Collection).

A BLIND BARGAIN was based on a book entitled "The Octave of Claudius" written by Barry Pain and published in America by Harper and Row and in England by Holden and Hardingham Ltd, in 1897. This period was a time when the gothic genre was quickly melting and reshaping it's ghosts, spectres and emotional monsters (locked up in it's obsessive madmen) into solid forms of fear; such as Bram Stoker's "Dracula" and H.G. Well's "The Invisible Man" published that same year.

Arthur Conan Doyle's Sherlock Holmes had changed what was left of the gothic mystery into scientific deduction. The third part of the gothic novel, the spiritual (you couldn't have an evil force like the devil without divine balance by the priests, clergy and monks of the time—even if they were a little mad themselves in these tales), the spiritual was being replaced by the metaphysical new age romances of Marie Corelli, "The Young Diana", "Sorrows of Satan", "Barabas" and "Ziska".

Barry Pain , who might also be Eric Odell, was best known as a short-story writer. He was born in Cambridge England on September 28, 1864 and he died on May 5, 1928. He was a journalist and a widely-read humorist. Examples of his gift of satire, although they do not hold up well today, are "Old Robinson Crusoe" (1907), in which a 300 year old Crusoe returns to Edwardian England, "The New Gulliver" (1913) followed the same theme. He also wrote early metaphysical romances such as "The Shadow of the Unseen", (1907), with James Blyth which dealt with witchcraft, "An Exchange of Souls", (1911) about a man with wings. He even dabbled in the supernatural in such short story collections as "Stories and Interludes" (1892), "Three Fantasies" (1904) and "Stories in the Dark" (1901). Being hailed as the greatest short story writer of his day was enough to attract the attention of Samuel Goldwyn.

The following uncredited synopsis of the novel Octave of Claudius is from the Goldwyn files: The octave referred to relates to Claudius' time allowed to live his life to the fullest (8 days) before he returns to Dr. Lamb's laboratory to submit himself to an experiment which might mean his life or worse, thus A BLIND BARGAIN:

1897 First Edition

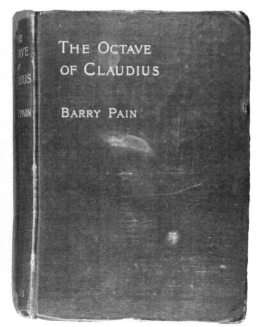

Cover of the American 1897 Edition

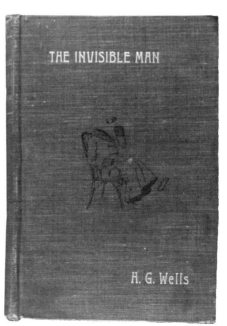

1897 First Edition

OCTAVE OF CLAUDIUS

Our story actually begins in Wimbledon Common, after a brief introduction to the Wycherley and their daughter Angela, who has her own ideas of the kind of man she wants to marry, but keeps it inside of her. But back to Wimbledon Common.

This is an area where Mr. Wycherley takes an evening stroll, but by Fate's strange workings, he has decided not to, and instead the opportunity to play the Good Samaritan has been given to a Dr. Gabriel Lamb. The good doctor has just returned from a brisk walk in the Common and has approached the garden-gate of his home, when he is stopped by the sight of a body lying in the grass. On closer examination, it is revealed to be that of a young man, half-conscious from starvation. As the book describes "he was clad in a well-cut tweed suit, worn to utter shabbiness. His boots were in holes. He was lying where he had fallen when he found that he could go no further; his hat was off, and had received from the fall, a damage with which it was already familiar. His face was thin, and at the present, quite colorless, but it had the tokens of refinement and strength." After a quick examination, Dr. Lamb heads for his own home to get his servant, Paul and return with some medicine in a glass. At first, the young man refuses to drink, but under Dr. Lamb's persistence, he drinks the liquid, which turns out to be part brandy. Then, with the aid of Paul, and another servant, Dr. Lamb gets the young man, who, it turns out, was educated at Eton and Cambridge Universities, to his home. It's described as "A house which seemed to have an old quiet in it—a quiet that had long been there. The colours in the interiors were low; it was lit softly without glare; one's footsteps were not heard on the thick carpets. The house was of red brick; but the red had been softened and shaded by time, and the walls partly covered with ivy. At the back of the house there was a modern addition which Dr. Lamb had erected for his own purposes. It was a long low building, and had a separate entrance into the garden."

The stranger awakens in a bedroom, and in a while, the valet returns, and brings some food, and then after the young man finishes eating, Dr. Lamb returns, gives him a cursory examination, and then finds out who the young fellow is. The stranger's name is Claudius Sandell (the Claudius of the title). Then the two engage in quiet discussion, during which Dr. Lamb explains that his wife is at church; she being devoted to religion to the point of fanaticism. Originally he had been a general practitioner, but after awhile, when he treated a patient who was drunk, he became discouraged with his work, and decided to devote himself to science for mankind's benefit. Seeing that Claudius is tired, the doctor leaves, but outside, the valet Paul tells Dr. Lamb that he knows Sandell, being that he worked at Eton and used to see Claudius there once in a while. But when Lamb hears this, he orders Paul to stay in the dressing-room next to Claudius's room. About then, Mrs. Lamb returns home, armed with several devotional books and a Bible. "She was a rather short woman with dark hair, and plain anaemic face and ecstatic eyes. She looked very young, twenty years younger than the doctor. Her rapture at the sermon of the day is shattered when her husband smiles strangely, frightening her. Then, they go to dinner. Then, after, he tells his wife, whose name is Hilda, about Claudius, and expresses his amazment at Claudius's sense of honor, which forces Claudius to insist on repaying him. In Dr. Lamb's words, "He says that he must repay me—cannot bear the obligation—is very strong on that point. "However, this is not very like her husband's nature. As we continue with their conversation we find that Dr. Lamb no longer loves his wife, but hasn't separated to keep up the appearance of domestic bliss. The wife is slowly going to the point of madness due to the loss

of her own child at birth. Lamb is sympathetic but that is all. At times, he despises her. As time passes, Lamb and Claudius start a friendship, and we learn more about this strange young man. At Dr. Lamb's request, he spends most of his time with Mrs. Lamb, and although Dr. Lamb suspects and begins to notice, Claudius does not realize that Mrs. Lamb, in attempting to replace the affection she has not gotten from her husband, has fallen in love with him. That night at dinner, Claudius tells his story to Mr. and Mrs. Lamb.

He is the only son of Sir Constantine Sandell, who has become estranged from his father. His dear old dad was always interested in religion, of any kind. "He is about due into Buddhism by now," as Claudius puts it. He was interested in spiritualism, and his fanaticism made him the easy prey of Miss Matilda Comby (at the mention of her name Dr. and Mrs. Lamb exchange glances). Miss Comby wormed her way into Sir Constantine's home, by masquerading as a medium, and was so convincing that she was fleecing the old man. Claudius did his own investigations into the tricks of the trade, and tried to expose her several times, but Miss Comby was clever, and had warned Sir Constantine about those very arguments. Sir Constantine was furious at his son, and the rift between them widened, as Miss Comby drove the wedge in deeper. Finally, the final blow came, when, one day at Cambridge, he received a letter from his father ordering him to marry Miss Comby in what was a union blessed by the spirit world. He refused, and soon letters came. Sir Constantine who had been convinced by Miss Comby that Claudius had been engaged secretly to another woman, and had trifled with Miss Comby's affections. Then, after Claudius told the old man off in a letter, and received one back, that he was to receive a check for one quarter's allowance, and that Sir Constantine never wanted to see him again. He was completely out of the old man's will, and Miss Comby accomplished her purpose; she was now the sole heir to the Sandell estate.

As Claudius stops his story, and the group goes to the library, Dr. Lamb and his wife talk for a moment and we learn why they exchanged glances. Miss Comby is Hilda Lamb's sister! Mrs. Lamb determines to write to Sir Constantine about Miss Comby, while her husband taunts her gently, and then she leaves him alone. Alone by the fireplace in the living before going into the library, Dr. Lamb chuckles to himself and smiles weirdly. He has something in mind, and says to himself, "I can finish my business with him to-night, tomorrow at the latest. After I have got him—once got him—bound by his word, after that there may be as much reconciliation as you please, my dear Hilda, because it will not make any difference." He is now certain that Hilda is in love with Claudius, and intends to use this factor plus the facts that Claudius is honorable, and that he has been kind to him. "We really progress," he says.

Later, Claudius tells more. After splitting with his father, he decided to go into writing, due to some friends he knew in Cambridge. But the novel he wrote was refused by publishers, and he had hocked the last thing of value that he had. By now he was almost in the position he was in when Dr. Lamb found him, and his own pride aided it. He could have fallen upon old friends, or a Lady Verrider, a rich woman of society, and they would have helped him. But no, his pride wouldn't let him. And so, his small amount of fifty pounds soon dwindled, until he only had enough money which could be spent on either food or lodging. The necessity of the moment prevailed, and he bought a loaf of bread, which he ate as he walked along. But his condition was too much, and he sat down at the spot where Dr. Lamb found him, until a strange drowsiness overcame him, and he was out like a light from weakness.

Time passes, and soon, Dr. Lamb and Claudius are talking about Dr. Lamb's work, which is now scientific research into mankind, which includes disection of animals. But Dr. Lamb has now decided to pull off his strange plan. Mrs. Lamb has been watching, and suspects what he has on his mind, but is powerless to do anything about it.

That night, after expounding on his idea at length, which is to help speed and improve evolution, and make mankind master of his own destiny, both physically and psychologically, Dr. Lamb springs his proposition. Knowing of the debt of gratitude that Claudius feeld toward him, and the young man's sense of honor, Dr. Lamb proposes literally, the almost selling of Claudius's soul, as repayment. He needed a human subject after animals, and found two other men, but couldn't trust them. But Claudius he can trust. This is how Claudius can repay his kindness. The terms are this: He will give Claudius an eight day holiday, an "octave" of the kind that the Church gives to it's saints (now you can guess what the "octave" in the title means), in addition to a sum of eight thousand pounds. On the eight day, at the end, Claudius will return to Lamb's home. By then the doctor will have liquidated all his holdings in England, and they will go to the country. Claudius will become the property of Dr. Lamb to do with as he please in his experiments. There you have it. Claudius agrees, and Dr. Lamb warns that he will not consider any getting out of the agreement, that it rests entirely on Claudius's word of honor, which to Claudius is like a firm chain.

Claudius leaves at Mightnight on Friday, to return on Saturday, eight days hence. He is taken to the railway station, and is off to London for his octave. But Mrs. Lamb begs Claudius to try and get out of it, before he leaves, out of Dr. Lamb's sight. She has really flipped for this boy!

After Claudius leaves, Mrs. Lamb's mental condition causes her to have hysterics which Dr. Lamb stops by beating her with a buggy whip, and then ordering her upstairs. And Dr. Lamb bides his time.

In London, Claudius has remade contact with acquaintances, and Lady Verrider, who has invited him to a party. And, as you can guess, love steps in. He meets the Wycherlys, and Angela, and falls for her. Mrs. Wycherley is hoping to get Angela to marry someone of social importance. She's pushy. The two young people talk during the banquet, and soon, they are meeting. They are in love. After their latest date, in the park, Claudius finds he has a few days left, and writes to Dr. Lamb trying to find a way to get out of the agreement, but in a return letter from Dr. Lamb, his hopes are dashed. And he also learns that a mare, who was also the favorite of Mrs. Lamb, was killed, for viciousness. We can already see, that Dr. Lamb cares nothing for other people, although he professes to love his fellow man, loves only his work, and seems to have a strange desire to torment his wife. Dr. Lamb's reply was made Claudius's decision. He has to tell Angela about the strange agreement. One night, he tells her about it, but not all of it. But this is enough to upset her. But she won't tell her folks, and she has every symptom of being ill. She is afraid to contact Claudius again, and his concern for her, prompts her to visit her home. He manages to see her, and is welcomed by Angela's mother. They spend a quiet day. Claudius must leave that night for his octave is over. That night, Angela has told her parents Claudius's strange pact. Mrs. Wycherley is upset, and Mr. Wycherley, a meek, mild-mannered little guy, is determined to do what he can to stop Claudius. He visits him, and finds out that Claudius is sure that he may die. After trying unsuccessfully to convince Claudius to get out of the agreement, he decides to

take the initiative, and visits the Abraham Penny Detective Agency, and hires one of their investigators to trail Claudius to Dr. Lamb's and find out where Lamb will move. Meanwhile, Claudius and his father have become reconcilled, after Miss Combs was thrown out after Sir Constantine received an anonymous letter. You can guess who it was sent by; Mrs. Lamb.

That night, Claudius returns by train to Wimbledon Common, and then goes by coach to Dr. Lamb's home. At the house, he is greeted by Dr. Lamb. It seems something new has been added; Mrs. Lamb's mind has snapped completely. Actually, Claudius is not met first by Mrs. Lamb, who in her demented condition, tells him not to go to see Dr. Lamb. "Gabriel's in there", she warns. "Not the angel Gabriel, but the devil Gabriel. He's getting ready to kill you, sharpening knives. Everynight I can hear sharpen knives, though he does not want me to hear. Always sharpening. It goes like this—brrrrrr-brrrrrr." It's a pretty gruesome imitation of a grindsome. But then a nurse appears and at the sight of her, Mrs. Lamb has a fit of kicking and screaming, as the nurse carries her to her room. After this touching little scene, Dr. Lamb appears, and explains to Claudius that Mrs. Lamb is plagued by the torment of believing that she hears her baby crawling around in her room, even though it is dead. She is hopelessly insane. The two men get down to business, as Claudius, tactfullly checks to see if Dr. Lamb will let out of the agreement. But Dr. Lamb has found in him the perfect subject, and explains what will happen. After they move into the country, he will operate on Claudius. Although he will be under anesthetic, Claudius will wake up for about fifty seconds, be in pain, and then go out for a second time, and never wake up. He will die, a martyr to Dr. Lamb's experiments. Dr. Lamb is also insane in his own way, for not only will he have a human guiena pig, but he will also be committing murder in a probable revenge for his wife falling for Claudius. But Dr. Lamb, cheerfully tells Claudius to settle up his affairs in the next few days before they move. That night, Claudius goes to sleep, and misses the horrifying events of the evening.

Mrs. Lamb, now dangerous, has been put in her. Dr. Lamb has told the nurse to take the night off and get some sleep since she has had to watch the deranged women for two nights without rest. Dr. Lamb will do it tonight, because the room is near the lab, and he can hear any sound from it. But Dr. Lamb has been working nights ceaselessly also, and so he starts to dose off, and does. Mrs. Lamb has gotten out of her room, and sneaks cunningly down the hall to the lab, and sees the doctor sleeping, and then opens the drawer where the surgical knifes are kept. She begins her hideous imitation of a grindstone as she picks a knife up, as Dr. Lamb begins to awaken, and as "Dr. Lamb began to move his head, she flung herself upon him, and thrust and hacked and pulled."

Claudius is awakened by someone hammering on his bedroom door, and finds the room filled with smoke, and voices yelling "Fire, fire." He escapes the blazing house, and hears people outside tell of a madwoman who was dragged back from repeated attemps to go back into the blazing inferno. But his suspicions are confirmed when he hears a policeman say, "I saw her myself, and there was blood on her hands and face. It'll be Broadmoor" (the insane asylum of it's day). With that bit of news, Claudius knows what happened. As we leave, Claudius orders a carriage to Ericston Square, where Angela and her family live. Thus goes the tale of the Octave of Claudius Sandell.

Not much of a plot for a Lon Chaney film. However, Goldwyn paid $2,000.00 for the story rights and the screenplay version was assigned to J.G. Hawks. Hawks was the perfect man for the job. He seems to have been a serious writer who paid close attention to current news headlines and could incorporate them into his then-current project. Keep in mind, while reading the sections of the script directing Claudius' reactions and motivations to his situation when he sees the wealthy patronizing a local night club, that the Bolshevik revolution had just taken place in Russia.

Hawks had been fascinated by the sensational, almost scandalous papers being published in Europe and the United States by a Dr. Serge Voronoff. Dr. Voronoff claimed that by surgically grafting the glands of animals into other animals and sometimes human subjects, he could correct birth defects and prolong life.

These excerpts are from the April, 1920 issue of Scientific American Monthly: an article written by May Tevis called "HUMAN GRAFTING, The Brilliant and Successful Experiments of Dr. Serge Voronoff":

"Out of the monstrous evil of the war is it (sic) comforting to reflect that at least some good has come in an enormous stimulus given to medical science and surgical skill. Nowhere is this more marked that in the marvels of human grafting, which have performed actual miracles for countless wounded, crippled and disfigured men.

A well-known European surgeon, Dr. S. Voronoff, formerly a pupil under the famous Dr. Alex Carrell of the Rockefeller Institute, and himself the author of the valuable work, "a Treatise Upon Human Grafting," contributes to a late number of La Revue (Paris), an article upon this vitally important subject. In 1913 I was able to give a convincing demonstration of the truth of my theory by exhibiting at the International Congress of Medicine a lamb which has been conceived by a ewe, whose reproductive organs have been transplanted from her sister sheep after her own had been removed."

Having thus proved his theory by animal experimentation, Dr. Voronoff proceeded to undertake human grafting. Shortly before the outbreak of the war he reported to the Academy of Medicine in Paris a remarkable case wherein he improved the condition of a child who was idiotic because of the atrophy of the thyroid gland by grafting upon it a thyroid gland of a monkey. Still more remarkable is the case where he grafted a portion of a thyroid gland of a mother upon her son with remarkable results. The latter, a youth of twenty, resembled a child of ten in appearance, having been born without a thyroid gland. He remained small, fat with a neck sunken in his shoulders and the cretinoid face which recalls an animal. This boy, dull and apathetic, able to pronounce only a few intelligible words, and hiding in corners like a frightened animal, presented a painful contrast to his brother only a year older, but a big vigorous fellow fighting bravely at the front. The operation was highly successful and at the end of a year an absolute marvelous change was found in the afflicted youth. He had begun to grow, gaining sixteen centimeters in the year, his head was no longer sunken between his shoulders. The bloated look had disappeared; best of all his mind had been awakened. He was able to talk distinctly and he is at present earning his living by working in a bakery."

The article then goes into details of skin grafting and graphic details of war operations that restored limbs and scar removals. He ends the article with:

"Bones will be grafted on to reconstruct jaws and eye sockets, and to make legs and arms serviceable; jaws will be grafted on to replace those which have been destroyed; skin will be grafted on to remove the disfiguration due to scars; tendons will be grafted to remedy contractions of the fingers; nerves will be grafted to cure paralysis on the limbs, and teeth and hair will be grafted to re-establish the harmony and beauty of the organism. It will be quite feasible to borrow bones from dead men to mend those of the living, since the death of the individual through the stopping of the heart and the cessation of the circulation of blood does not cause the immediate cessation of life in all the organs. Humanity in its ascending evolution acquired new creative forces, and we shall become more and more the masters of our own bodies."

A man ahead of his time? Maybe, but in 1920 most people thought he was a lunatic and couldn't take him serious. The combining of Barry Pain's character, Dr. Lamb, with the real life Dr. Voronoff was to give Chaney the basis of his character.

specified shall, however, be subject to the terms and conditions of this agreemtn.

TENTH: This agreement shall bind the parties hereto, and their heirs, executors, legal representatives, successors and assigns.

IN WITNESS WHEREOF, the AUTHOR has hereunto set his hand and seal, and the CORPORATION has caused this agreement to be executed by a properly designated officer, and its official seal to be affixed thereto, the day and year first above written.

In presence of

GOLDWYN PICTURES CORPORATION
BY

Last page of the writer's contract—also signed by Samuel Goldwyn.

ALICE KAUSER
DRAMATISTS' AGENT ❧ PLAYS
1402 BROADWAY, NEW YORK
CABLE ADDRESS: LINADORE, NEW YORK

MOTION PICTURE DEPARTMENT
R. L. GIFFEN
MANAGER

October 28, 1921

Mr. Gabriel L. Hess,
Goldwyn Pictures Corp.,
469 5th Avenue,
New York City.

Dear Gabe:-

Herewith three copies of contract for "THE OCTAVE OF CLAUDIUS", duly signed by Mr. Barry Pain and received from London this morning.

You are holding one copy which I signed as agent and this you will please return to me, together with one of the present copies, after it has been signed by Mr. Goldwyn, or whoever in this instance will do the honors.

Sincerely,

LEFT: *Senile, feeble and decrepit: A twelve-year-old ram before being grafted.* RIGHT: *The same old ram almost six years later, with his mate and third lamb*

Can Old Age Be Deferred?

An Interview with Dr. Serge Voronoff, the Famous Authority on the Possibilities of Gland Transplantation

HERE is a "Fountain of Eternal Youth." It lies in your glands. Through its life-giving flow old age may be postponed, if not avoided. Even death, save by accident, may become unknown. if the daring experiments of Dr. Serge Voronoff, brilliant French surgeon, continue to produce results such as have startled the world.

"My first determination to undertake this work," said Dr. Voronoff, "came from the realization of the dominant role of the endocrine glands in the human organism. Up to forty or fifty years ago physicians admitted that the energy which caused our organs to perform their various functions was an inherent one. They took it more or less for granted, however, that the secret of this energy never would be found—that the inherent energy that made the heart beat, for example, was a God-given motive power not to be tampered with."

Brain Not the Controlling Center of Life

These theories, Dr. Voronoff pointed out, were first shattered by the remarkable experiments and discoveries of Claude Bernard on the endocrinal value of the liver. Close on the heels of Bernard's research came the work of Brown-Sequard. For the first time the brain was found to be not the controlling center of life, but a peculiar combination of. gray flesh, capable of producing thought only when properly controlled by the chemical action of the liquid from the thyroid glands.

With improper functioning of this gland a young man became mentally old and feeble, useless to himself and to society. His physical condition, too, formerly strong and healthy, became weak and unsteady. Infants with congenital atrophy of the thyroid always show, both mentally and physically, the effects of such a condition, being puny in every way. Animals deprived of their thyroid glands soon after birth, according to experiments, are altogether outgrown by others of the same age within a period of eight to ten months.

On the other hand, it has been proved by experiment that a hypertrophy, or over-development, of the thyroid gland will cause such an over-excitation of the mental processes as to amount in some cases almost to insanity. Hypertrophy of other glands, such as the pituitary glands, which are situated at the base of the brain and which control the growth of the living cells, will cause occasional freak giants.

"Even the smallest glands sometimes play the largest roles," observed Dr. Voronoff. "Take away from an animal the four little para-thyroids, located beside the thyroid, and the effect is absolutely disastrous. The nervous system undergoes a terrific over-excitation, the muscles contract violently, and the subject dies in violent convulsions within a short time. The suprarenal glands, if removed, would cause death by a sort of strange lethargy, known as Addison's disease.

"But," continued the great surgeon, "it is, after all, the functions of the reproductive gland that have taken my entire attention since 1910.

"This remarkable and all important center, which has been regarded until recently as merely a mechanism for the prolongation of the life of the race on earth, plays one of the greatest and most important parts in our everyday normal physical existence."

Dr. Voronoff pointed to the many examples of men and animals deprived of these glands. Their

DR. SERGE VORONOFF
Well-known exponent of rejuvenation by gland-grafting

flesh becomes soft and flabby. Their mental energy wanes; their whole bodies sag and drop out of proper form; their blood is thin and poor. From latest observations it is entirely probable, says the doctor, that the work of the other glands may be distinctly affected and reduced by the loss of the secretions of these central glands.

As one remarkable example of the opposite effects caused by the over-development of the gland in question, Doctor Voronoff cited the case of a boy nine years old who was suffering from a hypertrophy of one genital gland. He had a full black beard and mustache, remarkably hairy arms and legs and the stockily settled appearance of a mature, though small man. When the extra growth was removed, the boy lost, within six months, all of his beard, except his mustache, as well as the heavy hair on his arms and legs. His mental condition, which previously had been far above normal for his age, dropped back nearly to that of other boys of his own years.

Results Not Immediate

"Here," said Doctor Voronoff, "was a remarkable demonstration that the glands play a part of primary importance in our mental and physical development. This does not mean that it is always the amount of glandular tissue present which can be called a hypertrophy, but it is evident from present knowledge of the construction of the glandular system that an over-growth makes itself felt upon the entire human system."

First attempts to change the conditions of men from this source were made, according to Dr. Voronoff, in 1869, when Brown-Sequard endeavored to inject into the glandular tissue of a man secretions from the glands of an animal. The experiment was successful at first, but the effects did not last for any length of time.

The experiment proved one thing, however—which is known also from other investigations—that the glandular secretions of both man and animal are chemically identical. The reactions observed are brought about, not through the energy of the fluid, but rather through the quality of the organism upon which the fluid acts. The thyroid gland of a man grafted into a sheep could not produce the mental activity of the man in the lower animal, nor would the thyroid gland of the sheep produce in the man that stupidity for which sheep are noted.

"The idea of the grafting of glands is not entirely novel, for as far back as 1767, an attempt was made by Hunter to change the glands of chickens," said Dr. Voronoff. "What is new? It is the practical realization of this grafting which is new, relatively speaking. In the past all efforts to graft glands in the higher animals and in man were failures, giving only a few weeks successful stimulation, at most, and then being reabsorbed into the dead tissue. The explanation of the failure is simple. These glands had merely been inserted under the skin or in the muscles, where they had been left to take root and grow, with no aid from the surgeons.

"In my own work I found that such a failure always followed such a method. The new glands never lasted long; they apparently expended only the slight residue of fluid which they contained, and then they gradually died. At last I realized that these grafted glands were not being properly fed by the new system into which they had been incorporated; thus it was impossible for them to produce any new fluid. It is only since 1917, that I have been able to realize a permanent effect."

The most practical manner of operation in these transfers, is to cut the gland itself into four parts, placing two of the "slices" in each of the "pockets" where in time the two will grow into one active unit. The results are not immediate, as the glands must have time to begin their normal functioning. In two or three months, he says, men who have had these grafts have come to him and reported that their first noticeable effect is that of a greatly improved memory. They are mentally stimulated; their color begins to come back into their cheeks; their eyes brighten; their muscles become elastic.

Startling Results With Animals

Another and more recent field of this research, which rivals in interest the grafting of glands in human beings, is the work Dr. Voronoff has been doing with animals. His chief activity along these lines has been the improvement of sheep, although he has operated upon horses, cattle, goats, pigs and other domestic stock. His experiments, which have been carefully recorded, reveal startling results.

In Algeria, for example, the French government owns a flock of about 3,000 sheep, whose wool, partly because of the warmer climate, but still more because of the elision of the germinal gland, was becoming less abundant. With this flock Dr. Voronoff grafted an extra gland into each of the young rams. The result has been an extra heavy coat of wool, an average increase of one pound per sheep being attained.

An interesting example of one of the doctor's earlier efforts to increase wool or hair production

F. M. Delano
AN OUTSTANDING EXAMPLE
The grafted kid on the right is twice as large as his ungrafted twin

is provided by the case of a young goat which was grafted at the age of six weeks. Another kid of the same age was left normal. The grafted animal increased in size far more rapidly than did the normal one until he was nearly twice the size of the latter. His hair, instead of remaining the fairly short length of the common goat, grew to nearly the length of the hair of an angora.

The doctor pointed to the photographs of three lambs upon which he had worked. The youngest, aged three months, he grafted with an extra gland. At the time the animal weighed about thirty-six pounds. The second animal, four months old and weighing forty-six pounds, he left normal, as a "witness." From the third lamb, five months old and weighing sixty pounds, he removed the germinal glands. Ten months later the youngest and smallest lamb had gained thirty-six pounds, the normal, twenty-six pounds and the third, only about nine pounds. When the animals were clipped it was found that the wool coat of the grafted animal weighed almost two and three-quarter pounds more than that of the third animal and was just a few grams short of the weight of the second animal, which was a month older than he. The length of the wool of the grafted animal, was one centimeter longer than that of the "witness."

One of Dr. Voronoff's most striking experiments was with an old ram. Rams generally live to the age of twelve or fourteen years. With considerable difficulty the doctor found a twelve-year-old ram so feeble that he could neither hold up his head nor walk without staggering.

"I grafted into this animal," said the scientist, "a gland taken from a ram two years old. In three months' time that old wreck of a beast became aggressive, heavy set, active and even splendid to look at. And eight months after this graft a lamb was borne by his mate.

"To avoid any imputation of 'autosuggestion' I removed the gland from this animal again. All my operations on animals, by the way, are done under a powerful, local anaesthetic so that they suffer no pain. Within three months this animal again became the old feeble tottering ram we had found at first. Again I provided him with an extra gland and again he regained his strength, vigor and aggressiveness. Today, six years after this animal by all known laws of sheep raising should have been dead, he remains alive, energetic and useful. He continues to produce a splendid coat of wool each year, in spite of the fact that he has passed by one-quarter the normal length of a ram's life.

"Consider the economic significance of gland grafting with sheep alone. Already we have gone far enough with our experiments to demonstrate that by continual grafting for several generations it is entirely possible to establish a superior race of animals with a heavier coat of wool, and so bring about a very great reduction in the price of woolen clothing." Bearing in mind the fact that in France, Algeria, Morocco, America, Canada, Argentina, Australia, and elsewhere, upwards of 150,000,000 of sheep are raised annually, the economic possibilities are indeed vast.

Shall We Live to be 125?

Just what may be done with the human race Dr. Voronoff is not yet prepared to predict with assurance. But his researches hint at startling developments. He has grafted many men; some of them are showing signs of reabsorption, but most of them still are in the prime of health and vigor. Diseases to which old and weakened frames succumb easily are shaken off by these young-old men invigorated by new glands. The various organs function as they should. The entire system is rejuvenated and strengthened.

"We must wait," says Dr. Voronoff. "If we consider one year of a ram's life equivalent to six years of a man's, then we may estimate that by grafting we can add thirty or forty years to a human life. We cannot tell yet just what results we will achieve, for we have been grafting glands successfully only for the last five years. When we have lengthened a man's age to ninety perhaps we will have done something. When a man will have lived to be one hundred and ten we probably will have accomplished something interesting. When he will have lived to be one hundred and twenty-five, we will at last have found the path toward the abolition of old age."

F. M. Delano

Hawks took it even farther and made his young hero a veteran of World War One to give attention to the millions of American soldiers who had returned home to reshape their lives. The hero not only becomes a soldier but as in the novel a writer.

But there was still not enough of a challenge for a Chaney story, so Hawks adapted an idea that had worked well for Chaney in previous films: that of playing two characters. Not only would he be the mad doctor but he would also become one of the doctor's failures in his experiments, of prolonging life by grafting ape gland and mixing monkey blood with human.

The completed script gave Chaney something with which to work. It isn't too obvious that he based his mad doctor character's appearance on the real Dr. Voronoff. The plot follows the novel with bits' of H.G. Well's Island of Dr. Moreau added for good cheer.

(Note to the film student—To see the exact order that the film was shot, follow the order on pages two and three of the script. EXAMPLE: The first 15 scenes of the film were Interiors and took place in the Tenement room. Scene 303 was shot along with scenes 41 listed through 303 in the library.

Here now is the script as it was presented to the cast in 1922. While all the other elements of movie making at Goldwyn began.

JACQUELINE LOGAN IN
GOLDWYN PICTURES

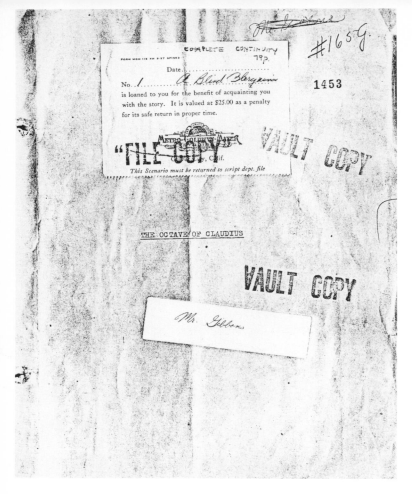

THE OCTAVE OF CLAUDIUS
CAST OF CHARACTERS

Claudius Sandell
Mrs. Sandell-his mother
Doctor Anthony Lamb
Mrs. Lamb
Angela
Angela's mother
Hunchback
Bessie-Dr. Lamb's Cook
Nurses
Beautifully gowned women
Well dressed men-Cafe scene
Ragged old man-tramp-
newsboy and bedraggled old woman
Taxi drivers
Italian flower vendor
Several surgeons
Professional spectators

It is earnestly requested by Mr. Lehr, that no changes of any nature be made in this scenario, either by the elimination of scenes, or the addition of scenes, or the changing of any of the action as described, or titles, without first consulting the editorial department.

THE OCTAVE OF CLAUDIUS
by Barry Pain
Screen Adaptation
by J.G. Hawks

SCENE 1   INT. TENEMENT ROOM
TITLE:
A CHAIN OF ADVERSE CIRCUMSTANCES HAD BROUGHT CLAUDIUS SANDELL TO DESTITUTE POVERTY.
FADE IN on a CLOSE UP on Claudius, a slight, dark student type of young fellow of about twenty-five. His face is haggard and drawn as he looks downward. It expresses apprehension and an intense anxiety. He is closely framed for the Close up kneeling by his mother's bed looking down while the doctor is examining his mother. (This out of scene of the close up)

SCENE 2   INT. TENEMENT ROOM
TITLE:
HIS MOTHER WASTED AWAY WITH A BAFFLING SICKNESS.
Shoot over the footboard of the bed and get Claudius and the doctor as they bend over the mother, a gentle faced, grey haired lady. The Doctor is the general practitioner type about forty-five. He is bending close studying Mrs. Sandell's face, her wrist in his hand. Just enough to plant the three and cut to:

SCENE 3   INT. TENEMENT ROOM
FULL SHOT of room—a cheap tenement bedroom but neat and clean. Gas bracket lit on wall. The Doctor concluding his examination—he rises after putting Mrs. Sandell's arm back under the bed clothing. She lies in a coma. Claudius gets to his feet—his eyes going from his mother to the doctor's face. The doctor frowns over the case as he replaces some bottles in his case and closes it. Claudius watches him, his concern making his face more drawn and haggard. He goes over to him around the footboard of the bed.

SCENE 4   INT. TENEMENT ROOM
Doctor in close up. Claudius coming into the picture to him. The doctor is still frowning over the case. Claudius puts his hand on his arm and asks anxiously, "Is she very bad, doctor?" What can we do to make her well again?" The doctor says shortly:
INSERT TITLE:
      "SHE MUST HAVE DELICACIES AND TONIC NOURISHMENT."
      Claudius' face grows more haggard and grim. The doctor continues:
INSERT TITLE:
      "TAKE HER TO A BRACING CLIMATE, THE SEA SHORE OR MOUNTAINS."
Back to them as Claudius' eyes turn to his mother and come back to the doctor. His face is tragic with his hopelessness. The doctor says matter of factly—"I can do nothing for her. She needs change and more oxygen." He looks at Claudius kindly and shakes his head and continues;
INSERT TITLE:
      "IT IS THE ONLY HOPE I CAN GIVE YOU.
      IF SHE STAYS HERE—"
He concludes the title with an expressive shrug. He takes his hat and case, ready to go. Claudius takes some coins from his pocket and pays him. It takes most all he has. The doctor thanks him and turns to leave the close up. Claudius goes with him.

SCENE 5   INT. TENEMENT ROOM
The doctor crossing to the door. Claudius opens it and the doctor nods and exits. Claudius closes the door and turns and stands looking at his mother.

SCENE 6   INT. TENEMENT ROOM
CLOSE UP on Claudius at the door. His face shows the hopelessness of complying with the doctor's orders. His eyes are off scene on his mother. His hand draws out the few remaining coins. His eyes drop to them—his jaw clenches and he rams them back fiercely in his pocket. From a side pocket he draws out a crumpled paper and straightens it out.
INSERT OF SLIP READING—
      The enclosed manuscript is not suitable for our purposes, but we thank you for submitting it and we shall be glad to consider more of your work.
            Very truly yours,
            The Editor
            Burton Publications.
A bitter smile just touches his lips and he tears the rejection slip across and stuffs it back into his pocket. He walks forward from the close up.

SCENE 7   INT. TENEMENT ROOM
CLOSE UP on bed with mother. Claudius coming into the close up from the door. He kneels and looks at his mother who lies quiet and still. His face is bitter and full of rebellion at their situation. As he looks, this changes to a tender smile of love for her and he puts his hand for a moment softly on her hair. This changes again to the bitter, haggard revolt at their situation.

SCENE 8   INT. TENEMENT ROOM
CLOSE UP on Claudius alone, shooting across the bed and framing him closely as he kneels beside the bed.
INSERT TITLE:
      THOUGHTS THAT GO BACK TO BETTER YEARS.
Back to him, and introspective look forming on his face.
FACE HIM OUT and LAP DISSOLVE INTO:

SCENE 9   A GARDEN
A garden backed by a handsome house. In the foreground, the mother, smiling and well, is knitting or embroidering in an easy chair under a shade tree. Claudius is sitting on the grass at her feet reading from a manuscript. A leather portfolio lies near. He is finishing the last page and looks up for her approbation. She smiles down at him and commends his work. He puts the manuscript in the portfolio and rises and looks off at the house next door and then back to his mother. He points and tells her, "I'm going to read it to Angela." His mother nods smiling. He runs down the background line diverging off toward the garden next door. As he leaves the picture in the background—out:

SCENE 10   ARBOR IN ANOTHER GARDEN
Angela seated in arbor with her mother. She starts as though she hears a call and looks from the arbor entrance toward the house next door. Into the background of the picture Claudius appears and comes running down foreground to her. She smiles and dimples and makes room for him on the seat beside her. He tells her of his story drawing it from the portfolio. She puts her book away and asks him to read it to her. He starts to read and she listens as he enthusiastically commences. LAP DISSOLVE BACK TO:

SCENE 11   INT. TENEMENT ROOM

CLOSE UP on Claudius as his face softens with his thoughts and a slight smile comes at his memories. This passes and his face grows bitter and hard again with his thoughts. FADE HIM OUT and LAP DISSOLVE IN:

SCENE 12   ARBOR IN ANOTHER GARDEN

Angela in different dress standing in entrance of arbor and watching the house across the garden. Her face is grave and sad. Claudius comes from the other garden down to her. He is dressed for traveling and carries a bag. He puts this down and comes down to the arbor to her. He takes off his cap and is evidently under great restraint as he tries to say a conventional good bye. He takes her hands and then his restraint gives away and he takes her in his arms. He holds her close for a moment—then draws back and looks into her eyes and says softly:
INSERT TITLE:

> "I'M GOING TO WORK NIGHT AND DAY AT MY WRITING AND SOME DAY I'LL COME BACK FOR YOU—A SUCCESS."

He presses her close again and then abruptly draws back and leaves the arbor, going back and picking up his bag and going toward the other garden. As he goes FADE OUT and LAP DISSOLVE BACK TO:

SCENE 13   INT. TENEMENT ROOM

Set up for this lap back to take in both Claudius and his mother and allow for his rising to his feet. As the scene comes up clear from the DISSOLVE, pick up Claudius, his face bitter with his memories. He rises to his feet:
INSERT TITLE:

> "BACK AGAIN AFTER A YEAR OF FAILURE TO WITHIN AN HOUR'S RIDE OF THEIR FORMER WORLD TO WHICH PRIDE FORBIDS AN APPEAL."

It is evident that he is coming to some determined resolution.

SCENE 14   INT. TENEMENT ROOM

A CLOSE UP on Claudius with a determined resolve forming in his face. His eyes burn and his jaws clench with desperate resolve. Just a FLASH.

SCENE 15   INT. TENEMENT ROOM

FULL SHOT as Claudius turns and looks down at his mother. The resolve strengthens on his face. He places the small stand nearer to the bed—to the reach of her hand. He bends and kisses her gently without rousing her. He turns down the gas bracket on half so that the room goes dim. He goes to the door and opens it letting in a light effect from the hall. As he goes out and closes the door behind him cutting down the set light again—FADE OUT.

SCENE 16   ENTRANCE TO CAFE. NIGHT
IRIS IN ON TITLE:
THE CREST—THE JADED, BLASE AND THOUGHTLESS.

FADE IN the front of a brightly lighted, elaborate cafe. Tip in the curb with a six foot uniformed auto attendant. A limousine rolls up and two men in fur overcoats over evening dress step out and assist two beautifully gowned women to the sidewalk. They are bored and languid in movement. They proceed into the cafe. Two couples emerge from the cafe and pass them coming out. They greet each other for a moment while the attendant is summoning their car by number. The limousine leaves the curb during this.

SCENE 17   NEAR ENTRANCE TO CAFE. NIGHT.
TITLE: THE SUBMERGED—THE WEARY, HOPELESS AND DESPERATE.

A group of three. A bent, ragged old man, a tramp and a shivering little newsboy with some papers. A bedraggled woman of the streets joins them. They are all looking off at the cafe entrance and the beautifully dressed people. After the woman has joined the group bring on Claudius. He halts unconscious of the group he has joined and stares with the others.

SCENE 18   ENTRANCE TO CAFE. NIGHT

The emerging couples coming to the edge of the curb. Their limousine driving up. The attendant opens the door and the men help their women in, the last man fumbles in his vest pocket and takes out a bill and hands it to the attendant, who touches his cap.

SCENE 19   NEAR ENTRANCE TO CAFE NIGHT

Back to a closeup on Claudius staring at the people of the cafe entrance. His face is a protest against it all. The careless money spenders and their luxury and the desperate condition at his own home.
INSERT TITLE:

> WHAT RIGHT HAD THESE WEARY PLEASURE LOVER TO FLAUNT THEIR LUXURY IN THE FACE OF DESPERATION?

Back to him, his face a mask of desperate protest. His jaw clenches with purpose again.

SCENE 20   NEAR ENTRANCE TO CAFE. NIGHT

Full shot of group of unfortunates as Claudius plunges away out of the picture leaving the others eyes still glued on the entrance. FADE OUT.

SCENE 21   PARK PATH. NIGHT. FADE IN.

A path through a park passing under trees. Patches of light and shadow leading down to foreground. Doctor Lamb in fur overcoat coming down foreground, a prosperous, assured figure. As he reaches foreground and is coming well into camera cut on him.

SCENE 22   INTERSECTION ON TWO PARK PATHS. NIGHT

Claudius, coming in from the side path and turning and coming down camera. When well in the lens he halts and stands for a moment staring by the camera, his eyes lighting with desperate resolve.

SCENE 23   PARK PATH NIGHT

Another flash of Doctor Lamb coming into camera. He halts close foreground to light a cigar. The flame lights his face and makes a big jewel on his finger flash for a moment. He comes on.

SCENE 24   INTERSECTION OF PARK PATHS. NIGHT

Back to Claudius as he furtively steps into a shadow behind a tree, his face watching the oncoming Doctor. The Doctor passes the camera coming into the scene and goes on down the background line. A moment later Claudius slips out from behind the tree and goes stealthily after him.

SCENE 25   PARK PATH NIGHT.

Reverse camera and get the Doctor coming into camera with Claudius slipping from tree to tree behind him following closely. When the Doctor is in close foreground Claudius tiptoes up swiftly and throws himself on his back trying to bear him to the gound. The Doctor staggers a moment, quickly recovers himself, throws his stick to one side and reaches up with both hands quickly getting his hands in the wrestlers grip over Claudius' head and fastening them locked about his neck. He brings them powerfully forward, stooping at the same time and shoots Claudius over his head. Cut.

SCENE 26   PARK PATH. NIGHT

Shooting down a bit as Claudius falls into the picture with the Doctor pouncing on him a second later. The Doctor fastens his fingers in Claudius' throat choking him violently. As he raises Claudius' head up by his grasp he sees his face clearly for the first time. Claudius, with white face and desperate glaring eyes staring up at him. The Doctor's hands stop and he stares at Claudius' face.

SCENE 27   PARK PATH. NIGHT.

Get the Doctor's face alone in this close up, angry and confused, staring down at Claudius. His face changes, a surprise comes and he bends a bit looking close—then suppressed excitement comes.

SCENE 28   PARK PATH. NIGHT

Set up to get the business. The Doctor looking closely at Claudius. Claudius head falls back limply as he swoons. INSERT TITLE:

THE TOLL OF DAYS OF MALNUTRITION AND SLEEPLESS NIGHTS.

The Doctor's face comes up camera. He is thinking deeply. He comes to a resolve.

SCENE 29   PARK PATH. NIGHT.

Full shot as the Doctor secures his hat and stick and stoops and raises Claudius from the path in his arms. He carries him off out of the picture.

SCENE 30   PARK DRIVE.

Lighted foreground. Headlights of taxi coming up from background. The Doctor carries Claudius into lighted foreground. He puts him down and steps out into driveway with uplifted stick hailing the approaching taxi. The headlights of the taxi swerve in toward him and stop. The driver stares then gets down from his seat to help the Doctor.

SCENE 31   PARK DRIVE—NIGHT.

CLOSE UP on side of taxi. The doctor makes a quick explanation to the taxi driver then bids him help him. The driver opens the door and the doctor enters the taxi and the driver lifts Claudius in to him. The doctor takes Claudius and places him on taxi seat. The driver closes the door and goes toward seat—CUT:

SCENE 32   PARK DRIVE—NIGHT

FULL SHOT—The taxi comes on and passes the camera—FADE OUT.

SCENE 33   EXT. DOCTOR'S HOUSE & GROUNDS—NIGHT
OPEN IRIS ON TITLE. . . .

DOCTOR ANTHONY LAMB, THE EMINENT SURGEON HAD HIS HOME ON THE OUTSKIRTS OF THE CITY.

Lighted drive entrance—grounds showing trees, through which the lighted upper windows of an old mansion show. The taxi turns into the drive and goes swiftly up it to the house entrance.

SCENE 34   HOUSE ENTRANCE & DRIVEWAY—NIGHT

The taxi halting before the entrance steps. The driver swings down and opens the door—the doctor emerges—he pays the driver and dismisses him though the driver offers to help the doctor with Claudius. The driver and doctor lift Claudius from the taxi. The doctor carries Claudius up the steps. The driver stands watching him.

SCENE 35   HOUSE ENTRANCE—NIGHT

The doctor carrying Claudius coming into scene—he frees one hand and rings and stands waiting with Claudius in his arms.

SCENE 36   HOUSE ENTRANCE & DRIVEWAY—NIGHT

Back to the taxi driver staring up at the entrance—his face frowning and troubled. His eyes go to a bronze plate at the foot of the entrance steps on a pillar—it reads:

ANTHONY LAMB
SURGEON

The taxi driver shrugs—reassured—and turns back and climbs to the driver's seat of his car—CUT:

SCENE 37   HOUSE ENTRANCE—NIGHT

The doctor standing with Claudius in his arms waiting—stands a little bit back from the door. The entrance door starts to open—CUT:

TITLE: INTRODUCING HUNCHBACK

SCENE 38   ENTRANCE DOOR—NIGHT

Cheat the doctor and Claudius out of this shot and show the door opening wider and a face coming out of the aperture when it is about eighteen inches wide—a face that peers out cautiously searching the entrance way outside. The hair short and coarse grows down alomost into the eyes, the upper lip is long and protuberant, the eyes small and secretive and the head sunk down with hardly any neck into powerful shoulders. Afer you have planted him he swings the door back further—as it moves—CUT:

SCENE 39   ENTRANCE HALL—SHOOTING TOWARD ENTRANCE DOOR

High ceilinged old fashioned paneled entrance hall—one light burning over the entrance door and one in globe held by bronze figure on newel post. The general effect is dim and gloomy but opulent. As you will have toreversecamera many times in this entrance hall—best make the entrance door a wild piece with a black backing for night and a park backing for day shots. PICK UP THE HUNCHBACK SWINGING THE DOOR BACK. He has his back to the camera and goes into deep shadow as he does so and the door opens wide.(double) His figure seen in this shot shows his shoulders bowed in a powerful sweep, his arms hanging with pendulous hands, his head sunk deep into his shoulders. As he swings into the shadow the doctor enters carrying Claudius. He passes under the entrance light and through the light of the newel post and passes the camera.

SCENE 40   ENTRANCE HALL

Reverse camera getting the library entrance—with heavy hangings—the hall running back to the entrance to another room, and the staircase. Pick the doctor up as he carries Claudius down the background line to the library entrance and enters it.

SCENE 41   LIBRARY

Big, high ceilinged room, the room of a scientist. Book cases lining walls with heavy ponderous columns of medical and surgical works. A massive table covered with books, manuscript and papers. A microscope prominent. Hooded light over table. Deep toned room, rich and old fashioned. A half light only as the doctor enters and walks quickly over, deposits Claudius in a big leather armchair and snaps on a light which lights Claudius and himself and the back of the room but which leaves foreground and middle distance in shadow. Quick tempo for this business. When the light comes up, CUT.

Note: The hangings of the arch to hall mask a heavy door which shows on this interior. It is open in this shot so that the doctor comes through the hangings.

SCENE 42   ENTRANCE HALL

Shot toward the entrance door. The hunchback is just turning from closing it, his face comes back toward the library entrance and he listens intently:

INSERT TITLE:
"A PATIENT, A SPECIAL CHARGE WHO HAS REMAINED A SERVANT IN THE SURGEON'S HOUSEHOLD UNDER HIS OBSERVATION.

Then comes softly down camera, his head forward, his arms swinging low and his legs showing a bit bowed giving just a suggestion of a big powerful ape. These is nothing ferocious in his face—in fact is is kindly and affectionate when in repose. It now shows a fear—an apprehension. Cautiously and softly he goes toward the library entrance passing the camera—a big foreground figure. If you can set up back far enough to tip in the library entrance—do so. This will be the real introduction of the hunchback, full figure and if you can give him the walk down the long hall in the dim light, pausing to listen as he comes it will plant him accurately. If you use this set up out when he reaches the library entrance.

SCENE 43   LIBRARY

CLOSE UP on Lamb and Claudius. Claudius still unconscious in the big chair with the doctor kneeling—looking keenly into his face and studying him intently.

SCENE 44   LIBRARY ENTRANCE

Shoot a close up on library entrance hangings with a spotlighting. The hanging is slowly drawn aside and the face of the hunchback appears peering into the room. His eyes fix themselves on the Doctor and Claudius (off scene) with a dread and apprehension.

SCENE 45   LIBRARY

Cutting in chair and library table. the doctor rises and comes down to table and makes swift preparations. He takes a slide from the microscope—takes a small case from the library drawer and opens it and takes a small bulb syringe from it—he goes back quickly toward Claudius. His face is full of suppressed excitement, smiling a bit and eager.

SCENE 46   LIBRARY ENTRANCE

CLOSE UP on library entrance hangings. The hunchback watching. Over his face comes a dawning look of horror and recognition as tho he sees a familiar act that makes him fear and instills aversion and repulsion in him.

SCENE 47   LIBRARY

CLOSE UP on Claudius and doctor at chair. The doctor kneeling has bared the arm of the unconscious boy and is taking a drop of blood from a vein in his forearm. He rises—CUT.

SCENE 48   LIBRARY

Shot with table foreground tipping in the chair with Claudius in background. The doctor coming eagerly to table with syringe. He squeezes out the blood on the microscope slide and waves it a few times to dry it and inserts it in the microscope. As he bends over it—CUT;

SCENE 49   LIBRARY

CLOSE UP on entrance hangings. The look of horror strengthening on the hunchback's face.

SCENE 50   LIBRARY
CLOSE UP on Lamb as he raises his face from bending over the microscope. Exultation and suppressed excitement as he smiles triumphantly.

SCENE 51   LIBRARY
CLOSE UP on entrance hangings as the hunchback slowly withdraws his face—the horror still on it.

SCENE 52   ENTRANCE HALL
Shooting toward the library entrance tipping in the foot of the stairs. Pick up the hunchback turning from the library entrance and coming softly and cat like down to the foot of the stairs. He stops and listens as he comes, the horror still on his face. As he starts to mount the stairs—CUT;

SCENE 53   DOCTOR'S GROUNDS
Shiny Ford Roadster is driven into the grounds by Bessie, the cook (comedy servant type)—and she is an inexperienced driver, and sits comically upright at the wheel. Dog on seat beside her. She intends to drive past front entrance around to side of house, but mishandles something and the car stops with a jerk. (Note: It should be a comic, impudent type of dog.)
TITLE: (if necessary)
THE NEW COOK, RETURNING FROM HER EVENING OUT.

SCENE 54   DOCTOR'S GROUNDS
SEMI CLOSE UP of Bessie and dog in front seat, as she determinedly tries to start car again. Does several wrong things before she gets action. Talks to the dog while trying to start car. As it starts with a jerk—CUT:

SCENE 55   DOCTOR'S GROUNDS
Same shot as Scene 53—Bessie driving roadster—disappears around side of house.

SCENE 56   LIBRARY
FULL SHOT—the doctor at a cabinet, takes out a bottle of liquid and wets his handkerchief with it—he goes over to Claudius and raises his drooping head and bathes his temple and holds the aromatic liquid to his nostrils.

SCENE 57   LIBRARY
CLOSE UP ON their chair as Claudius stirs and his eyes open weakly—the doctor continues to bathe his temples.

SCENE 58   HEAD OF STAIRCASE
This is the upper hallway and should match the entrance hall in deep tones and richness. It is dim except where an overhead light throws a lighting on the head of the staircase and railing. Pick up the hunchback coming to the staircase followed by Mrs. Lamb. She is a delicate lady of about thirty-five, slightly grey and with traces of great former beauty. The hunchback goes a couple of steps down and stands listening and peering. Mrs. Lamb just in rear of him looking down fearfully.
INSERT TITLE:

THE SURGEON'S WIFE, EVER DREADING THE CONSEQUENCE OF OPPOSING HER HUSBAND'S WILL.

Back to them as the hunchback takes a tablet from his pocket and writes a word on it and gives it to her—INSERT TITLE:
"THE SERVANT WAS DUMB WITH HEARING UNUSUALLY ACUTE.

She takes it and reads it in the light from above—INSET OF TABLET WITH:
ANOTHER.
Scrawled upon it. Back to scene as Mrs. Lamb stares at him with silent question. He nods solemnly—the consternation grows on her face and she clutches his shoulder. He pats her hand gloomily and they stand listening for sounds from below with a rapt, intent horror.

SCENE 59   LIBRARY
The doctor has drawn another chair up facing Claudius who, though weak, has recovered his senses. The doctor leaning forward watching him keenly asks—INSERT TITLE:
"YOU ARE NOT A THUG OR A THIEF. WHY DID YOU ATTACK ME?."

Back to them. The doctor nods and presses Claudius back in the chair again as he would have arisen to go. He says, smiling to give Claudius confidence, and not unkindly. INSERT TITLE:

"SUPPOSE YOU TELL ME ABOUT IT."

Claudius stares at the doctor who smiles back at him—the boy starts disconnectedly to tell the doctor his great trouble.

SCENE 60   HEAD OF STAIRCASE
Back to the hunchback and Mrs. Lamb at the head of the staircase. Mrs. Lamb gets a desperate courage and her lips set themselves and she takes a step downward as though to go down to the library. The hunchback stops her in terror. He shakes his head violently and writes on his tablet and hands it to her. An insert of the tablet with the word:
WAIT.
scrawled on it—back to scene as Mrs. Lamb stops and they both resume their listening attitude.

SCENE 61   LIBRARY
A FLASH of Claudius telling his story with the doctor listening attentively.

SCENE 62   LIBRARY
CLOSE UP on the doctor as he listens, his eyes show that the story is favorable to his planning, his mouth smiles a bit and his eyes gleam as he turns aside a bit so that Claudius does not observe it.

SCENE 63   HEAD OF STAIRCASE
Set up for this business. Shoot up the stairs. Back to Mrs. Lamb and the hunchback. They are looking down and listening as formerly. Mrs. Lamb again gets courage to descend, the hunchback protests by shaking his head but she goes by him and goes down half way where she halts again—her courage failing her. The hunchback has come down step by step with her.

SCENE 64   LIBRARY
Claudius finishing his story—the doctor makes a memorandum during his story of his mother's address—he ends with "I awoke here"—the doctor considers him a moment and rises—he stands before him and says musingly:
INSERT TITLE:
    "I WONDER JUST HOW FAR YOU'D GO FOR YOUR
    MOTHER?"
Claudius looks up at him and gets weakly to his feet—he says with an access of determination:
INSERT TITLE:
    "I'D DO ANYTHING — ANYTHING TO SAVE HER.
    SHE'S ALL I HAVE IN THE WORLD NOW."
Back to them as the doctor's face lights up and a smile comes to his face. He nods and presses Claudius back into his chair and goes down background to the cabinet and takes a graduate and bottle from it—as he measures out some of the liquid—
CUT:

SCENE 65   ENTRANCE HALL
NEAR LIBRARY DOOR. Bessie's dog runs playfully from rear of hall, sniffs at curtains, then noses his way into the library. Bessie appears from rear of hall just in time to see him disappear into library. She halts and looks much alarmed.

SCENE 66   ENTRANCE HALL
CLOSE UP on Bessie, frightened as she stands still and listens, first to the voices in the library, then to the uncanny footsteps on the front stairs. She crosses herself, then begins to reluctantly retreat by the way she came.

SCENE 67   ENTRANCE HALL
FOOT OF STAIRCASE. Mrs. Lamb and the hunchback coming down fearfully step by step to the foot of the staircase. They listen as they come.

SCENE 68
LIBRARY
The doctor presenting the graduate to Claudius. He tells him to drink it Claudius obeys. The doctor watches him with a trace of cunning.

SCENE 69
LIBRARY
CLOSE UP of the comic-looking dog belligerently barking at the doctor.

SCENE 70
LIBRARY
FULL SHOT showing Claudius leaning back in his chair, yielding to the influence of the drug. The doctor pays no atten-

tion to the still barking dog until he satisfies himself that Claudius is sleeping. Then, after rubbing his hands with the greatest satisfaction, he tries to pacify the dog, going towards it to pat it.

SCENE 71
LIBRARY
CLOSE VIEW of the doctor, approaching the dog, which backs underneath a low upholstered chair in order to avoid his touch.

SCENE 72
ENTRANCE HALL
Mrs. Lamb and the hunchback standing near the foot of the stairs their eyes on the library curtains. Mrs. Lamb gets another spasm of courage and putting aside the hunchback's remonstrance goes firmly toward the library. The hunchback stands watching, fear forming on his face.

SCENE 73   LIBRARY

Claudius falling into a deep sleep in the chair. The doctor straightens up sharply from his attentions to the dog as Mrs. Lamb enters the room. She comes down to him timidly, her eyes going from Claudius to him in appeal. She indicates the boy and says timidly, "Why is he here, Anthony? You are not going to—." He stops her sternly and coldly with upraised hand. She stops, quivering under his anger. He points silently and sternly to the doorway and she turns to go, as she does so her eyes fall on Claudius again and she stops, her eyes on him.

SCENE 74
LIBRARY
CLOSE UP of Claudius, with eyes closed, breathing heavily. Looking very young and helpless, and appealing.

SCENE 75   LIBRARY
CLOSE UP on Mrs. Lamb—her face and eyes fearful, looking at Claudius in the chair. Pity for him and renewed courage comes and she turns back to the doctor.

SCENE 76   LIBRARY
Mrs. Lamb pleading with the doctor. "You won't harm him, Anthony. Let him go. He's so young and good looking. Won't you send him away? The doctor glares at her with stony, cold fury. He points upward and says sternly,
INSET TITLE:
    "PREPARE A ROOM FOR HIM. HE'S UNDER MY
    CARE."
These words terrify her and she gasps, her hands flying to her heart. The doctor says sternly, "Go—attend to it!" she turns submissively and leaves the room turning at the curtains for a look at Claudius. The doctor waves her out. He goes to the wall and presses an electric call.

SCENE 77   ENTRANCE HALL
Mrs. Lamb coming to the foot of the staircase where the hunchback is standing. She makes a hopeless gesture pointing from the library to the upper part of the house. She motions the hunchback into the library to answer the call. He watches her as she ascends the staricase, then turns toward the library curtains.

SCENE 78   LIBRARY—DOUBLE EXPOSURE
Lamb standing at the electric call pressing it again impatiently. On the mat out Claudius asleep in the chair. The hunchback enters the mat out of the scene and stands his face toward Lamb. Lamb orders him to carry the boy upstairs and put him to bed. In the mat out the hunchback nods and goes to the chair and raises Claudius and carries him out through the entrance. Lamb's eyes follow him from the room. (I would take

my counts from action with the hunchback.) When the hunchback has made his exit the doctor goes to the table and takes out the memorandum and gets a number on his telephone.

SCENE 79   ENTRANCE HALL
The hunchback carrying Claudius through the hall and up the staircase. He looks down at the boy's face in foreground and shakes his head with forboding.

SCENE 80   LIBRARY
The doctor phoning. He is ordering an ambulance and bearers to bring Mrs. Sandell to his house. (I don't think this need be titled). He finishes and puts down the phone. He sinks into a seat and pulls the microscope toward him and studies the slide again.

SCENE 81   LIBRARY
CLOSE UP of the little dog peering out from under the chair, and cocking his head wisely at the doctor.

SCENE 82   BEDROOM
Door into upper hall and connecting door into another bedroom. This room to match in furnishings and decoration the other part of the house—somber but rich. Claudius lies on the bed partly disrobed and the hunchback is undressing him.

SCENE 83   LIBRARY
Back to the surgeon bending over the microscope. His eyes come up from it and for the first time we see something uncanny — almost demonical in his face. He bends over the microscope again.

SCENE 84   LIBRARRY
ANOTHER CLOSE UP of the little dog looking furtively at the doctor, as he (the dog) starts to come out from under the chair.

SCENE 85   BEDROOM
The hunchback pulling the covers up about Claudius. The door opens and Mrs. Lamb enters. She comes down to the bed and stands looking down at Claudius. The hunchback draws back from the bed as she bends over and smooths Claudius' hair back from his forehead. She murmurs pityingly.
INSERT TITLE:
     "YOU POOR, POOR BOY, SO YOUNG. JUST AS MY
     BOY WOULD HAVE BEEN HAD HE LIVED."
Back to them as Mrs. Lamb pities Claudius again. The hunchback is in nervous fear for her being in the room and urges her to go. His fear is communicated to her and she touches the covers quickly, arranging them for a moment as women do, then at another silent appeal from the hunchback she hurries out. He follows her.

SCENE 86   ENTRANCE HALL
CLOSE SHOT at library curtains. Bessie enters from direction of rear hall, tiptoeing with exaggerated anxiety and fear towards library curtains. Parts the curtains and peers through. Evidently sees the dog. She immediately kneels in front of parted curtains and begins to snap her fingers very softly, trying to coax the dog to come to her.

SCENE 87   LIBRARY
BIG CLOSE UP on the surgeon. He sits at the library table intently studying the microscope. His face comes up camera with an intensification of the cunning and uncanny and he says with suppressed triumph,

INSERT TITLE:
     "AT LAST! ALL THE ELEMENTS THAT I RE-
     QUIRE FOR MY SUPREME TEST."
He takes up a sheaf of manuscript and reads with satisfaction.
INSERT OF LONG HAND MANUSCRIPT:
     I am tired and my head aches. Medical scientists say it
     is death to attempt complete transfusion. Bah! the
     fools! I shall accomplish it.
Back to him—his face comes up smiling triumphantly.

SCENE 88   LIBRARY
CLOSE SHOT of the doctor's legs as the little dog makes a rush at him, and gets a mouth-hold on his ankle.

SCENE 89   LIBRARY
FULL SHOT as the doctor rises in sudden astonishment and pain, and Bessie rushes in and detaches the dog, which, held in her arms, continues to growl and snap at the doctor. As Bessie, who blames the doctor instead of the dog, shakes her fist venomously at the doctor. IRIS OUT.

SCENE 90   BEDROOM
IRIS IN ON TITLE:
     LATE MORNING.
FADE IN the bedroom with Claudius asleep in bed. The room dim as the curtains are drawn. Just enough light to plant Claudius on the bed.

SCENE 91   BEDROOM
Closeup on Claudius as his eyes open and he lies for a moment staring without consciousness—then realization comes to him and he sits up, the dazed look showing that he is trying to realize what has occured. He looks about and his eyes clear. He is weak and sick and dizzy from the chloral.

SCENE 92   BEDROOM
Full shot as he gets from the bed looking about the room dazedly. He goes unsteadily to the window and pulls the curtains and lets in the daylight. Come up full light on set. He looks about again for his clothing. There is a handsome dressing gown hanging near the bed and he goes to it and takes it, looking at it a bit stupidly. He puts it on and looks about again and then tries the knob of the connecting door. It is locked. His eyes go to the hall door and he goes over to it.

SCENE 93   BEDROOM
Closeup on hall door. As Claudius reaches it and looks for a call button. There is none there and he takes the knob of the door in his hand to open it when it swings wide and Doctor Lamb appears. Claudius sways back weakly and the doctor grasps him and leads him to the bed.

SCENE 94   BEDROOM
Mat out for double exposure. The surgeon seats Claudius on the bed. The hunchback comes through the door with a tray on which rests a small silver coffee urn, some toast, a bottle of effervescent water and a tall glass. He places it on a small stand near the bed. The surgeon dismisses him with a curt gesture. The hunchback leaves his eyes covertly on Claudius. The surgeon stands watching him with a frown until he has gone and closed the door. At this count the mat comes out and the surgeon crosses the stand and unwires the bottle and fills the tall glass and hands it to Claudius who drinks thirstily. It clears his head and he gives a gasp of relief passing his hand over his forehead and hair. The surgeon smiles.

SCENE 95 BEDROOM

Closeup on Claudius as his thoughts go to his mother. Concern and anxiety come into his face and he turns quickly toward the surgeon exclaiming, "My mother—I've left her alone."

SCENE 96 BEDROOM

Full shot as Claudius grasps the surgeon by the arms in his anxiety. He exclaims again,
INSERT TITLE:

> "MY MOTHER! I'VE LEFT HER ALONE UNCARED
> FOR ALL THIS TIME."

The surgeon smiles and shakes his head. Claudius in torment begs for his clothes. The surgeon walks to the connecting door and takes a key from his pocket and slips it in the spring lock and unlocks the door. He glances in and then bids Claudius come and look. Claudius goes toward him. Cut.

SCENE 97 BEDROOM

Set up close to the door so that you can tip in Claudius and the surgeon looking into the next room and getting for your background, the next room with Mrs. Sandell in bed tended by a trained nurse. Claudius starts to go forward but is prevented by the surgeon, who, smiling, shakes his head and firmly closes the door again. He leads Claudius back toward the bed. Cut.

SCENE 98 BEDROOM

Play these scenes without any heroics trying to get over the business naturally depending on the outbacks for the insinuation and inference. The surgeon leads Claudius back to the stand, makes him sit down and pours some black coffee for him. Claudius is naturally anxious to know about how his mother got there, but has been reassured by the sight of her in good hands. He says tremulously,
INSERT TITLE

> "I DON'T KNOW HOW TO THANK YOU. WHY
> HAVE YOU—"

The surgeon stops him with upraised hand and smile and bids him drink his coffee. This is an order given with a smile but in a manner that makes Claudius obey. He sips his coffee, his eyes anxiously on the surgeon's face. Do not tip the hall door into these shots.

SCENE 99 BEDROOM

Just a flash. CLOSEUP ON SURGEON? HIS EYES STUDYING Claudius from their corners, the busy thoughts crowding closely as he does so with just a trace of cunning planning. Cut.

SCENE 100 BEDROOM

Back to a close shot of the two as the surgeon turns and looks at Claudius, the smile leaving his face as he says gravely and a bit harshly, INSERT TITLE:

> "I HAD YOUR MOTHER BROUGHT HERE. I
> HAVE MADE A CAREFUL EXAMINATION."

He pauses and Claudius rises, his love and anxiety on his face, his hand outstretched in appeal—"What—What—?" The Surgeon concluded sternly,
INSERT TITLE:

> "YOUR MOTHER IS DYING!"

Claudius' face is struck by grief and horror. He sinks back in his chair and covers his face with his hands. The surgeon observes him keenly.

SCENE 101 BEDROOM

Closeup on surgeon. Just a flash of his face, keen and watchful, then just a trace of a cruel smile touches his lips. Cut.

SCENE 102 BEDROOM

Closeup on hall door. It swings open carefully and slowly. When the motion is planted, cut.

SCENE 103 BEDROOM

Back to the close shot on Claudius and the surgeon as the surgeon goes on, INSERT TITLE:

> AN IMMEDIATE OPERATION—A SKILLFUL, DE-
> LICATE ONE WILL SAVE HER."

Back to them as Claudius uncovers his eyes and stares wildly at the surgeon. The surgeon smiles down at him, power and surety in his face. Claudius gasps, rising and clutching the surgeon's arms.

SCENE 104 BEDROOM

Closeup on hall door. It has opened about a foot. It opens an inch or two more and the face of the hunchback appears in it, watching off scene the surgeon and Claudius.

SCENE 105 BEDROOM

Back to the close shot on the surgeon and Claudius. Claudius clutching his arm, staring into his face. The surgeon continues,

> "THAT OPERATION IS MY SPECIALTY. I HAVE
> PERFORMED IT A SCORE OF TIMES SUCCESS-
> FULLY. IT BEARS MY NAME,—THE LAMB OPER-
> ATION."

A wild hope flames in Claudius face. He says pleadingly,

> "YOU WILL PERFORM IT?—YOU WILL SAVE HER
> FOR ME?"

Back to him pleading. The Surgeon's face remains impassive as Claudius glares beseechingly at him.

SCENE 106 BEDROOM

Closeup on hall door. The hunchback watching the two, off scene. His face shows a dawning horror and understanding.

SCENE 107 BEDROOM

Back to a close shot of the two. The surgeon says with distinct stern meaning, watching Claudius hawklike as he does so,
INSERT TITLE:

> "I WILL OPERATE ON ONE CONDITION."

Claudius stares at him and then nods dumbly.

SCENE 108 BEDROOM

Just a flash of the hall door. The hunchback's face watching with suspense and horror.

SCENE 109 BEDROOM

Back to the close shot of the two as the surgeon says
INSERT TITLE:

> "I WILL SAVE YOUR MOTHER AND YOU SHALL
> HAVE THIRTY DAYS (whatever the period of time
> decided upon) OF THE FULLNESS OF LIFE WITH-
> OUT STINT OF MONEY IF—"

He pauses and Claudius begs him—"Yes—yes—go on—"

SCENE 110 BEDROOM

Just a flash of the hall door. The hunchback's face full of horror and protest.

SCENE 111 BEDROOM

Close shot of two as the surgeon says, INSERT TITLE:

> "IF YOU WILL LET ME MAKE A SURGICAL EX-
> PERIMENT ON YOU AT THE END OF THAT TIME.

Claudius' hands fall from his arm. He stares at the surgeon trying to understand, his eyes come camera a bit dazed and stricken.

SCENE 112   BEDROOM
Flash of hall door. The hunchback's face full of horrified protest. One hand comes from behind the door and is stretched out in appeal to Claudius not to agree. It is almost as though he was trying to will Claudius not to comply. His head is shaken in silent, horrified negation.

SCENE 113   BEDROOM
Back to a close shot of the two as Claudius eyes come back to the surgeon's and he falters—"An experiment—What experiment. The surgeon replies sternly and with suppressed quiet though he is hanging eagerly on Claudius' answer, INSERT TITLE:
    "THAT'S ALL I CAN TELL YOU NOW. DO YOU AGREE?"
He holds, waiting. Claudius's miserable eyes go toward the connecting door.

SCENE 114   BEDROOM
Just a flash of the hunchback as his face protests wildly and his outstretched hand pleads with Claudius not to agree.

SCENE 115   BEDROOM
Back to Claudius and the doctor. Claudius's eyes are coming back from the door. His jaw sets and his eyes flash and his eyes look right into the surgeon's and he says tensely, "Yes,— I agree!". The surgeon reaches into the breast of his coat and brings out a small Bible which he places on the stand without taking his eyes from Claudius. He says grimly,
INSERT TITLE:
    "DO YOU SOLEMNLY SWEAR THAT YOU WILL?"
Claudius puts his hand on the book, keeping his eyes on the doctor.

SCENE 116   BEDROOM
Very short flash of the hunchback's face in the door as he pleads silently with all the power of the horror and protest in his face and outstretched hand.

SCENE 117   BEDROOM
Back to the two looking steadily into each other's eyes as Claudius says firmly, "I solemnly swear that I will do so." They hold.

SCENE 118   BEDROOM
Closeup on hall door as the hunchback's face, full of terror and disappointment is withdrawn and the door begins to close slowly.

SCENE 119   BEDROOM
Back to the two as the surgeon steps to the connecting door and unlocks it. Claudius goes in to his mother, after standing for a moment to compose his face.

SCENE 120   SECOND BEDROOM
Pick up Claudius entering from the other room. The trained nurse is just leaving the room with some linen and Mrs. Sandel is awake and her head turns weakly as Claudius comes to her. Claudius kneels by her bed. The doctor can be seen watching from the other room.

SCENE 121   SECOND BEDROOM
Closeup on bed. Claudius, with his arms about his mother smiling into her eyes. He says softly, INSERT TITLE:
    "DOCTOR LAMB IS GOING TO SAVE YOU FROM ANY MORE PAIN, LITTLE MOTHER."

She weakly smoothes his hair back and her eyes are anxious as she says, INSERT TITLE:
    "WE ARE SO POOR, CLAUDIUS. HOW CAN YOU EVER PAY HIM?"
Back to them as she anxiously asks the question.

SCENE 122   SECOND BEDROOM
Close up on the surgeon standing in the half opened door watching and listening to them. He waits Claudius's answer with a frown.

SCENE 123   SECOND BEDROOM
Back to closeup of Claudius and his mother, as he answers, INSERT TITLE:
    "I HAVE FOUND A WAY TO PAY HIM."
He buries his face in the pillow beside hers.

SCENE 124   SECOND BEDROOM
IRIS OUT on the surgeon, smiling with the insane fire in his eyes as he softly closes the connecting door.

SCENE 125   OPERATING ROOM
IRIS IN ON TITLE:
    THE LAMB OPERATION AT THE COLLEGE OF SURGEONS.
FADE IN scene. Lamb, as surgeon operator, an anaesthetician, his assistant and two nurses with a half dozen of dignified surgeons and doctors as spectators. As you open the scene Lamb is finishing the operation. Get this business absolutely correct in detail. I would suggest sending for Doctor Conway of California Hospital who has acted before for you. (Location man note—would it be possible to take lights into a real operating room for these shots.)

SCENE 126   OPERATING ROOM
Closeup on Lamb as he raises his face from bending over Mrs. Sandell and turns camera toward the others. His face is smiling and sure. He says crisply,
INSERT TITLE:
    "GENTLEMEN, THE ARTERY WILL NOW STAND ANY BLOOD PRESSURE FOR THE REST OF HER NATURAL LIFE."
He gets the title over and bends over the patient again.

SCENE 127   OPERATING ROOM
Shoot a little group of three professional spectators. One, dignified grey type—one middle aged, spectacled, pointed beard type and one modern school surgeon with note book as they watch off scene with intent interest. The middle aged surgeon says to his senior,
INSERT TITLE:
    "MIRACLE SURGERY. THE DEVIATION OF ONE, ONE HUNDREDTH OF AN INCH WOULD HAVE MEANT DEATH."
The grey dignified surgeon nods and replies,
INSERT TITLE:
    "I PREDICT THAT HE WILL BE THE GREATEST SURGEON OF OUR TIME."
Back to them as the middle aged man replies, "In my opinion he is now."

SCENE 128   OPERATING ROOM
Tip in Lamb's head as he watches Mrs. Sandell's face. Get both their faces in this shot as he bends over watching the pulse in her temple. His face is sure and smiling.

69

SCENE 129   OPERATING ROOM
Full shot as Lamb straightens up from Mrs. Sandell. He turns to the surgeons. Here we want to get over what the praise and adulation of the profession mean to him. His assistant and the nurses close about the operating table while he receives the congratulations of the spectators. He expands under it with pride—his eyes glow. One of the nurses has taken his gloves and they shake his hand and praise his work.

SCENE 130   EXT. OPERATING ROOM
You won't need a set for this. Dress enough on both sides of the operating room door exterior so that you can place a chair or bench. On it, Claudius sits, tense and waiting, every nerve jumping as he twists a soft hat in his hands and his eyes keep going to the door and away.

SCENE 131   OPERATING ROOM
The surgeon takes leave of the surgeon spectators who go forward to the operating table to observe the patient. Lamb looks toward the door and smiles a bit and then steps toward it, Out.

SCENE 132   LIBRARY
FULL SHOT. Bessie with her dog clutches under one arm, is taking advantage of the doctor's absence to dust the library (with a feather duster) and see what she can see. She comes to his desk, notices the microscope and puts her eye to it.

SCENE 133   LIBRARY
Closeup of what Bessie sees through the lens. A lot of crawly things.

SCENE 134   LIBRARY
Closeup of Bessie's face as she draws away from the microscope in horror and ejaculates "Lord preserve us!"

SCENE 135   EXT. OPERATING ROOM.

Claudius comes quickly to his feet as the door opens and Lamb comes out. His face and eyes are a tremulous question and he puts his hand anxiously on the surgeon's arm. Lamb looks at him and at first does not reply to the boys appeal. The anguish doubles on Claudius' face and he grips the surgeon's arm with his fingers and then Lamb puts his hand over the boy's and smiles and nods. "She is safe—will live her natural span,—now." Claudius reels with the reaction and Lamb puts his arm about him quickly to prevent him from falling. IRIS OUT ON THEM.

SCENE 136   SECOND BEDROOM

IRIS IN ON TITLE:
    CONVALESCENCE

FADE IN the scene. Claudius very well dressed seated on the bed smiling down at his mother. His face is care worn as though he was under a continual mental strain, his eyes when they come from his mother's face lose their tenderness and become uneasy and anxious. The trained nurse, who should have been in the operating room scenes also is busy at a stand with some medicine. She brings it to the bedside and Claudius rises and draws back to allow her to administer it. The nurse's eyes and Claudius' eyes go to the door as though at a knock.

SCENE 137   SECOND BEDROOM
Just a FLASH CLOSE UP on Claudius' face, his eyes on the door as a dread and shrinking spring into them.

SCENE 138   SECOND BEDROOM
The nurse calling, "Come in". The door swings open and the hunchback comes in. He comes down to Claudius and smiles down at Mrs. Sandell who smiles weakly in reply. He takes his tablet out and presents it to Claudius. Claudius still uneasy takes it—as he reads it flash and INSERT ON THE TABLET:
    DR. LAMB — LIBRARY.
Back to them and cut.

SCENE 139   SECOND BEDROOM
CLOSE UP on Claudius holding the tablet. The dread and disquiet forms on his face.

SCENE 140   SECOND BEDROOM
Back to scene as Claudius asks the hunchback. "Doctor Lamb wants to see me in the library?" The hunchback nods. Claudius hands him back the tablet and the hunchback leaves the room. The gloom settles on Claudius' face again and Mrs. Sandell observes it. She says anxiously—"Is anything the matter, Claud?" Claudius starts, forces himself to laugh and shakes his head. He bends and kisses her and leaves the room, Mrs. Sandells' eyes following him. She is but partially reassured by his manner.

SCENE 141   DOCTOR'S GROUNDS
Near front entrance showing the name-plate on pillar. Postman, with a bag of mail over his shoulder, is being accosted by Bessie, who is delighted to receive a letter and a small flat square post package. Postman leaves. Bessie starts to open letter and package.

SCENE 142   HEAD OF STAIRCASE
The hunchback waiting at stairhead. He is nervous and his face shows that he is struggling to do something of which he is vastly afraid. Claudius comes on, coming from the bedroom. His face is gloomy again but he musters up a smile for the hunchback. (In all his encounters with the hunchback, Claudius' manner is kindly and considerate with pity for his affliction.) As he passes the hunchback to go downstairs, the hunchback with a nervous glance around tenders him the tablet but Claudius does not observe him. He goes on down the stairs and the hunchback withdraws his hand glancing down at the tablet that his still holds. INSERT OF TABLET:
    DR. LAMB — LIBRARY
    BE ON YOUR GUARD
The extra words have been scrawled below the original message. The hunchback musters courage to follow Claudius down the stairs.

SCENE 143   DOCTOR'S GROUNDS
Bessie is all swelled up with pride as she reads the letter, which is a certificate of membership in a fake detective agency:
INSERT CLOSE UP OF LETTER:
Back as Bessie takes a tin star out of the opened package, tries it on the bosom of her dress to see how it would look. Then pins it inside her dress, puts the letter in her bosom also, and begins to ponder what she shall do first, in her capacity of detective. As she registers that she has a bright idea—CUT.

Bessie Love's scenes were cut from the final release print.

SCENE 144   ENTRANCE HALL

Mrs. Lamb coming from the back of the hall as Claudius gets to the bottom of the staircase on his way to the library. He bows and smiles at her, the gloom leaving his face as he sees her. She detains him with her hand on his arm, her scared eyes going to the library entrance. She says, "You are going to see the doctor?" He nods, still smiling. She seems about to say something then her fear overcomes this and she sighs, her eyes going again to the library entrance. Claudius smiles again at her and bows slightly and then with a tightening of his lips turns again toward the library and goes on. Mrs. Lamb's hands fly to her breast as she watches him go. The hunchback has come to the bottom of the steps during this scene and stands watching Claudius into the library. Mrs. Lamb steps to him and grasps his arm and asks in a tense whisper, "Have you warned him?" The hunchback shakes his head, showing her the tablet and with a gesture of his hands getting over his fear to do so.

SCENE 145   LIBRARY

Shoot toward entrance with Doctor Lamb at the library table foreground absorbed in some work. He is writing with concentration and does not see Claudius who has stepped in through the hangings and stands waiting for his attention. The surgeon reads what he has been writing, INSERT LONGHAND MANUSCRIPT:

It is two weeks now since I infused the ape blood into the veins of my "study". He is already becoming a type.

SCENE 146   ENTRANCE HALL

Back to the foot of the staircase with Mrs. Lamb and the hunchback—their eyes off fearfully on the library entrance. Mrs. Lamb nervously bids the hunchback with a gesture to go to the library entrance. He goes with his dread and fear of the doctor showing in his face. She goes slowly upstairs her eyes following him as he goes down the hall.

SCENE 147   LIBRARY

Doctor Lamb concentrated on his writing with Claudius standing watching him, his face gloomy and disturbed. The doctor looks up conscious at last of a presence and starts to cover his manuscript hastily with some papers, his face showing a momentary confusion. He rises, his face frowning and says a bit sternly: INSERT TITLE:

"YOU MOVE TOO QUIETLY. IT ANNOYS ME TO BE STARTLED. SPEAK OR MAKE A NOISE OF SOME KIND WHEN YOU ENTER THIS ROOM AGAIN!"

Claudius draws himself up offended at this brusque greeting. The doctor observing this changes his manner immediately. He steps around the table and puts his hands on Claudius' shoulders and smiles at him.

SCENE 148   LIBRARY

CLOSE SHOT on two as the doctor clasps his hands on the boy's shoulders and says smilingly: INSERT TITLE:

"PAY NO ATTENTION TO MY IRRITATION. IT IS A MOMENTARY MOOD THAT COMES WHEN I AM TAKEN UNAWARES."

He continues to excuse himself and Claudius unbends a bit.

SCENE 149   DOCTOR'S GROUNDS

Rather full scene, showing Bessie with a jointed rule, taking measurements of the side of the house, trying to prove the existence of a secret corridor. Very laboriously and earnestly, she works her way to foreground, where she finishes measuring and registers triumph. Puts down the rule, and takes out a note-book, wherein she starts to record her findings.

SCENE 150   DOCTOR'S GROUNDS

CLOSE UP of Bessie's pudgy fingers laboriously writing in notebook these words:

EVIDENCE OF SECRET ROOM 20 FT. LONG BY 13 FT. WIDE.

(or whatever measurements are correct.)

SCENE 151   DOCTOR'S GROUNDS
Back to Bessie as she closes up the note-book, and sits down in a heap, leaning against the wall to rest herself after her arduous efforts. Perhaps fans herself with the note-book.

SCENE 152   ENTRANCE HALL
Just a FLASH of the hunchback drawing near to the library hangings.

SCENE 153   SECOND BEDROOM
Mrs. Lamb entering the room and going to Mrs. Sandell. I want to get over that Mrs. Lamb grows to love Mrs. Sandell and Claudius just as the hunchback gets a great liking for Claudius. She goes to the bedside, speaks kindly and affectionately to Mrs. Sandell, arranges the covers and takes up a magazine and seats herself to read to her.

SCENE 154   LIBRARY
Back to the surgeon and Claudius. The surgeon has succeeded in smoothing down the affront and is smiling and talking easily to Claudius whose face is grave and unsmiling but without indignation which it held before. The surgeon says smoothly, INSERT TITLE:
        "YOU HAVE HAD A YEAR OF MISERY AND POV-
        ERTY. YOU SHALL HAVE—OF PLENTY AND HAP-
        PINESS."
Claudius looks at him astonished. The surgeon takes a bank book and check book from the table and holding them says with a smile, INSERT TITLE:
        "IF YOU HAVE HAD A WISH THAT YOU COULD
        NOT GRATIFY—IF YOU HAVE A HOPE UNFULFIL-
        LED, THIS WILL HELP YOU TO A REALIZATION
        OF THEM."
He puts the books in Claudius' hands and stands smiling. As Claudius opens the bank book, this look changes to a keen and cunning scrutiny of his face.

SCENE 155   LIBRARY
Just a FLASH of the surgeon as he observes Claudius.

SCENE 156   LIBRARY
CLOSE UP on Claudius as he reads the amount in the bank book. His face shows his great surprise at the generosity of the surgeon. His face comes up to the surgeon again.

SCENE 157   LIBRARY
Just a FLASH as the surgeon's look changes from the keen and burning scrutiny to a smile.

SCENE 158   LIBRARY
Back to them as Claudius protests against the amount in the bank book and the surgeon waves his protestations aside.

SCENE 159   LIBRARY
A FLASH of the library hangings with the hunchback's face peering IN AT them.

SCENE 160   LIBRARY
Back to the surgeon and Claudius as the surgeon insists that Claudius put the bank book and check book in his pocket. He is masterly and dominating and Claudius says with an access of courage, INSERT TITLE:
        "WILL YOU TELL ME WHAT YOU REQUIRE OF
        ME? WHAT IS THE NATURE OF—"
Back to them as the surgeon stops Claudius with upraised hand. The smile has left his face and it is frowning and stern as he replies, INSERT TITLE:
        "WHEN THE TIME COMES I WILL MAKE IT
        KNOWN TO YOU. IN THE MEAN TIME, ENJOY
        YOURSELF TO THE UTMOST."
Back to them with Claudius far from satisfied with this.

SCENE 161   LIBRARY
A flash of the hunchback looking from the hangings at them (off scene). His face shows his dread for Claudius.

SCENE 162   LIBRARY
The surgeon dismissing Claudius. He accompanies him part way to the door and waves him out with apparently the best of feeling. As Claudius steps to the hangings, CUT;

SCENE 163   ENTRANCE HALL
The hunchback drawing back quickly from the curtains back into the dimness of the rear of the hall or through a door out of scene. Claudius comes from the library, his face gloomy and abstracted and comes down camera and past it. After he has left the scene the hunchback comes back stealthily and stopping to listen he goes back to the library hangings.

SCENE 164   LIBRARY
Back to the surgeon. His face has gone cunning and secretive, his eyes glaring a bit and a trace of his mania showing in his face as he stands smiling and thinking deeply. He makes up his mind to some action and goes quickly to the library hangings. He swings the heavy library door, locks it and puts key in his pocket.

SCENE 165   ENTRANCE HALL
Quick flash of the hunchback cowering back in terror as the library door closes behind the hangings.

SCENE 166   LIBRARY
The surgeon turning from the closed library door. He goes swiftly to the desk and takes the microscope slides and the instrument from the case—the same tiny syringe—that he used on Claudius. Takes revolver from drawer—looks at it and puts it in his pocket. As he crosses from the table to the book cases, CUT;

SCENE 167   ENTRANCE HALL
The hunchback behind the hangings of the library entrance fitting a key in the library door and swinging it a bit so that he can look in.

SCENE 168   LIBRARY
The surgeon standing before a book case. He takes out a volume and opens a book and takes a flat key out from the volume. Reaching in through the opening he presses a spring and the whole book case swings out and uncovers a panel of the wainscoting. The surgeon inserts the key and turns it and slides the panel to one side and discloses a flight of stone steps leading downward. He replaces the key in the volume, places the volume on the shelf and enters the panel and swings the book case back again so that every thing looks as it did before. (His manner is of one who goes into danger. He makes sure of the gun again before descending.)

SCENE 169   ENTRANCE HALL
The hunchback peering in through the library door. He swings it wider and enters the library.

SCENE 170   LIBRARY
The hunchback crosses swiftly to the book case. He is nervously eager, under a great fear but, urges his courage to sustain him in an evidently carefully planned task. He takes down the volumes searching them for the flat key. He finds it after trying two or three books and goes quickly to the library table with it. His manner during this is watchful, alert and listening always for noises from behind the panel.

AN EPISODE, A SEQUENCE OF TRIAL SCENES TO BE SHOT FOR SAFETY IN CASE OUR SUSPENSE AND MYSTERY IS STRAINED BEYOND THE PSYCHOLOGICAL STORY MOMENT.

72

SCENE 171   THE OPERATING ROOM
The surgeon crossing to the corridor door and preparing to enter it. He again assures himself that his gun is ready to his hand. He swings the door and enters the cage corridor.

SCENE 172   THE CAGE CORRIDOR
The surgeon entering and going past the first cage. When he is opposite it a great hairy arm shoots out between the bars and just falls short of grasping him. The surgeon draws back and then goes on keeping well out of reach. The grasping fingers and arm is withdrawn into the cage. He goes to the second cage and presses the light switch. The shadow of the ape appears on the opposite wall behind the bars. The surgeon swings the door open and closes it quickly behind him.

SCENE 173   THE CAGE CORRIDOR
Shoot the opposite wall alone and get the surgeon in shadow as he overcomes the ape and takes a test of his blood. CUT on it.

I feel that this is a mistake but am willing to concede it for safety. I think the proper story moment to disclose what is behind the panel should be when the boy sees it for the first time. To this end I have built the mystery and suspense as to what is there.

J.G.

SCENE 174   LIBRARY
CLOSE UP on library table as the hunchback takes a tablet of wax from his pocket and takes a careful impression of the key to the panel. He works under a pressure of terror and haste and after he has pressed the key into the wax and removed it, he carefully wipes the key with his handkerchief to remove any traces of the wax. As he starts back for the book case, CUT:

SCENE 175   LIBRARY
Angle that will get the hunchback as he crosses to the bookcase and replaces the key in the volume. He hurries to the hall door and exits all under the drive of fear and dread. The minute the door has closed behind him, CUT:

SCENE 176   LIBRARY
CLOSE UP on book case as it swings open and shows the surgeon standing in the open panel. His hair is tousled, his clothing disarranged and his tie is hanging and his collar crumpled. He is breathing heavily and sweat beads his forehead. His hands are stained with a dark fluid and he holds the slides and syringe. He steps out and the panel closes as he touches a spring. He comes into the room and closes the book case behind him. As he goes to the library table—CUT:

SCENE 177   LIBRARY
CLOSE UP on library table as the surgeon breathing heavily takes a handkerchief from his pocket and wipes the stains from his hands. He daubs at a spot on his cuff and arranges his collar and tie, then he eagerly turns to the microscope slides and ejects the contents of the tiny syringe on them and waves them to dry them. He inserts one in the microscope and bends eagerly over it. His face comes up camera, contorted with an almost insane triumph—IRIS OUT.

SCENE 178   A GARDEN PATH
IRIS IN ON TITLE. . .

ANGELA, THE WISH THAT IN THE PAST COULD NOT BE GRATIFIED — HOPE UNFULFILLED."

FADE IN a beautiful backlighted shot—a garden path and pick up Angela coming down foreground. She carries a canoe paddle and is dressed for the water. She passes the camera—CUT:

SCENE 179   LAKE LANDING
Two canoes and a skiff tied up to float. If you can get a location that has a boat house and an attendant on, it will help.

Angela comes on and the attendant helps her into one of the canoes. This should be a beautiful scene pictorially with a tree and water vista, back lighted if possible. The idea is to light all the scenes with Angela and Claudius and their love to contrast with the other episodes in the surgeon's house. This will give us great value when the dramatic crisis comes. As the attendant shoves her canoe out of the picture—CUT:

SCENE 180   LAKE
Shot of her paddling away from the camera. Same beautiful lighting with artistic composition. Frame it with a tree branch on shore—water middle distance and distant shore.

SCENE 181   ARBOR IN ANOTHER GARDEN
A comfortable looking matronly woman sitting sewing in the arbor. This is the location of the LAP DISSOLVE in the early part of the story in the grounds of Angela's home. Claudius comes into the middle distance of the picture and comes down to the arbor—his face slight with expectation. He enters the arbor and Angela's mother rises with an exclamation of pleasure. Claudius, though disappointed at not finding Angela greets her and she is manifestly glad to see him. Her eyes light up, at his evident prosperity, glad that his poverty has come to an end. She smiles as his glance wanders out to the garden searching for the girl. (I don't think the mother needs an introduction).

SCENE 182   LAKE
Another beautiful shot of the girl paddling toward the shore of an island in the lake.

SCENE 183   ARBOR IN ANOTHER GARDEN
Back to Angela's mother and Claudius. She is smiling teasingly as his eyes leave her and roam about in search of the girl. She takes pity on him and tells him, "Angela has gone to the boat house, Claudius." He is a bit confused but answers her smile and thanks her and takes his leave, going with a quick walk down the background line and off picture in middle distance.

SCENE 184   LAKE AND ISLAND
A pretty shot, with a beautiful lighting as the girl beaches her canoe and gets out and pulls it up on the beach.

SCENE 185   LIBRARY
Doctor finishes writing in diary. INSERT OF THE PARAGRAPH;

I AM GETTING READY. SOON I WILL NOTE FOR THE SCIENTIFIC WORLD THE CHANGES AS MY NEW "STUDY" REVERTS TO THAT OTHER SPECIES FROM WHICH WE EVOLVED.

Closes book, puts it away, locks drawer.

SCENE 186   LAKE LANDING
Claudius runs down to the boat house and asks the attendant if Angela is on the lake. The attendant points off across the lake and Claudius whips off his coat and gives it to the boatman and enters one of the canoes and shoves off into the lake.

SCENE 187   HOUSE ENTRANCE AND DRIVEWAY
Limousine waiting. The surgeon comes from the front door and descends the steps and enters the car. It drives off.

Cupid was to shoot an arrow through Robert's heart in these cut scenes.

SCENE 188   ENTRANCE HALL

Mrs. Lamb and the hunchback watching his departure from the front door. They turn camera and Mrs. Lamb urges the hunchback toward the library. He comes on by the camera while Mrs. Lamb stands watching him, her face full of a nervous tension.

SCENE 189   LIBRARY

The hunchback enters the room and goes quickly over toward the book case.

SCENE 190   LIBRARY

Closeup on book case as the hunchback takes out the volume and presses the spring and swings the bookcase back. He takes a key from his pocket and unlocks the panel and slides it. He steps inside, the panel closes and the bookcase swings back. Cut.

SCENE 191   ENTRANCE HALL

Mrs. Lamb on guard watching the driveway from the front door.

SCENE 192   LAKE AND ISLAND

Claudius, paddling his canoe to the beach where he runs it up beside the one that Angela has left. He gets out, pulls up the canoe and after a look about goes off in the direction Angela has taken.

SCENE 193   ISLAND

A pretty spot high on the island where the background can be the lake and other shore. Angela seated looking off across the water. Bring Claudius into the background of the picture. He comes down to her and standing near her says, "Angela— Angela." She starts and turns and a flood of happiness comes to her face. Claudius kneels beside her and takes her hands, repeating her name. Her eyes come up to his, shining with surrender and he takes her in his arms.

SCENE 194   LIBRARY

Close up on the book shelves as they swing back and disclose the hunchback in the open panel. He steps out and the panel slides back into place and the book shelves swing back and latch. Then hunchback hurries by the camera.

SCENE 195   LIBRARY

Full shot as the hunchback hurries from the library into the entrance hall.

SCENE 196   ENTRANCE HALL

Mrs. Lamb watching the driveway from the front door. The hunchback hurries to her. He writes on his tablet and gives it to her to read. As she reads it with gathering horror on her face, run the INSERT OF TABLET:

EVERYTHING IS READY. IT WILL BE SOON NOW.

Back to them as Mrs. Lamb's eyes come up from the tablet and meet the hunchbacks'. Both of full of horrified concern. Mrs. Lamb says tensely—"We must think—we must plan." The hunchback nods. Cut.

SCENE 197   LAKE

Beautiful shot with beautiful lighting. Claudius kneeling and paddling the canoe. Angela seated before him. They are towing the other canoe. He leans over and kisses the girl. She leans back against him and he paddles slowly on into camera, both their faces radiant with happiness.

SCENE 198   LAKE AND SHORE

Shoot from the shore and show the canoe coming toward it. As they near it Claudius bends to kiss the girl again. He leans a bit too far to one side and the canoe careens. Angela clasps him about the neck in her alarm and the canoe upsets shooting them both into the water. He gains his feet and picks her up in his arms and stands waist deep holding her.

SCENE 199   LAKE

Closeup on them streaming with water, both laughing. He kisses her and wades toward the shore. Cut.

SCENE 200   LAKE AND SHORE

Claudius wades ashore with Angela dripping wet and carries her into close foreground. They are still laughing and he does not put her down but stands holding her. He bends and kisses her again. Fade out on them.

SCENE 201   RECEPTION ROOM
IRIS ON TITLE:

> THE RECEPTION THAT ANNOUNCES THE ENGAGEMENT.

Fade in the room decorated profusely with flowers. Angela and her mother with Claudius in attendance receiving some guests that enter from the hall.

SCENE 202   RECEPTION ROOM

Closeup on Angela and Claudius, radiantly happy as they smile and receive the good wishes and congratulations of their guests. A young girl comes into the close up and, after greeting Angela and having Claudius presented to her, exclaims, INSERT TITLE:

> "WHAT LOVELY FLOWERS AND SUCH A PROFUSION OF THEM."

Angela indicates Claudius as the sender and tells the girl with happy vivacity, INSERT TITLE:

> "CLAUDIUS SENDS THEM. HE KNOWS HOW I LOVE THEM AND FAIRLY BURIES ME UNDER THEM."

She goes on to tell the girl friend of a happening that day, "Why as we were driving this afternoon. Fade out and lap dissolve in.

SCENE 203
DRIVEWAY

A driveway with an Italian flower vender and his wheeled cart foreground. A handsome roadster with Claudius and Angela drives up and stops in the driveway. Claudius jumps out and runs to the stand and laughingly waves the Italian away and wheels the flower cart alongside the roadster and commences to stack the flowers about Angela. The Italian protests but Claudius takes a handful of money from his pocket and silences him with it.

SCENE 204   DRIVEWAY

Closeup on roadster as Claudius heaps the flowers about the laughing and protesting girl. Fade out and lap dissolve back to.

SCENE 205   RECEPTION ROOM

Angela, the girl friend and Claudius laughing over the incident. A young fellow enters the closeup and claims the girl and Claudius whispers to Angela to steal away so that they can be by themselves.

SCENE 206   RECEPTION ROOM

Set up to get the business. Claudius and Angela steal away while her mother's attention is occupied with a guest. She turns around and finds them gone.

SCENE 207   SMOKING ROOM

Angela and Claudius steal on from the other room. They make sure they are not being followed then come down camera. Some pretty light hearted business here getting over their happiness.

SCENE 208   RECEPTION ROOM

Back to the mother of Angela receiving Doctor Lamb. He bows over her hand with old fashioned courtesy, chats a moment and then comes down camera, with a nod here and there to people he knows. His eyes are searching the room. He passes the camera going toward the smoking room.

SCENE 209   SMOKING ROOM

Back to Claudius and Angela as she holds a match for his cigarette. He puts his arm about her and she says, raising her eyes to his, INSERT TITLE:

> "I DID NOT KNOW THERE WAS SUCH HAPPINESS IN THE WORLD, CLAUDIUS."

He smiles happily and clasps her in his arms.

SCENE 210   SMOKING ROOM

Set up to get this. Angela's back is toward the smoking room door. Shoot to get Claudius face as it looks over her head. His eyes are down on her face and he raises them smiling tenderly. As he looks by the camera the smile is wiped from his face and he stares a bit, anxiety and a vague alarm coming. Cut.

SCENE 211   SMOKING ROOM

Reverse camera and show the smoking room door with Doctor Lamb standing in it, his eyes on them and a keen, mocking glare in his eyes—almost a sneer of derision. When this is planted show his face change to a smile as he starts forward.

SCENE 212   SMOKING ROOM

Full scene with Doctor Lamb coming down to them. They start apart quickly and the girl is prettily confused. The surgeon nods smilingly to Claudius and takes the girl's hands and smilingly congratulates her. Claudius is unsmiling and uneasy as the Doctor says smoothly, INSERT TITLE:

> "I HAVE BEEN TAKING THE PLACE OF FATHER TO CLAUDIUS, I AM GOING TO ADOPT ONE OF THE PRIVILEGES."

Angela smiles back at him, but just a little fearfully as if she senses something unpleasant about him. The surgeon bends and kisses her. She pulls back with aversion. Claudius starts forward involuntarily, but checks himself. Angela turns to them both and says, "I'll leave you to your cigarettes. Don't be long, Claudius." She runs to the door.

SCENE 213   SMOKING ROOM

Closeup on the door and she turns and blows a kiss to them and runs off smiling back at them.

SCENE 214   SMOKING ROOM

Back to the surgeon and Claudius. The surgeon lights a cigarette, his eyes on the boy. He exhales a puff of smoke and points his cigarette in the direction Angela has gone. He says gravely and smoothly, his keen eyes never leaving Claudius' face, INSERT TITLE:

    "DO YOU THINK THIS IS WISE?"

Claudius makes an appealing gesture. He steps to the surgeon and puts his hand on his arm and says tensely and with repressed feeling, INSERT TITLE:

    "I LOVE HER AND SHE—SHE LOVES ME. WON'T
    YOU EXTEND THE TIME?"

His eyes are appealing as they watch the surgeon anxiously.

SCENE 215   SMOKING ROOM

Closeup on surgeon as the mask drops for a moment and the cold, stern scientist with the trace of his mania appears and his eye glares a bit as it fixes Claudius and his jaw sets as he says in a low, harsh voice, INSERT TITLE:

    "YOUR TIME EXPIRES THREE NIGHTS FROM
    TONIGHT AS WE AGREED. ARE YOU GOING TO
    KEEP YOUR WORD?"

He gets the last of the title over as a cold threat.

SCENE 216   SMOKING ROOM

Lets give the boy some backbone here. His face grows as cold as the surgeons'— a stern dislike for him comes and he throws his head back and looks straight into the surgeon's eyes and says curtly, INSERT TITLE:

    "I WILL KEEP MY WORD!"

Back to them as the surgeon holds the boy a moment with his eyes, then tosses his cigarette into a receiver and walks from the room. Claudius watches him exit then slowly turns camera and the reaction comes. Over his face comes a look of almost hopeless misery. FADE OUT on him.

SCENE 217   RECEPTION ROOM

IRIS IN on TITLE:

    THE ANNOUNCEMENT.

FADE IN the scene. Angela's mother, with her arms about Claudius and Angela announcing their engagement. As she finishes the guests crowd forward. A pretty scene with the girls kissing Angela and the boys and young men shaking Claudius's hand. The usual social comedian insisting on kissing Angela and declaring that life holds nothing for him now, etc. A chance here to get of note of lightness in, that the director can guage better on his set when he has the people in the scene. Claudius forces himself to respond smilingly to the good wishes of the others. Split this scene up when you come to it.

SCENE 218   RECEPTION ROOM

Just a flash of the surgeon watching with folded arms a cynical, mocking smile just touching his lips. He starts forward. Cut.

SCENE 219   RECEPTION ROOM

CLOSE UP on Angela's mother, Angela and Claudius as the surgeon presses forward by the camera and congratulates them. He is smiling and sure and the forced smile is wiped from Claudius' face as the surgeon turns to Angela again after shaking his hand and patting his shoulder. As they stand fade the scene out.

SCENE 220   GROUNDS—NIGHT

OPEN IRIS ON TITLE. . .

    WHEN THE LAST GUEST HAD GONE.

Garden path and gate. Claudius with hat and overcoat accompanied by Angela coming down camera to the gate. They reach the gate—Angela says tenderly—

INSERT TITLE:

    "WHAT HAS COME OVER YOU? YOU HAVE LOST
    ALL YOUR GAY SPIRITS."

Back to them as he reassures her with an effort. He kisses her and she runs back up the walk. He stands watching her until she is out of sight then turns camera, his face grave and stern. He comes walking by camera. IRIS OUT.

IRIS IN ON TITLE:

    A DREAD THAT DRIVE HIM BACK ON FOOT TO
    HIS BARGAIN.

SCENE 221   ENTRANCE HALL

FADE IN the scene—same lighting as in first scenes of set. The front door opens and Claudius lets himself in. He is stern faced and grave. As he passes the hall stand he notices some mail and pauses, taking it up and running through the half dozen letters.

SCENE 222   ENTRANCE HALL

CLOSE UP on him as he stops at a letter and tosses the others back to the stand. He opens it with a trace of eagerness and unfolds and reads it.

INSERT OF LETTER:

    BURTON AND LAMB
    BOOK PUBLISHERS
    820 VINE ST. PHILADELPHIA.
      Mr. Claudius Sandell
      care Doctor Anthony Lamb
      My dear Mr. Sandell:
      Enclosed find check for—covering advance royalty
    on your story, THROUGH SILVER SEAS. Please sign
    enclosed contract and return at once. Daily proof of
    opening chapters will be mailed you to proof read
    within the next month. With many wishes for your
    continued success,
      Very truly yours,
      Proctor Wymns
      Editor

(Make two inserts of this by turning page and flashing the letter in two sections.)

Back to Claudius as he finishes reading. He holds the check up and reads it and then he laughs silently and bitterly at the success that has come to him too late. INSERT TITLE:

    THE IRONY OF FATE.

He crushes the letter and contract in his hand, the laugh leaving his face and the bitter mockery of it all, turning him grim and grave. As he turns toward the staircase, CUT:

SCENE 223   ENTRANCE HALL

Shoot the back of the entrance hall and show Mrs. Lamb tremulous and scared coming forward by the camera to him.

SCENE 224   ENTRANCE HALL

Claudius with his foot on the botton step to ascend as Mrs. Lamb comes quickly to him. His face is surprised and questioning at her appearance at the late hour. She begs him softly to come into the library with her. Her eyes keep going up the staircase and she makes a motion for caution and quiet. Wonderingly he follows her as she turns toward the library.

SCENE 225   ENTRANCE HALL
Set up to get Mrs. Lamb leading the way into the library. Claudius following. Mrs. Lamb moves with extreme caution, fear in her eyes—Claudius follows wondering at the summons.

SCENE 226   LIBRARY
Room dim with one light burning over library table. The hunchback waiting at the table. Mrs. Lamb enters followed by Claudius. They go down until they form a close group by the table.

SCENE 227   DOCTOR'S GROUNDS—NIGHT
Bessie, clad in an old-fashioned high-necked nightgown with a bathrobe over it—(and the tin star pinned to the bathrobe) is placing a ladder so that she can climb it and look in the library window. Note that the pockets of her bathrobe contain, among other weapons, a rolling-pin, which need not be specially registered in this scene.

SCENE 228   LIBRARY
CLOSE UP on the three as Mrs. Lamb turns to Claudius and says tensely and determinedly,
INSERT TITLE:

"YOU ARE IN GREAT DANGER. YOU MUST LEAVE THIS HOUSE TONIGHT—NOW!"
Claudius stares at her in the utmost surprise—his eyes go from her to the hunchback who nods once decidedly. His eyes go back to Mrs. Lamb and he says, "Why?"

SCENE 229   DOCTOR'S GROUNDS—NIGHT
CLOSE UP of Bessie at the open window, listening under intense excitement, with her hand cupped to her ear. Having heard what Mrs. Lamb said to Claudius, she pulls out her notebook and pencil to write it down.

SCENE 230   ENTRANCE HALL
Shoot the staircase and get the surgeon with a velvet house coat over his evening vest coming down the staircase, a sheaf of manuscript in his hand. Try for a thrill here as he comes on menacing and grim to the camera, his face set in strange, relaxed lines.

SCENE 231   LIBRARY
Back to the close group of the three as Mrs. Lamb begs Claudius to go. She points at the hunchback saying on the verge of hysterical horror, INSERT TITLE:
"DO YOU WANT TO BECOME LIKE HIM?"
Claudius looks quickly at the hunchback.

SCENE 232   LIBRARY
CLOSE UP on the hunchback, his face with all its simian characteristics magnified in the queer lighting looking back at him with intent suggestion.

SCENE 233   LIBRARY
Back to the three and Claudius says involuntarily, "My God! No." Mrs. Lamb turns to the hunchback and points toward the bookcase and says, "Show him." The hunchback leaves the scene toward the bookcase. He takes down the volume of Darwin, swings the book-case, and inserts the duplicate key.

SCENE 234   DOCTOR'S GROUNDS—NIGHT
CLOSE UP of Bessie at window, stretching her neck in great excitement as she watches the hunchback insert the key. She ejaculates "The secret room!" Then her gaze is swiftly diverted to the other room, with an expression of horror as she sees the doctor enter. She immediately draws herself to one side of window, so that he won't catch sight of her.

SCENE 235   LIBRARY
CLOSE UP on library entrance—Doctor Lamb turns in from the hall, stares and stands glaring.

SCENE 236   LIBRARY DOUBLE EXPOSURE.
The hunchback at the panel, starting to open it. Mrs. Lamb and Claudius watching him— the surgeon glaring at them from the doorway. He says harshly "Stop!" The hunchback stands frozen, Mrs. Lamb reels, and Claudius whirls towards the entrance. The surgeon stands for a moment then comes slowly down to Mrs. Lamb and Claudius. He turns and looks sternly and coldly at the hunchback (in the mat-out) and points toward the library door with a grim command—"Get Out". The Hunchback swings the book-case back, and replaces the book, but does not withdraw the key. Sidling and with fearful eyes on his master, he crosses toward the mat-out line. Cut as he reaches it.

SCENE 237   LIBRARY
Angle getting the entrance to the library as the hunchback enters the scene and with fear and dread on his face sidles and crawls to the entrance, his face turns back on his master. As he goes out the entrance into the hall, cut.

SCENE 238   LIBRARY
The surgeon turns back to his wife and Claudius, his eyes darkly watchful, his face grim and stern. he looks intently at Claudius for a moment then smiles easily and bows and says, INSERT TITLE:

"YOUR MOTHER IS LYING AWAKE WAITING TO SAY GOOD NIGHT TO YOU, CLAUDIUS."

Claudius' eyes go to Mrs. Lamb and she makes an appealing gesture to Claudius to go. Claudius bows to her and without turning to the surgeon again, leaves the scene toward the library entrance. The other two stand the surgeon watching Claudius go and Mrs. Lamb clutching the table for support, her eyes on the floor.

SCENE 239   LIBRARY ENTRANCE
Claudius, as he reaches the entrance, turns and looks back for a moment and then goes out.

SCENE 240   LIBRARY
The surgeon turns on Mrs. Lamb and grasps her arm fiercely. She shrinks and he twist it cruelly. She gives an involuntary cry. He quickly claps his hand over her mouth. Cut.

SCENE 241   ENTRANCE HALL

Shoot up the stairs. The hunchback halfway up and Claudius mounting the stairs to him. They both start and turn their faces toward the library at the cry. Claudius, with an exclamation turns to descend the stairs and go to the library again when the hunchback with a swift noiseless rush, comes down to him and holds him firmly, shaking his head in negation and preventing from descending.

SCENE 242   DOCTOR'S GROUNDS

Close view of Bessie, keying herself up to go to Mrs. Lamb's defense. She digs into one pocket and produces a revolver. Looks at it disdainfully, puts it back. Digs into the other pocket, produces a rolling-pin. Brandishes it.

SCENE 243   ENTRANCE HALL

Closeup on hunchback and Claudius. The hunchback with all the power at his dumb command urging Claudius to go upstairs and not to return to the library.

SCENE 244   LIBRARY

Close shot on the surgeon holding Mrs. Lamb firmly with his hand over her mouth, listening for sounds from the hall.

SCENE 245   ENTRANCE HALL

Back to the hunchback and Claudius. The hunchback holding Claudius firmly and both of them listening for sounds from the library. As none come, they both relax and Claudius nods to the hunchback who releases him. Claudius goes on up out of the picture reluctantly. The hunchback's face goes back toward the library door and a mask of hate and fear settle down over it.

SCENE 246   BEDROOM

Claudius enters the room. He removes his outer coat and throws it on the bed and passes his hands wearily over his face and head. After a moment he goes to the connecting door and softly opens it and looks in. A smile comes to his face and he moves back softly and strips off his evening coat and vest and collar and tie and dons the dressing gown and goes into the other room.

SCENE 247   SECOND BEDROOM

Claudius' mother, much better, lying on bed. The nurse making stand ready for the rest of the night. Claudius entering from his room. He goes to the bed and kneels by it and takes his mother in his arms. He tells the nurse to go to bed and get some rest. She makes one or two changes in the stand, indicates a medicine to Claudius and says "GOOD night" and leaves the room by the hall door. Claudius makes his mother comfortable and draws a chair up to her bed side.

SCENE 248   LIBRARY

The surgeon, holding his wife's wrists in one powerful hand while he sternly and angrily bids her keep out of his affair and says in a tense, harsh voice, INSERT TITLE:

> "I FORBID YOU TO SPEAK ANOTHER WORD TO HIM WHILE HE IS IN THIS HOUSE. WILL YOU OBEY?"

She pleads with her eyes but he grips her wrists more cruelly and she writhes and nods her head. He casts her brutally from him so that she staggers and then points sternly to the entrance. She creeps out smothering her sobs.

SCENE 249   ENTRANCE HALL

The hunchback waiting, his face twisted in its rage and fear. As Mrs. Lamb comes from the library he hastens softly to meet her and takes her hands and leads her to the staircase, his face changing to sympathy and love for her. As they start to mount the stairs, cut.

SCENE 250   LIBRARY

Back to the surgeon putting his sheets of manuscript away in an open drawer of the table. He stops to read one sheet. INSERT OF LONG HAND MANUSCRIPT IN THE SURGEON'S HAND.

> WHAT IS LIFE WHEN IT MEANS THE DEMONSTRATION OF A GREAT SCIENTIFIC TRUTH. I HAVE THE SUBJECT AND HE IS COMMITTED TO THE EXPERIMENT.

Back to him as he puts the sheet down with an insane smile and gleam of his eyes and closes and locks the drawer. He stands for a moment thinking, a triumph forming on his face, then he abruptly leaves the closeup toward the entrance.

SCENE 251   ENTRANCE HALL

Shoot the stairs and show Mrs. Lamb and the hunchback well up the flight, their faces in the light from the upper hallway as they bend over the stair rail and listen. Fear comes to them as they hear the surgeon leave the library and they quickly draw up out of sight. Hold the scene until the surgeon comes up from below and passes through the picture going to the upper hall.

SCENE 252   LIBRARY

Full shot as Bessie, armed with the rolling-pin, puts first one leg and then the other (in striped stockings, no doubt) over the window sill, and cautiously enters. Keeping one eye fearfully on the door where the doctor has just gone out, she tiptoes to the book-case, takes out the volume of Darwin, operates the key and the panel and, after a moment's hesitation, enters the secret chamber.

SCENE 253   SECOND BEDROOM
IRIS IN ON TITLE:

> WHEN AN HOUR HAD GONE.

Claudius sitting by his mother's bed reading a book to her. He stops and looks at her and sees that she is asleep. He closes the book, smiling at her and bends and kisses her. He lowers the light, the scene goes dim and he turns toward the connecting door.

SCENE 254   LIBRARY

Close view as Bessie emerges from the secret room in a state of wildest panic, and, throwing her rolling pin to one side, makes a leap in the direction of the window.

SCENE 255   DOCTOR'S GROUNDS

Bessie leaps from window, sliding rather than climbing down the stepladder. She picks herself up, and skedaddles around to the side of house, with her bathrobe flying out behind her.

SCENE 256   BEDROOM

The hall door opening and the hunchback coming furtively in. Claudius comes from the connecting door and sees him and stares in surprise. The hunchback makes a gesture for silence and caution and Claudius.

SCENE 257   HEAD OF STAIRCASE

Scene dim-one light above—The hunchback leading Claudius from the upper hall down the staircase out of the picture. A weird lighting.

SCENE 258   DOCTOR'S GROUNDS

Large view of house and grounds, as Bessie in her Ford, comes whirling around the side of house and towards roadway. She is evidently going for help. The dog is on the seat beside her.

SCENE 259   BEDROOM DOOR

Frame closely. The door swings and Mrs. Lamb's face looks out, listening. She hears them descending, raises her face and says a silent prayer and withdraws her head. The door closes softly. A light effect here will help.

SCENE 260   ROADWAY-NIGHT

Close shot (from hood of car) of Bessie, whizzing along at a great rate and yelling "Help!" every few seconds. There are no other cars in sight. "This scene is for comedy effect, more than for suspense".

SCENE 261   LIBRARY

The hunchback and Claudius entering the dim library. The hunchback leads Claudius over to the bookcase. The panel is open. closes the connecting door and goes to him. The hunchback takes his tablet from his pocket and puts it in Claudius hand. Claudius reads it. INSERT OF TABLE. (IN WOMAN'S HAND)

        GO WITH HIM.
        MRS LAMB.

Back to them as Claudius raises his eyes from the tablet and looks enquiringly at the hunchback. The hunchback nods and though under the stress of fear and horror, he takes Claudius by the sleeve and leads him toward the door into the hall. Claudius follows. As the hunchback goes he tears the leaf from the tablet and puts it in his mouth and chews it.

SCENE 262   LIBRARY

CLOSE UP at bookcase-Claudius draws back his face questioning the hunchback. The hunchback stands for a moment listening intently then urges Claudius into the panel. After a moment Claudius' sets his jaw and enters it. The hunchback follows. The panel closes and the book case swings but fails to latch and settles back half open. CUT;

SCENE 263   OPERATING ROOM

Scene dark at first, then it flashes up light, showing Claudius and the hunchback on steps. The hunchback's fingers just leaving a light switch in the staircase wall.

Staircase leading down from above (narrow—width of panel) Door into corridor. Two operating tables side by side connected by a series of tubes and straps ready for some operation. A stand with surgical knives and instruments in white enameled trays under a glass cover. Shelves with tubes and retorts,—a recess in which surgeon's gowns, linen and gauze are ready. Pick up Claudius coming down the narrow stairs with the hunchback following. Claudius stares at the operating tables with a shudder. His eyes go all about the room—the hunchback stands with his eyes on Claudius' face. Claudius turns to him with staring eyes and the hunchback urges him toward the corridor door. Claudius draws back—CUT:

SCENE 264   BEDROOM

From here on you want to step with quick tempo and short footage scenes as the situation grows.

The hall door opening slowly and softly. Dr. Lamb's face looks into the room—it grows baleful as he sees the room empty. Try for a thrill here.

SCENE 265   OPERATING ROOM

The hunchback urging Claudius toward the corridor—they are both under a tense strain. The hunchback swings the door open and motions Claudius to enter. Claudius goes in and the hunchback follows.

SCENE 266   BEDROOM

The surgeon softly entering the bedroom—he crosses to the connecting door and opens it carefully without making any noise and looks into the mother's bedroom.

SCENE 267   SECOND BEDROOM

Tipping the surgeon into foreground looking into the room and showing through the door the second bedroom with Claudius' mother asleep and alone in the room.

SCENE 268   BEDROOM

The surgeon closing the connecting door and turning camera from it. His face is hideous in its maniacal anger,—his eyes gleam with anger and his jaw sets—he takes an automatic from his pocket and examines it—as he passes camera toward the hall door.

SCENE 269   HEAD OF STAIRCASE

The surgeon has face set with a terrible anger coming from upper hall to staircase and down.

SCENE 270   BEDROOM DOOR

It swings open again and Mrs. Lamb looks out listening with a face on which horror and anguish forms.

SCENE 271   CORRIDOR OF CAGES

A corridor which shows two cage fronts. It goes off at right angles from the operating room. So that anyone descending the stairs cannot see into it. Door into operating room opens showing brightly lighted operating room beyond. The hunchback placing Claudius before the first cage—he presses a light switch in the front of the cage and the interior springs up into bright light. Claudius glares and then staggers back with horror his hands shielding his eyes. The light from the cage throws a shadow of the bars and the inmate of the cage on the opposite corridor wall.

SCENE 272   CORRIDOR WALL

A huge misshapen creature in shadow uncoiling and rising from the cell floor. It rushes to the bars and clutches them and weaves and sways from the side to side (All in shadow projected on the opposite wall.)

SCENE 273   LIBRARY

The surgeon entering the library—his scowling eyes look all about and rest on the half opened bookcase—he starts and an insane anger flashes into his face. He goes over toward the book case and swings it full open and unlocks and slides the panel. He stands, his head in the panel—listening—CUT:

SCENE 274   CORRIDOR OF CAGES

Claudius standing with covered eyes his face full of horror. The shadow still projected on the opposite corridor wall. The hunchback snaps out the cage light and the shadow disappears. He touches Claudius who starts violently. He points to the cage and then to himself significantly. Claudius shudders and puts his arm over the hunchback's shoulders in pity. The hunchback points to the other cage and starts to lead Claudius toward it. Claudius draws back shaking his head. The hunchback nods vehemently—and Claudius allows himself to be drawn to the front of the cage. The hunchback presses another light and the interior of the cage lights up—they look within.

SCENE 275   INTERIOR SECOND CAGE
An ape rising from a pallet in the corner of the cage and coming down to the bars. CUT:

SCENE 276   LIBRARY
The surgeon standing with his head in the panel listening. He steps into the panel and turns to descend the stairs. He halts listening intently again.

SCENE 277   CORRIDOR OF CAGES
The hunchback and Claudius before the second cage. The hunchback throws his head up listening intently—his eyes going to the operating room. INSERT A FLASH CLOSE UP on him as terror comes to him as he hears a noise from the stairs into the operating room. Back to scene as he grasps Claudius—pulls him down to operating room door and thrusts him through and closes the door after him. He leans against it for a moment panting heavily in terror.

SCENE 277-A   OPERATING ROOM
Claudius wondering and exclaiming at the hunchback's action. He starts and his eyes fly to the staircase and his whole body tenses and the surgeon comes walking down the narrow staircase from the panel. The surgeon halts before he reaches the bottom and stares at Claudius. Claudius, his facinated eye on him, stares back his body half crouched, his fists involuntarily clenched.

SCENE 278   OPERATING ROOM
CLOSE UP on the surgeon his eyes on Claudius with a baleful glare under their scowling brows.

SCENE 279   OPERATING ROOM
Back to scene as the surgeon descends the remaining steps and Claudius comes form his momentary daze. He makes a passionate gesture toward the corridor door and then to the double operating table and says with excited protest,
INSERT TITLE:
    "TELL ME—TELL-ME, YOU MONSTER! AM I GOING TO BE LIKE HIM? — THAT CAGED CREATURE IN THERE THAT WAS ONCE A MAN?"
His arm goes back pointing with repugnance to the corridor door again.

SCENE 280   OPERATING ROOM
CLOSE UP on the surgeon, his face coldly, insanely furious. Then his cunning brain forces him to become the suave scientist and a smile comes placating and cunning and he replies:
INSERT TITLE:
    "HE WAS THE FIRST SACRIFICE THAT SCIENE DEMANDED IN A MARVELOUS BIOLOGIC EXPERIMENT."
Back to him his face studying Claudius keenly as he continues:
INSERT TITLE:
    "I TOOK HIM ONE HOUR FROM DEATH, A WASTED MANIAC AND GAVE HIM THE LIFE AND VIRILITY OF A POWERFUL ANIMAL."
Back to him as exaltation comes and he leans forward and says with enthusiasm and ferver,
INSERT TITLE:
    "THIS TIME I WILL REVERSE THE PROCESS OF TRANSFUSION. THE BLOOD IN YOUR VEINS SHALL FLOW IN THE APES!"
Back to him smiling triumphantly.

SCENE 281   ROAD
Another close shot of Bessie in the Ford, whizzing along and shouting "Help" and getting more and more frantic every minute. Her hat, if she had one, is now over one eye, or she is otherwise comical in appearance.

SCENE 282   OPERATING ROOM
Back to them as the full horror of it clutches Claudius. His face grows desperate and wild as the surgeon goes on with the same wild enthusiam. INSERT TITLE:
    "IT IS YOUR GREAT PRIVILEGE TO ASSIST IN THIS MAGNIFICENT WORK."
BACK TO THEM as Claudius with a great effort calms himself. He effects a nonchalance he is far from feeling as he tries to say calmly, INSERT TITLE:
    "THEN I'LL GO AND GET MY AFFAIRS IN ORDER. I HAVE ONLY THREE DAYS MORE."
He advances to the steps, the surgeon watching him with cunning eyes, drawing slightly to one side. As Claudius puts his foot on the bottom step the surgeon seizes him and hurls him back into the room.

SCENE 283   OPERATING ROOM
Another angle as the surgeon bending over with extended fingers, pointing at Claudius as he says tensely and insanely,
    "YOU HAVEN'T THREE DAYS MORE. YOU HAVE ABOUT THREE MINUTES."
Back to them as the surgeon throws himself at Claudius. Claudius strips his dressing gown off and throws it from him at the title. They struggle, the surgeon seizing Claudius by the throat with his great strength.

SCENE 284   ROAD
View from side of road, as the Ford heads straight for a tree or post.

SCENE 285   ROAD
CLOSEUP of Bessie as she gets the shock of the impact: the windshield in front of her is shattered. Bessie now gives up in despair, bursts into tears, tells the dog what a rotten detective she is, and throws away her tin star. Slumps down into the seat, beaten.

SCENE 286   CORRIDOR OF CAGES
The hunchback crouched at the operating room door, listening with wild eyes and terror.

SCENE 287   ENTRANCE HALL
Mrs. Lamb as she steals down the stairs one at a time, listening and fearful as she comes.

SCENE 288   OPERATING ROOM
The surgeon choking Claudius until he is limp. He drags him over and bends him back over the operating table and wrenches one of his arms over so that he can strap it.

SCENE 289   LIBRARY
Mrs. Lamb timidly and fearfully entering the library. She gasps in fear as she sees the open bookcase and panel.

SCENE 290   OPERATING ROOM
The surgeon straping Claudius to the operating table. He takes a surgical scissors from the tray and commences to cut the evening shirt and undershirt from Claudius.

SCENE 291   CORRIDOR OF CAGES

The hunchback crouched against the operating room door opening it an inch and looking through. He draws back with a gasp of horror.

SCENE 292   OPERATING ROOM

Claudius naked to the waist as the surgeon strips off the last shreds of his shirt. The surgeon whips off his velvet house coat and takes down the surgical gown. He transfers the automatic from the side pocket of the coat to his back trousers pocket. As he starts to don the surgical gown, Cut.

SCENE 293   CORRIDOR OF CAGES

Back to the hunchback as he nerves himself to peer through the crack of the door again, his face showing his terror and horror of what he sees.

SCENE 294   OPERATING ROOM

Seen through the narrow crack of the door as the surgeon, now in his surgical gown, rolls the tray of surgical knives close and takes off the glass cover. He places the other cones handy and lays out the tubing and connecting apparatus for the operation. He turns toward the corridor door bringing with him some straps to bind the ape.

SCENE 295   CORRIDOR OF CAGES

The hunchback, closing the door and drawing back from it and retreating down the corridor. His eyes glaring on the door.

SCENE 296   CORRIDOR OF CAGES

The door opens and the surgeon stands in it. He sees the hunchback off scene and an insane snarl lights his face and he closes the door and goes slowly forward, his hands outstretched to clutch him, the straps dangling from them.

SCENE 297   CORRIDOR OF CAGES

The hunchback, backing away, comes opposite the cage with the abnormal man in it. His eyes are wild and his face terrorized as he throws up his hand for the surgeon to stop.

SCENE 298   CORRIDOR OF CAGES

A flash of the surgeon coming steadily on, an insane angry light in his eyes and face, his hands outstretched to grasp the hunchback.

SCENE 299   CORRIDOR OF CAGES

The hunchback throws up the latch of the first cage and the horrible figure of the man ape leaps out into the corridor, glares around and crouches threateningly toward the surgeon, off scene.

SCENE 300   CORRIDOR OF CAGES

The surgeon, drawing back from the danger, terror replacing the crazed malignity in his face. His hand fumbles under his surgeon's robe and brings out the automatic. He levels it by the camera cringing back with his other hand upflung as he does so. Now the big shape of the man ape rushes by the camera at him. The surgeon fires twice and the creature reels and turns half around clutching and tearing at his breast and then turns and throws himself on the surgeon and bears him to the corridor floor and holds him for a moment gnashing his teeth over him, then sinks his teeth in the surgeon's neck. Cut. Get enough here to cut back and forth in flashes with succeeding scene.

SCENE 301   CORRIDOR OF CAGES

The hunchback crouched in the corner of the corridor drawing back and cringing away from the horror he sees (offscene by the

camera). He shudders, staring horribly, then covers his face with his forearms, pressing back farther into the corner. Get enough here for your cutter to cut back and forth in flashes with preceding scene.

SCENE 302   OPERATING ROOM

Closeup on Claudius strapped to the table. He raises his head as far as his bonds will allow and calls for help.

SCENE 303   LIBRARY

Mrs. Lamb, terror stricken at panel. One by one, scared and trembling, aroused by the shots from the hall entrance come the trained nurse, the cook, an unmistakable type, stout and wrapped in a flannel wraper, a maid, hair in curl papers in a kimona, and group about Mrs. Lamb. The trained nurse has the most composure and grasps Mrs. Lamb's arm. Mrs. Lamb nerves herself into a desperate courage and enters the panel and goes down the staircase. The trained nurse follows and the other two trembling and afraid, prepare to follow. Cut.

SCENE 304   OPERATING ROOM

Mrs. Lamb coming down toward the bottom of the stairs, her horrified eyes going from Claudius to the corridor door. She rushes over to Claudius and starts to unstrap him. The trained nurse goes to her assistance while the other two huddle, scared and trembling, their eyes going to the door also. They all stop and shrink their eyes all on the door when a great growl and shout comes from the corridor. (I'd rather get this over by inference than by cutting to the struggle again—but if this is necessary, just a quick flash of it before the movement in the operating room.

SCENE 305   OPERATING ROOM

Now set up for another angle that will give you the operating table foreground with the corridor door tipped in the background. Claudius is just slipping from the operating table, shaken and trembling from his experience. The nurse picks up the surgeon's velvet house coat and holds it while he slips into it. Their eyes all this time never leave the corridor door. When Claudius has the coat on they all tense,—still and motionless watching the door. Hold this just a moment and then the door swings open and the hunchback slips into the room, closing the door after him. He stands for a moment looking at them and then comes slowly down to them. His face has a great awe and calm on it. Their faces question him. He points to the door and shuddersand covers his face with his hands.

SCENE 306   OPERATING ROOM

Close shot on Claudius and Mrs. Lamb. Their eyes coming to each other. Claudius sets his jaw firmly and starts forward in the closeup. Cut

SCENE 307   OPERATING ROOM

The corridor door. Shoot from a high tripod and show Claudius coming into the closeup followed a moment later by Mrs. Lamb. You should just get their heads. Claudius opens the door. The camera shooting beyond them gets the corridor and there in middle distance on the corridor floor lies the surgeon, his face upturned, dead, while lying across his body is the great hairy shape of the ape man, blood from the bullet wounds in his chest making a dark pool about them. He is lying half turned, one powerful hand on the doctor's throat. He is dead also. Don't hold onto this shot. Just as soon as it is planted IRIS OUT ON SHOT.

SCENE 308   BOOK STALL

OPEN IRIS ON TITLE:
        ONE OF THE BEST SELLERS OF THE YEAR.
FADE IN THE SCENE. A book stall open to the street. A shelf of books, with same publication prominent in the shot with a placard reading: THROUGH SILVER SEAS by CLAUDIUS SANDELL. Flash an insert closeup of about four of the volumes with their superscriptions. Back to full shot with a couple of customers buying the book from the bookseller and CUT.

SCENE 309   GARDEN

The garden of the first lap dissolve. Fade in the scene and show Mrs. Sandell, now recovered, with Mrs. Lamb sitting in comfortable easy chairs with the hunchback coming from the house with shawls for them. He covers Mrs. Lamb's shoulders and then Mrs. Sandell's. They smile and speak kindly to him and he gathers up some tea things from a stand and turns toward the house with them.

SCENE 310   ARBOR—ANOTHER GARDEN

The arbor of the first lap dissolve. Pretty picture of Angela seated in the arbor with Claudius seated on the ground at her feet. She is reading and he is writing on a sheaf of manuscript. He finishes and looks up and says, "See how this sounds, Angela—I'm afraid my descriptive phrasing is too florid." She closes her book with a smile and nods. He reads a couple of lines and looks up for her approval. She says, "I think they're splendid." He smiles back at her and puts his head against her knee comfortably. She rumples his hair. IRIS OUT ON THEM.

CHANGES ON "OCTAVE OF CLAUDIUS"

SCENE 36

Change this insert from "Anthony Lamb, Surgeon," to "Anthony Lamb, M.D."

SCENE 175   BALLROOM

IRIS IN ON TITLE: THE BALL AND RECEPTION THAT ANNOUNCED THE ENGAGEMENT WAS THE MOST BRILLIANT EVENT OF THE SEASON.
FADE IN the ballroom thronged with well dressed couples and decorated profusely with flowers. Near the ballroom entrance Angela's mother receives with Claudius and Angela. A gorgeous shot that will bear out the title. Orchestra on dias and space railed off with velvet cord for dance number. (Break with closeups of orchestra, dancers, various angles on room, etc. This whole episode should be played with a great deal of sparkle and vitality.)

SCENE 176   BALLROOM

CLOSE UP on Angela and Claudius, radiantly happy as they smilingly receive their guests and receive the good will and congratulations of the arriving guests. A young girl comes into the close up and after greeting Angela and having Claudius presented to her indicates the profusion of flowers and exclaims, INSERT TITLE:
        "WHAT A PROFUSION OF LOVELY FLOWERS!"
Angela indicates Claudius as the sender and tells the girl with happy vivacity, INSERT TITLE:
        "HE KNOWS HOW I LOVE FLOWERS AND FAIRLY BURIES ME UNDER THEM."
BACK to them laughing over this. Angela goes on to tell the girl of a happening of the day before.

SCENE 176 A   BALLROOM

Frame just Angela and the girl friend for this as Angela says, INSERT TITLE:
        "WE DROVE OUT TO LAKESIDE YESTERDAY,— ——"
FADE OUT on them and LAP DISSOLVE IN

SCENE 177   DRIVEWAY

A driveway with an Italian flower vendor and his wheeled cart foreground. A handsome roadster with Claudius and Angela drives up and Claudius brings it to a stop in the driveway. He jumps out and runs to the stand and laughingly waves the Italian away and wheels the flower cart alongside the roadster and commences to stack the flowers about Angela. The Italian excitedly protests but Claudius takes a handful of money from his pocket and silences him with it.

SCENE 178   DRIVEWAY

CLOSE UP on roadster as Claudius heaps the flowers about the laughing and protesting girl. Get a pretty piece of business and FADE OUT and LAP DISSOLVE BACK TO—

SCENE 179   BALLROOM

BACK to Angela and her girl friend laughing over the incident. A young fellow enters the CLOSE UP and claims the girl and leaves with her. CUT

SCENE 179A   BALLROOM

BACK to FULL SHOT as a herald appears on the musicians dias and blows a call on a trumpet.

SCENE 179B   BALLROOM

CLOSE UP on herald.

SCENE 179C   BALLROOM

BACK to FULL SCENE to get the movement as the guests form about the open space before the musicians. The orchestra plays and dancers in costume run on and the group in the open space.

SCENE 179D   BALLROOM

Open space. The dance. I would suggest something appropriate, a well rehearsed minuet in costume—a Russian folk dance—a Hungarian dance—a Dutch number or a Spanish cachuca—not the naked numbers that the Morgan and St. Denis dancers do. Get enough to cut back and forth with.

SCENE 179E   BALLROOM

CUTBACK SHOT on group. Claudius, Angela and the mother framed by guests watching the dance.

SCENE 179F   BALLROOM
The dance ending. The herald makes another announcement as there is a movement of the applauding guests to disperse. The guests reform and the herald blows the trumpet again and eight tiny cupids run on drawing a little flower bedecked chariot. They wheel and go through a circle of the cleared space, the little coachman driving them finally up to where Claudius and Angela stand and pulling up the chariot before them.

SCENE 179G   BALLROOM
CLOSE SHOT on Claudius, Angela and the chariot. On the chariot body is a huge conch shell closed. This opens and discovers another little cupid kneeling inside with a cushion, on which a casket rests. The Cupid rises and jumps down to the ballroom floor and kneels.

SCENE 179H   BALLROOM
LONGER SHOT tipping in guests framed about the couple as Claudius puts the ring on Angela's finger and kisses her. The guests applaud and congratulate them after Angela's mother has kissed her.

SCENE 179I   BALLROOM
FULL SHOT as the Cupid mounts the chariot again and the little coachman drives his team and chariot from the scene. Claudius raises his hand to the orchestra. They play and the guests break up into a waltz.

(Now from here on play the business of the script as it starts at Scene 180, but take Claudius and Angela into the conservatory instead of the smoking room. Play it out up to Scene 190. Eliminate Scenes 191-192-193.)

SCENE 303   In this scene, better leave out the cook as well as the maid,—certainly the cook since she is at this time in a different location and probably in different clothes.

SCENE 305   Someone, preferably Mrs. Lamb, should help Claudius get off the operating-table.

SCENE 307   (NEW SCENE)
CLOSEUP Mrs. Lamb and Claudius. Mrs. Lamb is half hysterical but quiets quickly under the soothing words of Claudius. He asks her a few questions, and she answers, INSERT TITLE:
> "THIS HAS BEEN HIS OBSESSION FOR YEARS, AND I ALWAYS FEARED IT WOULD TURN OUT TRAGICALLY."

BACK TO SCENE. Claudius comforts her and tells her not to worry—that things might have been much worse. She smiles at him appreciatively for his comfort. He speaks title, INSERT TITLE:

> "YOU MUST COME WITH MY MOTHER AND WITH ME. WE ARE STARTING LIFE ALL OVER AGAIN."

BACK: to scene. Mrs. Lamb dries her tears and smiles at him as he continues speaking, INSERT TITLE:
> "YES, I'M GETTING MARRIED AT ONCE."

BACK TO SCENE, as he explains enthusiastically about Angela. Mrs. Lamb forgets her own tragedy and listens to him with great interest as we FADE OUT.

While Chaney was preparing his characterizations of Dr. Lamb and the hunchback, based on the script the rest of the cast and crew also began their work.

Director Wallace Worsley had a reputation for bringing in pictures under budget and on time. Wallace Worsley remains one of the biggest names of the silent era and yet very little is known about him or what happened to his career following the HUNCHBACK OF NOTRE DAME.

In fact very little would be known to this day had not Wallace Worsley Jr. kept a garage full of memories of his and his parent's careers. Here is a short biography based on the notes from Wallace Worsley Jr.:

Wallace Worsley was born on December 10, 1878 at his Aunt Mattie Goring's estate at Wappingers Falls, New York. The family residence was in Washington D.C. where his father, Ashley Sanders Worsley was the electrical engineer who installed the original electrical system in the United States Senate.

Wallace grew up in Washington society, where he attended high school, excelling as a sprinter on the track team as well as participating in drama activities. In 1896 he entered Brown University in Providence Rhode Island. In his sophomore year he volunteered for the Army and on July 20, 1898 he was wounded in battle at Puerto Rico during the Spanish American War.

After returning home he decided to be an actor and entered the American Academy of Dramatic Arts in New York City, where in 1901 he met his future wife, Julia Marie Taylor. After graduation they both became successful, Wallace starring as the juvenile with Willie Collier and Julia the leading lady with Richard Mansfield's traveling Shakesperean company.

They were married in 1904 and their first child Wallace Jr. was born in 1908. For three years from 1912 to 1914 they had a summer stock company in Pittsfield, Massachusetts at the Colonial Theatre. At that time there was little theatrical activity during the summer month's in New York City.

His talent was quickly recognized and he became a producer and director of vaudeville and theatrical productions for the Shuberts and Charles Frohman. In 1916 whle producing shows for the Kirke-Lashell Stock Company he was asked by Robert Brunton of the Brunton Studios (later Paramount) to come to Hollywood as a contract actor. Within a year he was made a director.

From 1917 to 1923 he was continually working and was soon one of the most successful directors in the industry. (See appendix A for titles).

It is highly possible that his relationship with Lon Chaney began early in the century for Chaney was working as a scene shifter for Mansfield's company at the same time that Mrs. Worsley was touring as his leading lady. Ten years later, from 1920 to 1923, they were to make four films together and would have undoubtably continued had he followed Thalberg to MGM as had Chaney after the completion on THE HUNCHBACK, when he received offers to direct.

But he was ill advised by his agent to take a long vacation abroad before signing anything.

By the time he returned from his vacation some of the fire had died down. He found that his agent was insisting on an excessive salary. This worked against him, for Hollywood was in the middle of it's first big shake-up. Smaller studios were failing, larger studio's were merging.

There followed a period when the quality of scripts offered were declining and finally he did go to work but, as he had feared, his pictures were less than they should have been and his image was tarnished.

When sound pictures came in, stage directors were brought from New York. Again, his agent, to whom he was still loyal, didn't know how to sell Wallace's talents—although he was just the kind of director the industry was frantically haunting the New York stage to sign.

In 1927 an Australian friend asked him to come to Australia to start a studio of his own. After a year the deal fell through when the original investors of the project failed to secure financing.

He returned to Hollywood where he had a succession of excellent projects but could not sell them. A few years later he became ill and entered compulsory retirement, a thoroughly disillusioned artist, where he died on March 7, 1944.

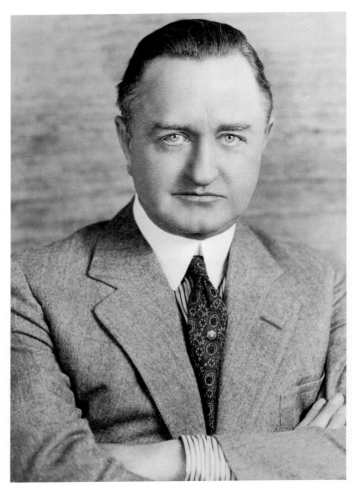

Wallace Worsley

Loud Speaker for Movie Mob Scenes

Western Electric Apparatus Plays Important Part in Direction of "The Hunchback of Notre Dame"

Right—Wallace Worsley directing crowd of 2,500 actors by "Loud Speakers" at Universal City, Cal.

IT HAS been found that the installation of loud speakers in moving picture productions enables the handling of great "mob" scenes with perfect ease, and assures perfect co-ordination of principal players and the many groups of "extras." As a time and trouble saver, the device is one of the greatest boons which has come to motion picture directors.

Its first practical use on a large scale occurred recently during the filming of "The Hunchback of Notre Dame," the screen adaptation of Victor Hugo's celebrated novel recently made at Universal City, Cal., by the Universal Pictures Corporation.

Wallace Worsley, the director, was faced with handling more than 2,500 people scattered over a ten-acre lot. Even with a large corps of assistants, rushing here and there with megaphones and bawling orders first at one group and then another, the best Worsley could have hoped to get without endless rehearsals would have been just a "mob" scene, with "extra" players milling around.

But Worsley is a detailist. His motto is "Verisimilitude," which, translated into words comprehensible to the least erudite member of his production staff, means "life-like." He determined to make his crowd scenes absolutely natural—even to the point of detailed instruction and rehearsing for each of the several thousand players.

Here is the problem which confronted him:

"The Hunchback of Notre Dame" is a story of love and adventure in Paris in the 15th Century. Much of the action takes place in the big square in front of the Cathedral of Notre Dame de

Below—A close-up of part of the amplifying apparatus set up by the Western Electric Company.

Paris. This square, the Place du Parvis, has been exactly reproduced at Universal City, just as it was in 1482 A.D. The massive cathedral has been reconstructed with remarkable fidelity, even to the hundreds of statues and decorative figures on its ornate façade.

In order to get a comprehensive camera view of this square, with its quaint houses, inns and market places, towered over by the great gothic edifice of Notre Dame, it was necessary for Worsley to put his motion picture cameras on a structure six stories high and almost a quarter of a mile away from the cathedral doors. Worsley himself had to be on this distant camera stand.

It was at this juncture that the director thought of applying "loud speakers" to the task of handling such a scattered multitude at such a distance. Nathan Levinson, specialist of the Western Electric Company, was consulted and at his recommendation the latest improved style of public speaking amplifying devices was installed.

Four "loud speaker" horns were arranged to command the vast set from various angles, so that every person within range of the camera might hear the director's instructions. One was concealed behind the figure of a portly saint on the face of the cathedral, another near the portals of the garrison building which housed the King's guards a quarter of a mile away. A third

found its place under the eves of a quaint medieval dwelling and the fourth, four squares south, threw its strident tones from beneath the pillory in the center of the Place du Parvis across the huge courtyard.

These horns, twelve inches in diameter, speaking with one voice, each magnified Worsley's words fifty times.

The initial use of the "loud speakers" was an event unique in filmdom. The scene to be photographed was the famous Festival of Fools, the Epiphany celebration in which the townspeople of 15th Century Paris made merry with parades, music, dancing, fakirs and the big event of the day—the crowning of the King of Fools—the annual king of the carnival.

The great courtyard presented a motley appearance, the vari-colored costumes of the olden times matching the brilliant flags and pennants strung between the house tops. There was a strange calm as the host of players awaited

instructions. They stood in groups idly chatting of high prices in the Hollywood meat markets or temperature of the water at nearby beach resorts, as they made final adjustments of doublets and other strange fitting garments of four centuries ago.

Then Worsley took up his manuscript and turned to the small transmitting microphone on the table before him. Without raising his voice, he began to direct.

The four monster voices of the "louder speaker" system roared out his commands and the actors jumped. Only a few of them knew of the installation. In an instant, however, they had recovered from their surprise over being thus roared at, and quickly moved to their designated places.

So perfect was the co-ordination between the director and the many players, that many thousands of dollars were saved in time alone.

One of the odd features of the "loud speaker" system is its

adaptability. During its use on subsequent days, it was connected up with a room housing a small orchestra, so that lilting carnival music could be amplified and sent to the far corners of the vast set, to inspire the players to a better emulation of the gay carnival spirit. With this music, six times more powerful than a big brass band, the festival scene took on a true holiday movement and spontaneity.

Still another unique use of the "loud speaker" system is an arrangement by which it can be used to catch and amplify radio telephone broadcasting. During the making of the picture, and during the lunch hour, the "loud speaker" operator amused the crowd by tuning in to Los Angeles and other broadcasting stations. It may interest radio "fans" to learn that the "loud speaker" system used at Universal City employs vacuum tubes for amplification, much the same as the radiotrons used in wireless telephony.

A "mob scene" from the Hunchback of Notre Dame. All these people are playing their parts under the direction of one man. Western Electric Loud Speaking apparatus made this possible.

242

243

Director Worsley (on platform wearing hat) and crew filming THE ACE OF HEARTS with Lon Chaney (center table).

He appears not to have been a total director, such as Tod Browning or Eric Von Stroheim, rather he acted more like an executive who hires the right people for the right job and entrusts them to carry their own. From my own observations this was a great way to go prematurely gray, however if you have the right personality and hadn't already gone into politics you do end up with a product filled with care and professionalism. Giving the actors and technicians free run of the talents the incentive to work even harder and become personally involved makes it more than just a job.

His notes and scripts suggest that he did extensive research and intense planning. Having every detail and angle already complete in his mind before the camera began to role, thus saving the producers hundreds of thousands of dollars staying within budget.

His imagery in THE HUNCHBACK such as the spider spinning its web while Norman Kerry tries to seduce Pasty Ruth Miller and his ability to create a suspension of disbelief in lesser budgeted films such as THE PENALTY with its simple sets and story full of holes. Worsley's skill is evident in producing a disturbing mood which keeps you riveted to the action.

And he hired the best. Cedric Gibbons was already known as the best man in Art Direction. He would continue on in this position throughout the golden years of MGM.

Norbert Brobin was assigned as Cinematographer. To best describe his working method I would like to reprint an article that he wrote around the time of A BLIND BARGAIN.

The greatest action ever developed from the greatest plot ever written by the best actors and the best director in the business would mean nothing if the cameraman was not efficient enough to record it properly, so it isn't exactly egotistical to assert that the cameraman is a very important unit in motion pictures even though the public never knows much about him. If the photography is good, people seldom notice it but if it's bad and one's eyes smart from looking at a picture intently then the cameraman gets all of the credit in the world—for being terrible.

Truthfully, one of the greatest advances made in motion pictures has been that in photography and it is not braggadocio to say that today the photographic artists of the world get more ideas from the motion picture than from any other source. Motion picture photography has become foremost of the commercial arts because of hard work and careful study on the part of a few men who have seen the possibilities for the development of screen photography and have been tireless in their efforts. Perhaps the motion picture is perfect photographically more than in any other sense yet there is much to be done in the future.

People often ask if eventually the screen lighting will not be exactly like natural lighting—people in a room, for instance, being lighted through the one window of the room. It does not seem that this condition will ever arrive. What the screen loses in voice it must make up in gesture and traveling as it must always, at a steady, fast rate, there must not be anything lost that will aid the plot and the development of it. Furthermore, it seems more important to photograph scenes advantageously from the angle of the subject, and the audience, too, rather than to be just correct in lighting. Every day we come closer to photographing scenes as they really are but never will we discard the art of photographing people and objects in the backgrounds for certain pleasing effects.

Some people have the idea that the cameraman must merely know how to turn a crank steadily, after he focuses his lenses and loads his film magazine. Such is not the case. The cameraman today must not only be a master craftsman so far as his photographic apparatus and its use are concerned but he must be a master of lighting. He must know how, by the use of reflectors, to switch the natural rays of the sun to suit his purpose, to bring light where there naturally is none, to high light and graduate the natural rays, as he wills. He must know the absolute values of various types of manufactured light. He must know how close lights may be set to an object to get an accurate photographic result and he must know how many lights he can use for photographing at a certain speed. He must know how to eliminate cross shadows when rays of light strike objects from several different sides and most of all he must muster the art of making an object appear to have three dimensions when it really has two. He must be an artist in every sense of the word. Unlike the artist he may never have to draw anything or model anything from clay or wax but he must know the value of light and shade and of composition. He must know how to mold a face or figure, how to overcome natural defects consistently and to photograph things to their decided advantage.

The cameraman cannot retouch his negative and because of the present day vast fortune invested in every production he must be accurate. An alibi wouldn't save an expensive scene incorrectly filmed. He must be positive of every move he makes before he has a chance to see how it will look. He must visualize accurately in order to photograph accurately. And he must work quickly. When a motion picture director orders a thousand people for certain scenes and all of the scenes must be completed in a certain time the cameraman must make the best of the situation and get the best results always. He can't take all the time he should, in many instances.

Some day motion pictures are not going to be made on schedule. When the era arrives the cameraman may show the world many photographic advances he hasn't been able to thus far because of the handicap of time.

NORBERT F. BRODIN
A.S.C.

The original editor was Paul Bern, who was given screen credit. However, the revised cutting continuity gives Frank Hull credit on the cover, but not on the screen. Paul Bern was known mostly as a writer-director. He was said to have been one of the most well-respected and liked men in Hollywood and would go on to become a major force at MGM until his tragic death in 1933 only a short time after marrying Jean Harlow.

The title man on this film is listed only by his last name—Mayer*.

For his cast Worsley hired Raymond McKee for the role of Claudius, Jacqueline Logan as Angela, Fontaine LaRue as Mrs. Lamb, Virginia True Boardman as Mrs. Sandell, Aggie Herring as Bessie the maid and Virginia Madsen as Angela's mother. No credit was given to the maid's little dog as mentioned throughout the script. But he didn't even make it to the first uncut print which was previewed on November 22, 1922.

Either Bern or Hull made drastic cuts in the film following two sneak previews where the picture was received with little or no positive response from the audience. The theme of the picture caused a major uproar.

Not only that a Doctor was portrayed as being mad and playing at God (Doctors had spent the last twenty years building up the position of power that they still hold today and the public was just beginning to trust in modern medicines as treatments); Not only at the thought of humans as the subject of scientific experiments—vivisection being a guaranteed topic for violent arguments as far back as the 1870's—but mostly because the public thought it favored evolution and Darwinism.

Fundamentalist church groups had begun to grow in power in the United States around the turn of the century. They had, by the 20's, published a 17-volume book of dogma and rules banning all but the strictest interpretation of the Bible.

It finally reached it's peak in the People of Tennessee vs. John Scopes trial in 1925. Scopes was nothing more than a substitute summerschool teacher. It was reported that he agreed to be the patsy in the trial so that it could be written down in the record and tested by law. The trial achieved the exact result that the instigators of the trial had wanted. The right of free speech and separation of church and state was upheld. But in 1922 there was a little more caution. The picture was withdrawn to the editing room and recut**. However, even for Goldwyn, who used his own money in his productions, it was even more risky since just the year before Chaney and Worsley's film THE NIGHT ROSE was banned in New York because of its themes of drugs, prostitution and underworld figures. Possibly because there was a certain New York politician who felt that one of the characters was a little too close for comfort. Event the name was very similar.

Some of the best scenes of the film were cut to avoid the vivisection theme. Almost all the footage of the 8 days Claudius*** had had to live it up, were cut. Claudius' book SILVER SEAS was changed to A SACRIFICE FOR SCIENCE and the acceptance of the book moved to the end so that his motives for breaking his promise to the Doctor were inspired by survival instincts and not the sudden wealth brought about by being a published author. Without these scenes Virginia Madison's part as Angela's mother was cut as was Aggie Herrings comedy relief. Without this footage the total running time of the picture was only 52 minutes so additional scenes were added to the grand ball. These scenes were hand-colored but still made the final release print only 5 reels.

As the actors and director prepared for their scenes the technicians began their work.

Paul Bern (Courtesy Marc Wanamaker-Bison Archives)

Cedric Gibbons
Art Director

*Presumably Edwin Justin Mayer

**Had Sam Goldwyn still been in production the end result would have been a good feature. He would have found a way to bring his golden touch to the feature. But Godsel, the new president, or who ever he placed in charge of production must have had little knowledge of movie making.

***Now, Robert Sandell

87

APPROVED AND ACCEPTED:

[signature]

(Cedric Gibbons)

[signature: Harry Pain]

[signature: Wallace Beery]

[signature: Wallace Worsley]

CAST AND CREW

[signature: Paul Bern]

[signature: Lon Chaney]

[signature: Raymond McKee]

GOLDWYN PICTURES CORPORATION

BY *[signature]*

[signature: Jacqueline Logan]

[signature: Norbert Brodine]

(Norbert Brodine)

[signature: Fontaine La Rue]

88

J.J. Cohn and crew prepare the bubble machine for the hand-colored scenes with dancing girls at Robert's and Angela's engagement ball.

While the filming progressed the cast posed for publicity photographs with visiting literary, political and studio personalities.

Wallace Beery and Lon Chaney clowning during a break from filming.

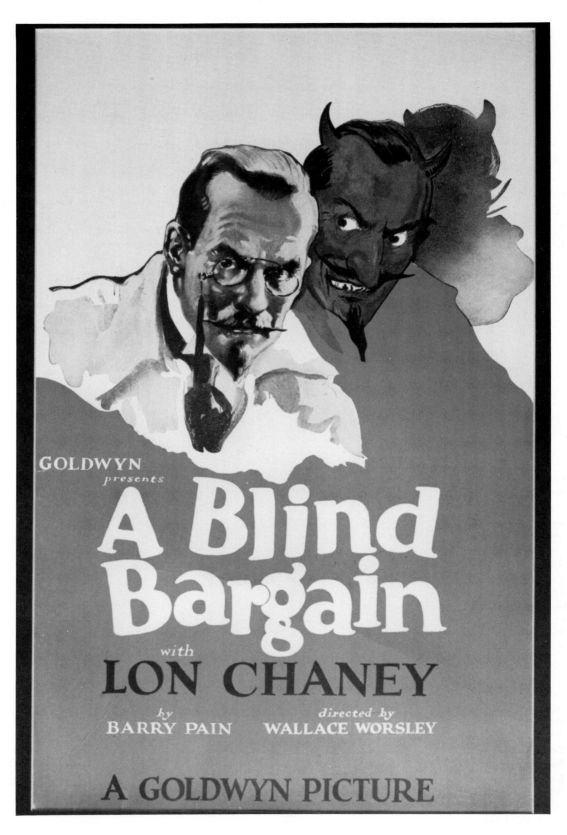

The following pages are a combination of the British and American Pressbook prepared for the publicity campaign.

STORY

ROBERT SANDELL (Raymond McKee), despondent over his ill luck as a writer, and his mother's declining health, attacks a theatregoer, Dr. Lamb, (Lon Chaney) a sinister, fanatical physician living in the suburbs of New York. Lamb takes the boy to his home, learns his story, and agrees to perform an operation on Mrs. Sandell (Virginia True Boardman) on one consideration—that Robert shall at the end of eight days, deliver himself to the doctor to do with as he will, for experimental purposes. Frantic with worry over his dying mother's condition, Robert agrees.

Mother and son take up their residence in the Lamb home, where Robert is closely watched, not only by the doctor, but by his wife, (Fontaine La Rue) and a grotesque being (Lon Chaney) whom Robert afterwards learns is the result of one of the doctor's experiments.

Dr. Lamb, anxious to keep his hold on Robert, not only gives him freely of spending money, but assists him in having his book published through Wytcherly, head of a publishing concern. Robert meets Wytcherly's daughter, Angela (Jacqueline Logan) and promptly falls in love.

In the meantime the days are slipping by to the time of the experiment. Robert has been warned by Mrs. Lamb and the hunchback that great danger threatens him. He is told these are the doctor's experiments. In agony and fear, Robert goes to the physician and tries to buy himself out of the bargain—for his book has been published, and he is now a successful writer. There is yet one day before the time limit is up, but the doctor, realizing his victim may try to escape, seizes him, and straps him to the operating table. He is rescued by Mrs. Lamb, and the doctor is himself brought to a horrible end at the hands of a man wrecked mentally by the doctor's experiments.

MUSICAL SUGGESTIONS for "A BLIND BARGAIN"

By J. BERCOVITCH

	Titles or Scenes.	Style of Music.	Music Suggested.	Composer.	Publisher.
1.	At Screening	Dramatic	"Misterioso Dramatic"	A. Morris	Fox
2.	In another port	Sad	"Sorrow Theme"	Roberts	Fox
3.	The oldest	Hurry	"Hurry"	Zamecnik	Fox
4.	After struggle	Repeat 1			
5.	See garden	Light	"Gossamer"	Bord	Hawkes
6.	After father's death	Sad	"Tears"	Zamecnik	Fox
7.	She comes in	Repeat 1			
8.	Late morning	Flowing	"Romance"	Wood	Bosworth
9.	Your mother	Dramatic	"Andante"	Berge	Hawkes
10.	He goes to mother	Sad	"Pour vous les larmes"	Chopin	Hawkes
11.	Within a week	Flowing	"Berceus"	Ambrose	Lafleur
12.	Holding mother	Flowing	"Romance"	Cauget	Lafleur
13.	Doctor locks door	Repeat 1			
14.	Knowing that	Flowing	"Love Song"	Wood	Hawkes
15.	The scientist	Repeat 1			
16.	At a fashionable	Ragtime	"Ten Little Singers"		Feldman
17.	See Hunchback	Repeat 1			
18.	At change	Rag	"The Gaby Glide"	Hirch	Enoch
19.	Doctor enters	Repeat 1			
20.	A foreboding	Sad	"The Last Goodbye"	Bennet	Hawkes
21.	Resigned to his fate	Dramatic	"Dramatic Tension"	Simon	Lafleur
22.	After Doctor Lamb	Repeat 1			
23.	See animals	Gruesome	"Terreur"	Liodire	Chester
24.	See doctor	Dramatic	"Dramatic Reproach"	Berge	Hawkes
25.	I was willing	Allegro	"Agitato"	Noyes	Fox
26.	After fight	Mysterious	"Misterioso"	Zamecnik	Fox
27.	At change	Repeat 23			
28.	When the horror	Light	"Idris"	Nevin	Lafleur

Goldwyn *presents*

A Blind Bargain

with **Lon Chaney**

and a wonderful cast

directed by **Wallace Worsley**   *by* **Barry Pain**   A **Goldwyn Picture**

The Story

Robert Sandell, a young author in desperate circumstances is overcome by a powerful stranger he seeks to rob. He wakes to consciousness in a mysterious mansion, the home of the eminent surgeon, Dr. Lamb.

Attending the doctor is a hunchback mute who observes Robert's presence with horror. Dr. Lamb offers to perform an immediate operation to save the life of Robert's invalid mother, also to give the boy unlimited resources provided that Robert deliver himself blindly for experimental purposes in humanity's behalf.

At the height of a brilliant reception which Robert is attending with his fiancee, Dr. Lamb appears. The surgeon announces that on the following morning their bargain must be fulfilled.

At dawn the hunchback mute rouses Robert and shows him as warning a mysterious underground vault in which is a complete operating room and a tunnel of cages in which are strange prisoners. Suddenly Dr. Lamb appears, enraged at the duplicity of his servant. He approaches the mute but the latter quickly releases a cage door and the surgeon meets a horrible end in the powerful arms of an ape monster.

Finally freed from the terms of his blind bargain, Robert returns to his home to learn that his writings have met with success and that Angela awaits him for the marriage ceremony.

To Exhibitors!

This is a Mystery Year! The tense thriller has taken hold of the public imagination and is drawing the real money today.

Legitimate producers who have followed the trend of the times with mystery pieces are packing them in for the thrills.

And now Goldwyn is first in the national field with a sensational, thrill-packed film subject that promises to make the kind of financial records in picture houses that "The Bat" did and is still doing in legitimate theatres.

"A Blind Bargain" is built directly for the thousands who have been waiting for this type of subject to come to the screen. It is Big in story, Big in the quality of its direction, Big in respect of cast and Big in the lavishness of its production. It is a worthy pioneer of the Mystery vogue, and will draw the crowds that have been hearing about this new style of offering.

Other mystery plays will come, but the first smashing thriller takes the cream of the business. "A Blind Bargain" should be heralded everywhere as the first Big Mystery Sensation to reach the screen.

Lon Chaney, doubling in the two principal roles creates a new record for himself. His performance is canny, baffling, absorbing. And the rest of the all-star cast: Raymond McKee, Jacqueline Logan, Fontaine LaRue, Virginia True Boardman carry the fast mystery tempo to perfection.

Get the mystery atmosphere going strong for this sensation. Let them know the feature is packed with thrills, chills, gasps, action. It's the kind of attraction they'll stand in line for. And you'll get your thrill in the final count at the box-office.

LON CHANEY in two thrilling roles

As the hunchback servant   *As the mad scientist Dr. Lamb*

Jacqueline Logan brings beauty and action to an appealing part.

Virginia True Boardman contributes a beautiful mother role.

Raymond McKee is a two-fisted hero who fights overwhelming odds—and wins.

Fontaine LaRue is the fascinating Mistress of the strange grey mansion.

Catchlines

Three human lives in the crafty hands of a mad genius of surgery!

———

A vital mystery drama, brimming with suspense and adventuring into the vast unknown.

———

Lon Chaney's greatest contribution to the screen!

———

A powerful drama in which love emerges triumphant from the toils of villainy and cruel circumstance.

———

A masterpiece of mystery in which a mad scientist learns that life forces are superior to the feeble theories of humanity.

———

Lon Chaney in two powerful roles offers the most superbly thrilling dramatic acting of his career.

———

A surgeon who laughed at God's creation is assailed by life's inscrutable forces.

———

The great love of a girl redeems a soul bartered for money.

———

An emotional hurricane in which Lon Chaney reaches the pinnacle of artistic triumph.

———

The most amazing picture of the year!

———

Wherein a young author, to save his mother's life, binds himself to an unknown fate in a mystery mansion.

———

A mad physician tears the veil of secrecy from life's profoundest secrets.

———

The gripping story of a man who forgot his God in his love for science.

———

Will the gland of the Ape bring humanity eternal Youth?

———

Has science found the way to double the span of human life?

Two Promotion Letters

(1)

(Send the following to physicians, surgeons, medical students, etc.)

Dear Doctor:

You will doubtless be interested to know of an exceptionally interesting photodrama built around the fascinating subject of renewed youth through the agency of the Steinach gland operation which we take pleasure in presenting at the Alamo Theatre next week.

This absorbing mystery play, "A Blind Bargain," was adapted from a short story by Barry Pain and concerns the efforts of a great imaginative surgeon to tear back the veil of human origin and by radical experimentation to prove it is possible to alter human forms by the grafting of glands from an anthropoid ape. Aside from the diverting character of the medical research you will find this picture wonderful entertainment as an ingenious and thrilling mystery drama.

Respectfully and sincerely yours,
Manager, Alamo Theatre.

(2)

(A strong sales letter for your regular patron list. Direct-by-mail appeal is a promotion aid of real value.)

Dear Friend:

We are delighted to inform you of a real surprise for next week's program at the Alamo Theatre.

We have just booked "A Blind Bargain," with Lon Chaney in the principal role and our advice is Come Early and Avoid the Crowds! This is the year's greatest mystery sensation. It is different from any mystery drama you ever saw, no spooks, no crooks, no murders, but a thrilling surprise plot in which a young author in desperate circumstances signs his life away blindly to a fanatic surgeon.

You will gasp at the hidden door behind the book-case that leads to a secret chamber of mysteries under the great surgeon's palatial residence. In these underground passages take place some of the most breath-taking incidents ever flashed on the screen.

"A Blind Bargain" will keep you guessing. It's the big mystery thriller of the year. And it's got a love story too! If you miss this one you'll miss one of the very best.

Yours truly,
Manager, Alamo Theatre.

Features—Shorts—General Stories

GOLDWYN'S FILM, "A BLIND BARGAIN", IS THRILLING, TINGLING MELODRAMA

Lon Chaney Has Two Roles in the Photoplay Which Challenge Comparison with the Most Vivid and Compelling Screen Characterizations Ever Seen — "Follies" Beauty Is Leading Woman

There is coming to the ---------- theatre on ---------- for ------ days a screen play that is so out of the ordinary run of feature films it startles and, on occasion, even terrifies the spectator. It is Goldwyn's picture, "A Blind Bargain," based on a story by Barry Pain, one of England's best and most popular writers of short stories, called "The Octave of Claudius." The story is melodramatic, unusual, thrilling and tingling. Seldom, if ever, has the screen been able to induce so creepy a sensation in the nervous systems of spectators as "A Blind Bargain." It is melodrama that reaches the brain as well as the spinal column.

The story concerns one Dr. Lamb, a half-mad surgeon who believes that he can demonstrate the truth of evolution by turning men back into ancestral physical and mental conditions through grafting monkey glands into their bodies. He is attacked by a half-starved struggling author Robert Sandell, but easily overcomes him and takes him home. There he learns young Sandell's story—he cannot make enough money to give his sick mother the medical and hospital treatment she needs to save her life. Dr. Lamb says he will restore Mrs. Sandell to health, furnish the youth with plenty of money on the condition that, at the end of a stated time, he deliver himself over to the surgeon to do with as he will in the pursuance of his experiments. Frantic with worry about his mother, the youth consents.

Dr. Lamb introduces Sandell to a publisher who accepts one of the struggling author's manuscrips for publication. Sandell falls in love with the publisher's daughter, Angela, and the days slip by until the time for the experimental operation approaches. The young man has been warned by the doctor's wife and by the hunchback, the victim of one of Dr. Lamb's previous experiments, that great danger to both mind and body threaten him as a result of the experiment; they show him horrible wrecks of human beings locked in cells in the surgeon's private dungeon. The youth tries to buy his release from Dr. Lamb but in vain. Almost immediately after the great ball at which his engagement to Angela is annqunced, Dr. Lamb, believing Sandell may try to escape, seizes and straps him to the operating table, but as he goes into the dungeon to get the monkey from whose body the glands are to be taken, one of his former victims breaks the bars of his cell, seizes and crushes the mad surgeon to death. Sandell is rescued from the operating table just a few minutes earlier by Mrs. Lamb and the hunchback. Sandell is restored to his mother and to Angela.

The story has been directed by Wallace Worsley, the man who directed two earlier Goldwyn pictures with Lon Chaney, "The Penalty" and "Ace of Hearts," with infinite attention to the details that make for the uncanny, creepy thrills that such a melodrama should produce. It is the biggest screen feature Mr. Worsley has yet made and one that should give him rank among the ablest men in his profession.

Goldwyn selected Lon Chaney for the roles of Dr. Lamb and of the hunchback victim of one of the doctor's experiments. In each role he gives a characterization that is truly startling in its vivid, uncanny power, and in striking contrast to any of his screen roles. The struggling author is acted by Raymond McKee, while Angela is portrayed by Jacqueline Logan, one of the most beautiful girls ever seen in Ziegfeld's "Follies," who has rapidly been making a name for herself in motion pictures. Others in the cast are Virginia True Boardman, Aggie Herring and Virginia Madison.

The soap-bubble ballet in the ballroom scene is one o fthe most magnificent spectacles ever soreened. Two hundred barrels of soap were required to make the clouds of bubbles amid which a doezn diaphanously clad beauties pirouet. Cedric Gibbons, Goldwyn's art director, proves his genius for film stagecraft in this gorgeous spectacle.

BRIEFS

Lon Chaney plays one of the most, if not the most remarkable role of his spectacular career, in "A Blind Bargain," directed by Wallace Worsley, who also directed Chaney in "The Penalty."

In this Goldwyn photo-drama, coming to the ------------ theatre, for ------ days, commencing ---------- Chaney plays two roles—one a polished suave physician, whose exterior hides a maniacal nature, and the other a hunchback. When Worsley, his director, read this story, he said: "There is only one man in pictures who can play these roles! That man is Lon Chaney!"

Fontaine La Rue, who plays one of the leading feminine roles in "A Blind Bargain," a Goldwyn photo-drama coming to the ------------ theatre on ---------- for ------------ days, is a screen recruit from the Orpheum vaudeville circuit, where she was noted as a toe dancer. Miss La Rue suffered an accident to her right foot, which made it impossible for her to con. tinue dancing, and has since then proved herself a versatile actress. Miss La Rue is as Frnech as her name, with all the artistic expression for which the French are noted. The character she portrays in "A Blind Bargain" is one of the most interesting ever shown on the screen, and would be an absorbing study in psycho-analysis. The picture was directed by Wallace Worsley. In the cast are Lon Chaney, Jacqueline Logan, Raymond McKee, Virginia True Boardman and Virginia Madison.

THE PLAYERS

Dr. Lamb and Hunchback	Lon Chaney
Robert	Raymond McKee
Angela	Jacqueline Logan
Mrs. Lamb	Fontaine LaRue
Mrs. Sandell	Virginia True Boardman
Bessie	Aggie Herring
Angela's Mother	Virginia Madison

Director: Wallace Worsley
Author: Barry Pain
Continuity: J. G. Hawks
Asst. Director: James Dugan
Gameraman: Norbert Brodin
Art Director: Cedric Gibbons
Editorial Credit: Paul Bern.

THE STORY

"A Blind Bargain," a production extraordinary by the Goldwyn Studios, coming to the ---------- theatre on --------, for ------ days, shows Lon Chaney in the triumph of his art. Raymond McKee, and Jacqueline Logan are the two other principal figures in the picture, which is built around the secret ambitions of an unbalanced physician.

Robert Sandell, (Raymond McKee) despondent over his ill luck as a writer, and his mother's declining health, decides to wrest from the rich the funds he so sorely needs. He attacks a theatregoer, who happens to be Dr. Lamb,(Lon Chaney) a sinister, fanatical physician living in the suburbs of New York. Lamb takes the boy to his home, learns his story, and agrees to perform an operation on Mrs. Sandell (Virginia True Boardman) on one consideration—that Robert shall at the end of eight days, deliver himself to the doctor to do with as he will, for experimental purposes. Frantic with worry over his dying mother's condition, Robert agrees. Mother and son take up their residence in the Lamb home, where Robert is closely watched, not only by the doctor, but his wife, (Fontain La Rue) and a grotesque being (Lon Chaney) whom Robert afterwards learns is the result of one of the doctor's experiments.

Dr. Lamb, anxious to keep his hold on Robert, not only gives him freely of spending money, but assists him in having his book published, through Wytcherly, head of a publishing concern. Robert meets Wytcherly's daughter, Angela (Jacqueline Logan) and promptly falls in love.

Iu the meantime the days are slipping by to the time of the experiment. Robert has been warned by Mrs. Lamb and the hunchback that great danger threatens him. He is told these are the doctor's experiments. In agony and fear, Robert goes to the physician and tries to buy himself out of the bargain—for his book has been published, and he is now a successful writer. There is yet one day before the time limit is up, but the doctor, realizing his victim may try to escape, seizes him, and straps him to the operating table. He is rescued by Mrs. Lamb, and the doctor is himself brought to a horrible end at the hands of a man wrecked mentally by the Doctor's experiments.

The experiment Dr. Lamb intended to try on Sandell was the transplanting of monkey glands into his body. The laboratory scenes are strictly scientific.

A special feature of the production is a spectacular ball scene, which cost a fortune in itself, and was filmed in a vast pavillion erected for the purpose. The affair marks the engagement of Angela and Robert, for of course the love episode in the story ends happily.

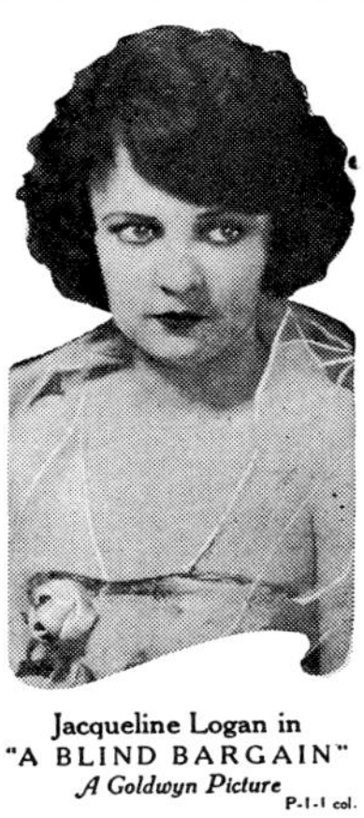

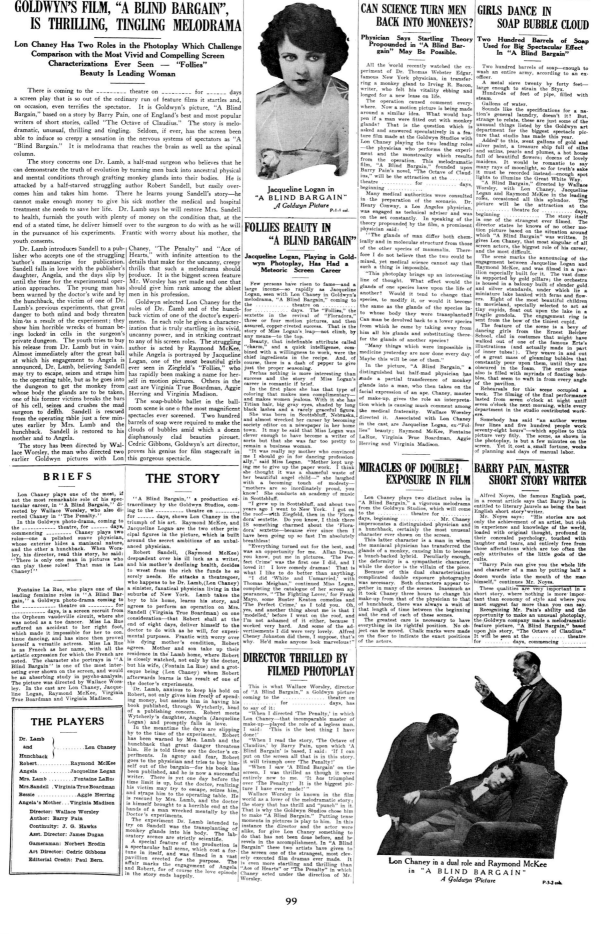

Jacqueline Logan in
"A BLIND BARGAIN"
A Goldwyn Picture
P-1-1 col.

FOLLIES BEAUTY IN "A BLIND BARGAIN"

Jacqueline Logan, Playing in Goldwyn Photoplay, Has Had a Meteoric Screen Career

Few persons have risen to fame—and a large income—so rapidly as Jacqueline Logan, seen with Lon Chaney in Goldwyn's melodrama, "A Blind Bargain," coming to the .... theatre on .... for .... days. The "Follies," the sextette in the revival of "Floradora," three or four motion pictures, and then assured, copper-riveted success. That is the story of Miss Logan's leap—not climb, by any means—to the top.

Beauty, that indefinable attribute called "charm," and a quick intelligence, combined with a willingness to work, were the chief ingredients in the recipe. And, of course, there is a dash of pepper to give just the proper seasoning.

Perhas nothing is more interesting than success and the story of Miss Logan's career is romantic if brief.

In the first place she has that type of coloring that makes men complimentary—and makes women jealous. With it she has Titian hair, big gray eyes, shaded by long black lashes and a rarely graceful figure.

She was born in Scottsbluff, Nebraska, and almost wrecked her career by becoming society editor on a newspaper in her home town. It may be said that Miss Logan was clever enough to have become a writer of sorts but that she was far too pretty to remain a business woman.

"It was really my mother who convinced me I should go in for dancing professionally," said Miss Logan. "Mother kept urging me to give up the paper work. I think she thought it was a shameful waste of her beautiful angel child—" she laughed with a becoming touch of modesty—"mothers are so inordinately proud, you know! She conducts an academy of music in Scottsbluff.

"I grew up in Scottsbluff, and about two years ago I went to New York. I got on the roof—with Ziegfeld, then in the 'Floradora' sextette. Do you know, I think there IS something charmed about the 'Floradora' sextette—because ever since then I have been going up so fast I'm absolutely breathless!

"Everything turned out for the best, and was an opportunity for me. Allan Dwan, you know, put me in pictures. 'The Perfect Crime' was the first one I did, and I loved it! I love comedy dramas! That is what I like to do better than anything.

"I did 'White and Unmarried,' with Thomas Meighan," continued Miss Logan, completing the catalogue of her screen appearances, "'The Fighting Lover,' for Frank Mayo, some Buster Keaton comedies and 'The Perfect Crime,' as I told you. Oh, yes, and another thing about me is that I 'modelled,' before I went on the roof, and I'm not ashamed of it either, because I worked very hard. And some of the advertisements I did were very lovely. Alfred Cheney Johnston did them, I suppose, that's why. He'd make anyone look marvelous!"

DIRECTOR THRILLED BY FILMED PHOTOPLAY

This is what Wallace Worsley, director of "A Blind Bargain," a Goldwyn picture coming to the .... theatre on .... for .... days, has to say of it:

"When I directed 'The Penalty,' in which Lon Chaney—that incomparable master of make-up—played the role of a legless man, I said: 'This is the best thing I have done!'

"When I read the story, 'The Octave of Claudius,' by Barry Pain, upon which 'A Blind Bargain' is based, I said: 'If I can put on the screen all that is in this story, it will triumph over 'The Penalty!'

"When I saw 'A Blind Bargain' on the screen, I was thrilled as though it were entirely new to me. 'It *has* triumphed over 'The Penalty!' It is the biggest picture I have ever made!'"

Wallace Worsley is known in the film world as a lover of the melodramatic story; the story that has thrill and "punch" in it. That is why the Goldwyn Studios chose him to make "A Blind Bargain." Putting tense moments in pictures is play to him. In this instance the director and the actor were alike, for give Lon Chaney something to do that has not been done before, and he revels in the accomplishment. In "A Blind Bargain" these two artists have given to the screen one of the strangest, most cleverly executed film dramas ever made. It is even more startling and thrilling than "Ace of Hearts" or "The Penalty" in which Chaney acted under the direction of Mr. Worsley.

CAN SCIENCE TURN MEN BACK INTO MONKEYS?

Physician Says Startling Theory Propounded in "A Blind Bargain" May Be Possible.

All the world recently watched the experiment of Dr. Thomas Webster Edgar, famous New York physician, in transferring a monkey gland to Irving R. Bacon, writer, who felt his vitality ebbing and longed for a new lease on life.

The operation caused comment everywhere. Now a motion picture is being made around a similar idea. What would happen if a man were fitted out with monkey glands? That is the question which is asked and answered speculatively in a feature film made at the Goldwyn Studios with Lon Chaney playing the two leading roles—the physician who performs the experiment and the monstrosity which results from the operation. This melodramatic film, "A Blind Bargain," founded upon Barry Pain's novel, "The Octave of Claudius," will be the attraction at the .... theatre .... for .... days, beginning ....

Many medical authorities were consulted in the preparation of the scenario. Dr. Henry Conway, a Los Angeles physician, was engaged as technical adviser and was on the set constantly. In speaking of the theory propounded by the film, a prominent physician said:

"The glands of man differ both chemically and in molecular structure from those of the other species of mammalia. Therefore I do not believe that the two could be mixed, yet medical science cannot say that such a thing is impossible.

"This photoplay brings up an interesting line of thought. What effect would the glands of one species have upon the life of another? Would it tend to change that species, to modify it, or would it become the same as the glands of the species into whose body they were transplanted? Can man be devolved back to a lower species from which he came by taking away from him all his glands and substituting therefor the glands of another species?

"Many things which were impossible in medicine yesterday are now done every day. Maybe this will be one of them."

In the picture, "A Blind Bargain," a distinguished but half-mad physician has made a partial transference of monkey glands into a man, who then takes on the facial expression of an ape. Chaney, master of make-up, gives the role an interpretation which is causing much comment among the medical fraternity. Wallace Worsley directed it. Associated with Lon Chaney in the cast are Jacqueline Logan, ex-"Follies" beauty; Raymond McKee, Fontaine LaRue, Virginia True Boardman, Aggie Herring and Virginia Madison.

MIRACLES OF DOUBLE EXPOSURE IN FILM

Lon Chaney plays two distinct roles in "A Blind Bargain," a vigorous melodrama from the Goldwyn Studios, which will come to the .... theatre for .... days, beginning .... Mr. Chaney impersonates a distinguished physician and a hunchback, certainly the most unusual character ever shown on the screen.

This latter character is a man in whom the maniacal physician has transferred the glands of a monkey, causing him to become a hunch-backed hybrid. Peculiarly enough, the deformity is a sympathetic character, while the doctor is the villain of the piece.

Because of this dual characterization complicated double exposure photography was necessary. Both characters appear together in many of the scenes. Inasmuch as it took Chaney three hours to change his make-up from that of the physician to that of hunchback, there was always a wait of that length of time between the beginning and the end of each of these scenes.

The greatest care is necessary to have everything in its rightful position. No object can be moved. Chalk marks were made on the floor to indicate the exact positions of the actors.

GIRLS DANCE IN SOAP BUBBLE CLOUD

Two Hundred Barrels of Soap Used for Big Spectacular Effect In "A Blind Bargain"

Two hundred barrels of soap—enough to wash an entire army, according to an ex-officer.

A metal sieve twenty by forty feet—large enough to strain the Styx.

Hundreds of feet of pipe, filled with steam.

Gallons of water.

Sounds like the specifications for a nation's general laundry, doesn't it? But, strange to relate, these are just some of the unusual things listed by the Goldwyn art department for the biggest spectacle picture that studio has made this year.

Added to this, went gallons of gold and silver paint, a treasure ship full of silks and satins, pearls and plumes, a hot house full of beautiful flowers; dozens of lovely maidens. It would be romantic to say many rays of moonlight, so for truth's sake it must be recorded instead—enough spot lights to illumine the Great White Way.

"A Blind Bargain," directed by Wallace Worsley, with Lon Chaney, Jacqueline Logan and Raymond McKee in the leading roles, occasioned all this splendor. The picture will be the attraction at the .... theatre for .... days, beginning .... The story itself is one of the strangest ever filmed. The director states he knows of no other motion picture based on the situation around which "A Blind Bargain" was written. It gives Lon Chaney, that most singular of all screen actors, the biggest role of his career, and the most difficult.

The scene marks the announcing of the engagement between Jacqueline Logan and Raymond McKee, and was filmed in a pavilion especially built for it. The vast dome is supported by gold pillars; the orchestra is housed in a balcony built of slender gold and silver standards, under which lie a miniature lake banked with ferns and flowers. Eight of the most beautiful children in movieland, specially selected to act as tiny cupids, float out upon the lake in a fragile gondola. The engagement ring is sent from the bow of the tiniest cupid.

The feature of the scene is a bevy of dancing girls from the Ernest Belcher School, clad in costumes that might have walked out of one of the famous Erte's illustrations (and actually made in part of inner tubes!). They weave in and out of a great mass of gleaming bubbles that constantly pour upon them, until they are obscured in the foam. The entire scene also is filled with myriads of floating bubbles, that seem to waft in from every angle of the pavilion.

Rehearsals for this scene occupied a week. The filming of the final performance lasted from seven o'clock at night until seven o'clock the next morning, while every department in the studio contributed workers.

Somebody has said "an author writes four lines and five hundred people work seventy-eight hours"—which applies to this picture very fitly. The scene, as shown in the photoplay, is but a few minutes on the screen. Yet it cost a small fortune, weeks of planning and days of manual labor.

BARRY PAIN, MASTER SHORT STORY WRITER

Alfred Noyes, the famous English poet, in a recent article says that Barry Pain is entitled to literary laurels as being the best English short story writer.

Mr. Noyes says: "His stories are not only the achievement of an artist, but rich in experience and knowledge of the world, loaded with original thought, profound in their concealed psychology, touched with laughter and tears, and entirely free from those affectations which are too often the only attributes of the little gods of the cults.

"Barry Pain can give you the whole life and character of a man by putting half a dozen words into the mouth of the man himself," continues Mr. Noyes.

These qualities are very important in a short story, where nothing is more important than economy of style and where you must suggest far more than you can say.

Recognizing Mr. Pain's ability and the opportunity to make an unusual photoplay, the Goldwyn company made a melodramatic feature picture, "A Blind Bargain," based upon his story, "The Octave of Claudius." It will be seen at the .... theatre for .... days, commencing ....

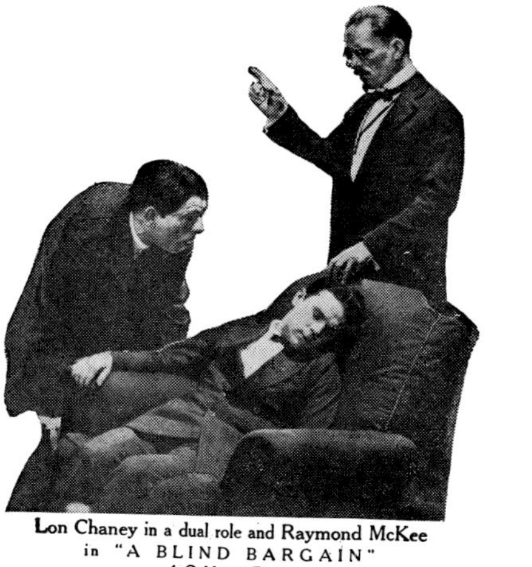

Lon Chaney in a dual role and Raymond McKee
in "A BLIND BARGAIN"
A Goldwyn Picture
P-3-2 col.

Advance Notices—Reviews—Who's Who

IT'S THE CLEANEST FILM EVER MADE

Tons and Tons of Soap Used for the Spectacular Soap Bubble Ballet In "A Blind Bargain"

The cleanest picture ever made is going the rounds of these United States.

It is "A Blind Bargain," the Goldwyn photoplay which will be seen at the .... theatre for .... days, beginning .... No one should miss the chance of seeing what a little soap and water can do for a perfectly good picture.

When Barry Pain wrote the story from which "A Blind Bargain" was made, he never thought that his "Octave of Claudius" could be cleaned up the way the Goldwyn Company did the job. They didn't use any moral suasion; there was no need for that. Barry saw to it that the Censors wouldn't have a chance to get at him before he signed his name to the original manuscript. But Goldwyn used tons and tons of soap and water.

It all happened like this.

Barry Pain thought out a unique kind of ball, something that had never been seen in a book or a magazine before. Now the Goldwyn Company has put over all kinds of costume balls, jazz included, but they struck a snag—temporarily—when they learned all the fancy details Barry Pain had put into his own private little ball. That's where the author has it on the motion picture producer. He can just say—a million dollar palace—and the producer has got to find one. Authors haven't earned their spendthrift reputations without good cause.

But to get back to this ball of Barry Pain's imagination that Goldwyn made into a fact. The scene demanded that, as part of the entertainment, a half dozen barefoot dancers gowned in flyaway nothings, sport about for the guests amid a shower of soap bubbles.

Here's the how of it.

The floor in the centre of the ball room in which the dancers were to appear, was cut out; and in place of a hard-wood floor, appeared a zinc square with hundreds of air holes in it. This zinc flooring was really the roof of a huge gas tank beneath the stage. On top of the zinc the Goldwyn mud slingers smeared a few tons of soap and water. This was prepared in huge vats from several barrels of washing soap. The next step was to harness a gas engine to the tank and blow air into the soapy mixture spread over the zinc, air-cooled, dance floor.

Result: Thousands of irridescent soap bubbles bouncing about in the air. All about the edge of the zinc floor, mountains of soap suds were banked.

When everything was ready, the director, Wallace Worsley, called: "Bring on the fairies;" and on they came. They rose out of the banks of suds, high-kicked, smiled, pretended to enjoy earning their salaries. It was the first time fairies had ever danced amid flying soap bubbles for the delight of screen audiences. And the mechanical effects were perfectly carried out. The best proof of this is that they are never in evidence; and the entire scene is sure to baffle anyone who doesn't know how it has been made. To say the least, it is a clean job.

Another, and an even more interesting event associated with the production of "A Blind Bargain," is the first appearance of beautiful Jacqueline Logan as the leading lady in a Goldwyn picture. Lon Chaney, the man who can look like anything or anybody, will be seen in his thousand and first transformation. The picture is a powerful melodrama, carefully made and exceptionally well acted.

Young Actor Builds Log Cabin in Screen Colony

One of the reasons why many speaking stage actors turn to motion pictures, is because it gives them a greater opportunity for home life. The motion picture actor may get a contract for several years with one studio, and make his home in the vicinity, while the speaking stage actor often is months "on the road."

Raymond McKee, who plays in "A Blind Bargain," a Goldwyn photo-drama coming to the .... theatre for .... days, commencing ...., not only loves his home, but he made it, in the literal sense of the word. While the majority of homes in Hollywood, the popular screen actor's habitat, are Italian villas, Colonial, or old Spanish, McKee built himself a log house, with a huge fireplace, and a general atmosphere of the wilds about it.

Mr. McKee in "A Blind Bargain" plays the role of a struggling young author driven to desperation by lack of success. He waylays a belated theatregoer returning home, but is overcome by his intended victim, a half-mad physician who believes he can turn a man back into a monkey by transplanting monkey glands into his body. He forces the young author to agree to submit himself to be experimented upon in exchange for the means of giving his mother the medical and hospital attention she needs to save her life.

Lon Chaney plays the role of the Doctor; also that of one of the victims of his experiments. Jacqueline Logan is the leading woman. Others in the cast are Virginia True Boardman, Aggie Herring and Virginia Madison. Wallace Worsley, who directed Chaney in two previous big photoplays made by Goldwyn, "Ace of Hearts" and "The Penalty," was in charge of the production. Barry Pain, upon whose story, "The Octave of Claudius," the picture was founded, is one of the best known short story writers of England.

HOW 'MOVIES' BEAT THE MILLIONAIRES

"Get married?"

"What for?"

That's the way Jacqueline Logan, who will be seen in Goldwyn's spectacular melodrama, "A Blind Bargain," which comes to the .... theatre for ....days, commencing.........., answers the expectation that the members of the revived "Floradora" sextette will follow in the celebrated footsteps of the original, and all capture millionaires.

"We don't have to marry millions any more. We make 'em!" says Miss Logan further, and tosses her Titian head saucily, and asserts further:

"I guess the millionaires feel pretty inadequate when they try to compete with 'the movies.'

"Years ago poor girls went into the chorus because it gave them a chance at the millionaires. Now they do it because it gives them a chance at the 'movies.'

"The original 'Floradora' girls did all they could in their day—every one married a millionaire,—but now they would probably be motion picture stars!

"I know a millionaire's wife, and I want to tell you her allowance isn't any bigger than my salary is going to be.

"Men used to think all they had to do was to pile up a million or so—but now—"

Miss Logan has to date: One very handsome automobile. One man to drive it. One expensive bungalow in Hollywood, Cal. (where they're all expensive.) One maid. One gorgeous personal wordrobe. One blue ribbon chow dog.

All inside of a few months.

Millionaires? Well, they'll have to offer something more attractive than millions!

TOOK CHANEY THREE HOURS TO MAKE UP

Lon Chaney and E. A. Warren, peers of make-up men, both chanced to be playing at the Goldwyn Studios at the same time recently, and both took three hours to apply their individual make-ups. It will be remembered that Warren and Chaney played in "Outside the Law," in which they did Chinese characterizations.

In "A Blind Bargain," coming to the ....theatre, for............. days, commencing ...., Mr. Chaney plays a dual role, while Warren at the same time was working in "Hungry Hearts," also a Goldwyn picture. Before many days had passed the studio folk were betting on the two as to which would break the three hour record, and there was a lot of good natured rivalry between the two professionals, as it takes a very complicated and different make-up to consume three hours.

Wallace Worsley, who directed Chaney in his two previous big Goldwyn photoplays, "Ace of Hearts" and "The Penalty," held the megaphone on "A Blind Bargain." It's just the sort of rapid action story he likes to film and he made an excellent job of it. In the cast, besides Lon Chaney are Jacqueline Logan, a screen recruit from the "Follies" beauties; Raymond McKee, Virginia True Boardman, Aggie Herring and Virginia Madison.

"Two hundred barrels of soap! Say, *that's* going to be a clean picture, all right!"

The salesman of a soap house was talking to the production department of the Goldwyn Studios. The salesman had never had an order like that from a motion picture studio. It stunned him.

"A Blind Bargain" is the picture for which this unprecedented soap order was given. It will come to the .... theatre, for .... days, commencing .... When the soap is projected onto the screen, it will be in the form of white foam, and radiant bubbles, in one of the most impressive ballroom scenes ever filmed. Beautiful girls dance in the foam.

Jacqueline Logan, screen beauty, is a shooting star. When three men tried to steal her auto from the garage of her residence in Hollywood, she grabbed a rifle and drove them off.

Miss Logan was awakened by noises in the yard. She went to the porch, turned on the lights and saw two men attempting to make off with her car, and a third trying to pry his way into the house. Miss Logan began shooting, and the burglars fled in their own auto. Miss Logan believes one of her shots hit the side of their car. After all the fireworks were over, the actress notified the Hollywood police, who counselled her hereafter to notify the department first and shoot afterwards.

Miss Logan plays the feminine lead in "A Blind Bargain," which will be seen at the .... theatre .... for ....days, commencing .... Lon Chaney and Raymond McKee will also be seen in this Goldwyn picture.

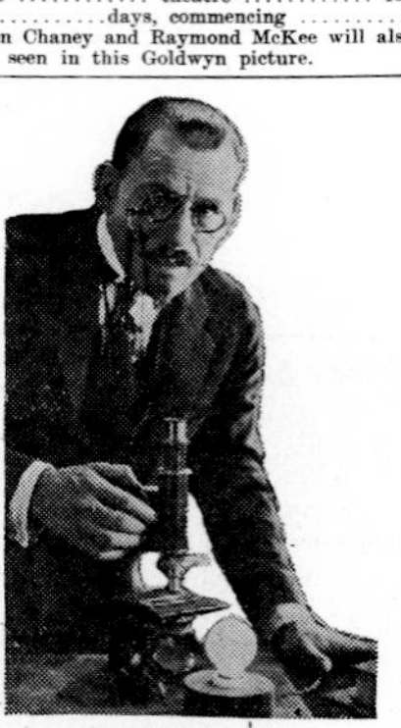

Lon Chaney in
"A BLIND BARGAIN"
A Goldwyn Picture
P-2-1 col.

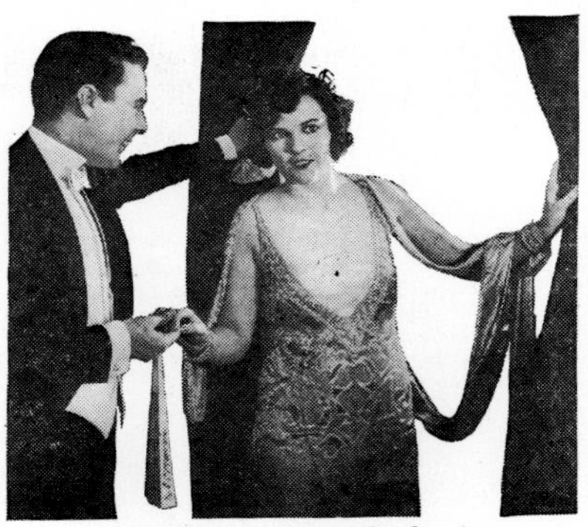

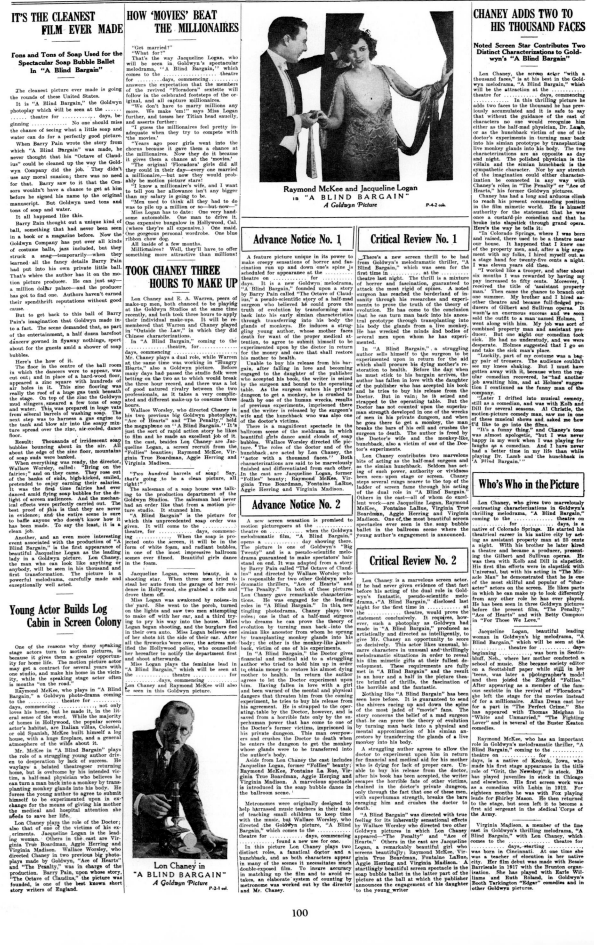

Raymond McKee and Jacqueline Logan
in "A BLIND BARGAIN"
A Goldwyn Picture
P-4-2 col.

Advance Notice No. 1

A feature picture unique in its power to make creepy sensations of horror and fascination run up and down one's spine is scheduled for appearanec at the .... theatre on .... for .... days. It is a new Goldwyn melodrama, "A Blind Bargain," founded upon a story by Barry Pain called "The Octave of Claudius," a pseudo-scientific story of a half-mad surgeon who believed he could prove the truth of evolution by transforming man back into his early simian characteristics through transferring into his body the glands of monkeys. He induces a struggling young author, whose mother faces death for want of the proper medical attention, to agree to submit himself to be experimented upon by the doctor in return for the money and care that shall restore his mother to health.

Unable to buy his release from his bargain, after falling in love and becoming engaged to the daughter of the publisher who accepted his book, the writer is seized by the surgeon and bound to the operating table. As the surgeon enters his private dungeon to get a monkey, he is crushed to death by one of the human wrecks, results of previous experiments, imprisoned there and the writer is released by the surgeon's wife and the hunchback who was also one of the doctor's victims.

There is a magnificent spectacle in the ballroom scene of the meldrama in which beautiful girls dance amid clouds of soap bubbles. Wallace Worsley directed the picture. The roles of the doctor and of the hunchback are acted by Lon Chaney, the "actor with a thousand faces." Both characterizations are said to be marvelously finished and differentiated from each other. In the cast are Jacqueline Logan, former "Follies" beauty; Raymond McKee, Virginia True Boardman, Fontaine LaRue, Aggie Herring and Virginia Madison.

Advance Notice No. 2

A new screen sensation is promised to motion picturegoers at the .... theatre on .... when the Goldwyn melodramatic film, "A Blind Bargain," opens a .... day showing there. The picture is one of Goldwyn's "Big Twenty" and is a pseudo-scientific melodrama guaranteed to make spectators' hair stand on end. It was adapted from a story by Barry Pain called "The Octave of Claudius" and directed by Wallace Worsley who is responsible for two other Goldwyn melodramatic thrillers, "Ace of Hearts" and "The Penalty." In both of these pictures Lon Chaney gave remarkable characterizations. He was engaged for the leading roles in "A Blind Bargain." In this new tingling photodrama, Chaney plays two roles; one is that of a half-mad surgeon who dreams he can prove the theory of evolution by turning man back into the simian like ancestor from whom he sprung by transplanting monkey glands into his body; the other is the monkey-like hunchback, victim of one of his experiments.

In "A Blind Bargain," the Doctor gives financial and medical aid to a struggling author who tried to hold him up in order to obtain money to restore his almost dying mother to health. In return the author agrees to let the Doctor experiment upon him. Having fallen in love with a girl and been warned of the mental and physical dangers that threaten him from the coming experiment, he tries to buy his release from his agreement. He is strapped to the operating table by the Doctor, however, and is saved from a horrible fate only by the superhuman power that has come to one of the Doctor's former victims, imprisoned in his private dungeon. This man overpowers and crushes the Doctor to death when he enters the dungeon to get the monkey whose glands were to be transferred into the author's body.

Aside from Lon Chaney the cast includes Jacqueline Logan, former "Follies" beauty; Raymond McKee, Fontaine La Rue, Virginia True Boardman, Aggie Herring and Virginia Madison. A marvelous spectacle is introduced in the soap bubble dance in the ballroom scene.

Metronomes were originally designed to help harrassed music teachers in their task of teaching small children to keep time with the music, but Wallace Worsley, who directed the Goldwyn picture, "A Blind Bargain," which comes to the .... theatre for .... days, commencing ...., found a new use for one.

In this picture Lon Chaney plays two distinct roles, a fanatical doctor and a hunchback, and as both characters appear in many of the scenes it necessitates much double-exposed film. To insure accuracy in matching up the film and to avoid retakes, an elaborate system of counting by metronome was worked out by the director and Mr. Chaney.

Critical Review No. 1

There's a new screen thrill to be had from Goldwyn's melodramatic thriller, "A Blind Bargain," which was seen for the first time in .... at the .... theatre last night. The thrill is a mixture of horror and fascination, guaranteed to attack the most rigid of spines. A noted surgeon has reached the borderland of insanity through his researches and experiments to prove the truth of the theory of evolution. He has come to the conclusion that he can turn man back into his ancestral prototype through transplanting into his body the glands from a live monkey. He has wrecked the minds and bodies of several men upon whom he has experimented.

In "A Blind Bargain," a struggling author sells himself to the surgeon to be experimented upon in return for the aid which shall procure his dying mother's restoration to health. Before the day when he must stick to his bargain arrives, the author has fallen in love with the daughter of the publisher who has accepted his book and he tries to buy his release from the Doctor. But in vain; he is seized and strapped to the operating table. But the Doctor has not counted upon the superhuman strength developed in one of the wrecks of men in his private dungeon, and when he goes there to get a monkey, the man breaks the bars of his cell and crushes the surgeon to death. The author is freed by the Doctor's wife and the monkey-like hunchback, also a victim of one of the Doctor's experiments.

Lon Chaney contributes two marvelous bits of acting as the half-mad surgeon and as the simian hunchback. Seldom has acting of such power, authority or vividness been seen upon stage or screen. Chaney steps several rungs nearer to the top of the ladder of screen fame through his acting of the dual role in "A Blind Bargain." Others in the cast—all of whom do excellent work—are Jacqueline Logan, Raymond McKee, Fontaine LaRue, Virginia True Boardman, Aggie Herring and Virginia Madison. One of the most beautiful screen spectacles ever seen is the soap bubble ballet in the ballroom scene where the young author's engagement is announced.

Critical Review No. 2

Lon Chaney is a marvelous screen actor. If he had never given evidence of that fact before his acting of the dual role in Goldwyn's fantastic, pseudo-scientific melodrama, "A Blind Bargain," disclosed last night for the first time in .... at the .... theatre, would prove the statement conclusively. It requires, however, such a photoplay as Goldwyn had made in "A Blind Bargain," produced as artistically and directed as intelligently, to give Mr. Chaney an opportunity to score so decisively. This actor likes unusual, bizarre characters in unusual and thrillingly melodramatic situations in order to reveal his film mimetic gifts at their fullest development. These requirements are fully met in "A Blind Bargain" and the result is an hour and a half in the picture theatre brimful of thrills, the fascination of the horrible and the fantastic.

Nothing like "A Blind Bargain" has been seen here before. It is guaranteed to send the shivers racing up and down the spine of the most jaded of "movie" fans. The story concerns the belief of a mad surgeon that he can prove the theory of evolution by turning man back into a physical and mental approximation of his simian ancestors by transferring the glands of a live monkey into his body.

A struggling author agrees to allow the doctor to experiment upon him in return for financial and medical aid for his mother who is dying for lack of proper care. Unable to buy his release from the doctor, after his book has been accepted, the writer escapes the horrible fate of other victims, chained in the doctor's private dungeon, only through the fact that one of these men, with superhuman strength, breaks the bars encaging him and crushes the doctor to death.

"A Blind Bargain" was directed with true feeling for its inherently sensational effects by Wallace Worsley who directed two other Goldwyn pictures in which Lon Chaney appeared—"The Penalty" and "Ace of Hearts." Others in the cast are Jacqueline Logan, a remarkably beautiful girl who screens beautifully; Raymond McKee, Virginia True Boardman, Fontaine LaRue, Aggie Herring and Virginia Madison. A startlingly beautiful screen spectacle is the soap bubble ballet in the latter part of the picture at the ball at which the publisher announces the engagement of his daughter to the young writer

CHANEY ADDS TWO TO HIS THOUSAND FACES

Noted Screen Star Contributes Two Distinct Characterizations to Goldwyn's "A Blind Bargain"

Lon Chaney, the screen actor "with a thousand faces," is at his best in the Goldwyn melodrama, "A Blind Bargain," which will be the attraction at the .... theatre for .... days, commencing .... In this thrilling picture he adds two faces to the thousand he has previously accumulated and it is safe to say that without the guidance of the cast of characters no one would recognize him either as the half-mad physician, Dr. Lamb, or as the hunchback victim of one of the doctor's experiments in turning man back into his simian prototype by transplanting live monkey glands into his body. The two characterizations are as opposite as day and night. The polished physician is the villain and the simian hunchback is the sympathetic character. Nor by any stretch of the imagination could either characterization be connected in any way with Chaney's roles in "The Penalty" or "Ace of Hearts," his former Goldwyn pictures.

Chaney has had a long and arduous climb to reach his present commanding position in the film mimetic world. He is himself authority for the statement that he was once a custard-pie comedian and that he broke into slapstick through grand opera. Here's the way he tells it:

"In Colorado Springs, where I was born and raised, there used to be a theatre near our house. It happened that I knew one of the property men, and, after a big argument with my folks, I hired myself out as a stage hand for twenty-five cents a night. I was eleven years old then.

"I worked like a trooper, and after about six months I was rewarded by having my pay increased to fifty cents. Moreover, I received the title of 'assistant property man.' Then came the chance to branch out one summer. My brother and I hired another theatre and became full-fledged producers of Gilbert and Sullivan operas. It wasn't an enormous success and we soon sold the outfit to a man named Holmes, I went along with him. My job was sort of combined property man and assistant producer. But one night our comedian took sick. He had no understudy, and we were desperate. Holmes suggested that I go on and take the sick man's place.

"Luckily, part of my costume was a baggy pair of trousers. The audience couldn't see my knees shaking. But I must have gotten away with it, because when the regular comedian recovered, he had another job awaiting him, and at Holmes' suggestion I continued as the funny man of the company.

"Later I drifted into musical comedy, still as a comedian, and was with Kolb and Dill for several seasons. Al Christie, the motion-picture comedy man, saw me in one of these musical shows and asked me how I'd like to go into the films.

"It's a funny thing," and Chaney's tone was almost apologetic, "but I was never happy in my work when I was playing for laughs as a comedian. And I have never had a better time in my life than while playing Dr. Lamb and the hunchback in 'A Blind Bargain.'"

Who's Who in the Picture

Lon Chaney, who gives two marvelously contrasting characterizations in Goldwyn's thrilling melodrama, "A Blind Bargain," coming to the .... theatre on .... for .... days, is a native of Colorado Springs. He started his theatrical career in his native city by acting as assistant property man at 25 cents a night. With his brother he later hired a theatre and became a producer, presenting the Gilbert and Sullivan operas. He was then with Kolb and Dill in slapstick. His first film efforts were in slapstick with Universal, but with his acting in "The Miracle Man" he demonstrated that he is one of the most skilful and popular of "character" actors on the screen. He likes parts in which he can make up to look differently from any other role he has ever played. He has been seen in three Goldwyn pictures before the present film, "The Penalty," "Ace of Hearts" and with Betty Compson in "For Those We Love."

Jacqueline Logan, beautiful leading woman in Goldwyn's big melodrama, "A Blind Bargain," which will be seen at the .... theatre for .... days beginning ...., was born in Scottsbluff, Neb., where her mother conducted a school of music. She became society editor on a Scottsbluff paper while still in her 'teens, was later a photographer's model and then joined the Ziegfeld "Follies." After appearing as a member of the famous sextette in the revival of "Floradora" she left the stage for the movies instead of for a millionaire. Allan Dwan cast her for a part in "The Perfect Crime." She has appeared with Thomas Meighan in "White and Unmarried," "The Fighting Lover" and in several of the Buster Keaton comedies.

Raymond McKee, who has an important role in Goldwyn's melodramatic thriller, "A Blind Bargain," coming to the .... theatre on .... for .... days, is a native of Keokuk, Iowa, who made his first stage appearance in the title role of "Grit, the Newsboy," in stock. He has played juveniles in stock in Chicago and elsewhere. His first screen work was as a comedian with Lubin in 1912. For eighteen months he was with Fox playing leads for Shirley Mason. He then returned to the stage, but soon left it to become a first aid sergeant in the Medical Corps of the Army.

Virginia Madison, a member of the fine cast in Goldwyn's thrilling melodrama, "A Blind Bargain," with Lon Chaney, which comes to the .... theatre for .... days, starting ...., was born in Cincinnati. At one time she was a teacher of elocution in her native city. Her film debut was made with Bessie Barriscale in 1917 with the Brunton organization. She has played with Earle Williams and Ruth Roland, in Goldwyn's Booth Tarkington "Edgar" comedies and in other Goldwyn pictures.

Ads

Fontaine LaRue as the mad doctor's wife

Lon Chaney as the mute servant

Lon Chaney as the fanatic Dr. Lamb

Raymond McKee as Robert Sandell, the young author

Jacqueline Logan as Angela, Robert's sweetheart

THE MOST AMAZING MYSTERY PLAY OF THE YEAR!

What dark Fate, cruel, monstrous, lay behind the door of the secret underground chamber?

Every moment of this picture will thrill you and surprise you. You will want to see it all over again!

with LON CHANEY

GOLDWYN presents A,5-3 COL.

A Blind Bargain

by BARRY PAIN   Directed by WALLACE WORSLEY

Beyond the door—
—hidden dangers
—a horde of apes
—countless thrills

You will gasp at the YEAR'S BIGGEST THRILLER!

GOLDWYN presents

A Blind Bargain

with LON CHANEY AND AN ALL STAR CAST
by BARRY PAIN
directed by WALLACE WORSLEY

A GOLDWYN PICTURE

NOTE: Above are five 1-col. portrait cuts for general use. Below is a suggestion for a teaser campaign taking advantage of the widespread interest in the monkey gland experiments of which the newspapers are full. Set up the type as indicated using the names of physicians prominent in your town.

DR. JOHN SMITH:
—Do you believe that monkey glands transferred to Man restore Youth and promise a new Civilization of Man?

DR. F. EVANS:
—Is it true that the much discussed monkey gland operations to restore Youth and Vitality are being done successfully today?

DR. SAUL ROBOT:
—Would you advise a young man for humanity's sake to enter in a BLIND BARGAIN and submit himself to an experiment to prove the monkey gland theory.

HAS SCIENCE FOUND THE WAY?
—To prolong life?
—To make old men young?
—To build a new race of giants?

THE WORLD IS THRILLED by the great experiments taking place today to determine whether the transferring of glands from Ape to Man will save the human race.

IS IT HUMANE to permit desperate men to sell themselves as subjects for these experiments?

The story of a young man who entered into a blind pack with a mad genius of surgery is one of the most amazing, thrilling and gripping mystery themes ever brought to the screen.

The Year's Big Thriller,

A BLIND BARGAIN

with LON CHANEY

A Doctor, a mute servant, an Ape-Man and a brave girl are mysterious figures in this absorbing drama.

You will want to see it all over again!

Never before has the screen offered a more thrilling or baffling mystery picture. Clever, diabolic, startling, it will make you gasp. You will want to be thrilled all over again!

Goldwyn presents

A BLIND BARGAIN

with Lon Chaney by Barry Pain

directed by Wallace Worsley

a GOLDWYN PICTURE

Lon Chaney, as the mad Dr. Lamb

Lon Chaney, as the servant, half man, half ape

Mysteriously called away to face the unknown

The strange occupant of the mystery mansion

Don't Miss The Year's Greatest Mystery Picture!

A-7-3 Col.

Ad Copy

Dr. Lamb thought he could create a new race of men by grafting monkey glands to humans.

Eminent surgeon, mad with the brilliance of his theory, he forgot God and soul in the pursuit of a scientific belief. Into the shadow of his mystery mansion came a youth, desperate for money, and a blind bargain was sealed between them. You will gasp at this thrilling story. You will be amazed at the train of mysteries that lie behind the secret panel of the surgeon's wall. If you like thrills and mystery and romance you will call this photoplay one of the most entertaining you have ever seen.

A dumb man-servant, half human half ape, bore mute testimony to the fact that living beings became toys in the power of this mad genius of surgery.

What sinister fate, cruel, monstrous, lay behind the stout doors of the hidden chamber of human experimentation?

NOTE: Below are six strong ad slugs that command attention. They are exceptional for advance advertising and also admirably fill the small space needs during run.

The Year's Greatest Mystery Thriller!

What Sacrifice Would You Make For A Loved One?

—Is Life itself too much to give, unhesitatingly, blindly!

—A young author makes a strange agreement with a mad genius of surgery. Gripping events occur in a mystery mansion.

—Don't miss this amazing picture-play!

Lon Chaney in A Blind Bargain

by Barry Pain
directed by Wallace Worsley

A Goldwyn Picture

A,15-2 COL.

Thrills! Chills! Suspense! Danger! Daring! Love! Romance!
A BLIND BARGAIN
with LON CHANEY — The Year's Big Mystery Film!

The Year's Most Gripping Mystery Film!
A BLIND BARGAIN
with LON CHANEY   A gasp in every reel!

The Year's Big Thrill!
A BLIND BARGAIN
It's a Mystery Picture!

T.1- 1 COL.

The Year's Most Gripping Mystery Film!
A BLIND BARGAIN
with LON CHANEY   A gasp in every reel!

T.6 2 COL.

Thrills! Chills! Suspense! Danger! Daring! Love! Romance!
A BLIND BARGAIN
with LON CHANEY — The Year's Big Mystery Film!

T.2 - 3 COL.

The Year's Big Thrill!
A BLIND BARGAIN
It's a Mystery Picture!

T.4 - 1 COL.

Robert dearly loved Angela
But alas!
Too soon they have to part, for shortly he must leave her

How they loved each other - while dire fate, like a spectre hovered over their future.

to fulfill a Blind Bargain with a Mad Genius of

Surgery - to be the victim of a great scientific operation aimed to create a race possessed of eternal youth.

The story of the Doctor, the Devil, the Man, the Ape.

What a thrilling picture this is !! It will hold your attention every second

Goldwyn presents

with

Lon Chaney

A BLIND BARGAIN

by **Barry Pain** directed by **Wallace Worsley**

A,16 - 6 COL.

A Goldwyn Picture

(Theatre Name)

Exploitation – Lobby Ideas, Contests, Window Displays, Other Tie-ups

Lobby Miniature Stage

To the right are two designs for a miniature stage suggested as a vivid and arresting lobby attractor for this mystery subject. The secret of selling entertainment is to let them know by a graphic presentation what you've got for them inside the house. The box is easy to build and can be made over time after time for other productions.

DIRECTIONS: Enlarge or decrease dimensions to suit special needs of your lobby. Take two wooden uprights 5 feet long (A). Join them by three horizontal bars 6 feet long (B). Cut a piece of compo board 2 by 6 feet and make an oval panel as in sketch, this being for the transparent sheet bearing the title (X). Nail this to lower portion of the frame. Nail two simple columns (Y) to uprights. Cut a second piece of compo-board for the top, making five circular openings for transparent sheets bearing the words: WHAT LIES BEYOND THE DOOR! (Z). Separate each panel by a small square of board (C) so that each word will be illuminated separately when the flasher is installed. For the sides of the display join two wooden uprights (A) with three cross pieces 2 feet long (E). Run a piece of board (F) along center of frame for drop illumination of (X) panel. Similarly a strip of board (G) on upper section to support illumination of upper panel. Separate the middle and top section and the middle and bottom section by strips of thick material so that the lighting in the three sections will not interfere with each other. At the middle left affix a wooden support (H) for a bulb. At middle right place another support for a bulb (I).

Complete the stage with a back-drop to support the three cut-out figures looking into open door, as in sketch. By means of a flasher which should be installed by your electrician the lighting is as follows: Bulb (J) three white lights are steady to illuminate title. Bulb (I) blue light should flash every few seconds. Bulb (H) red light should be steady, creating mystery atmosphere. Bulbs (K) of which there are five are white and should flash from left to right, illuminating each word in succession; then all out; then complete sentence; then repeat. Dress up miniature stage with plush curtain effect (W.) Build foot-board (V) to stabilize display. Cover back and sides with compo board and the attractor is complete.

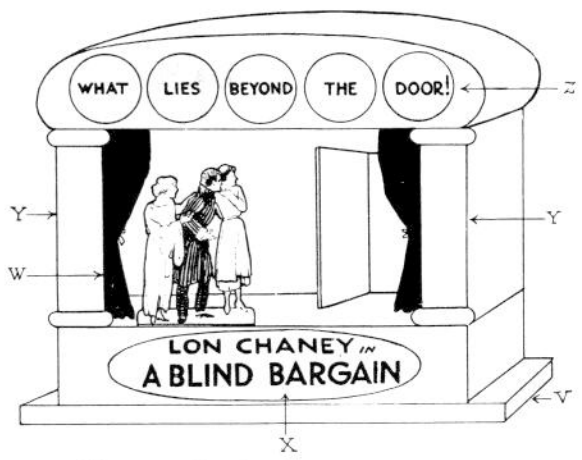

WHAT
LIES
BEYOND
THE
DOOR!
Z
Y
W
LON CHANEY in
A BLIND BARGAIN
V
X

The completed miniature lobby stage.

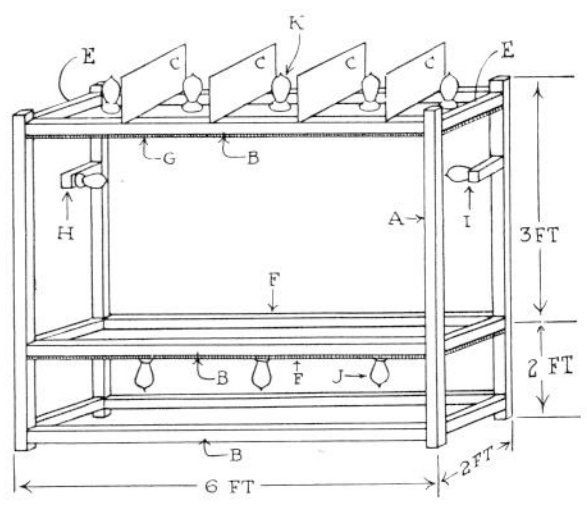

E
K
C
G
B
H
A
I
3 FT
F
B
J
2 FT
6 FT
2 FT

Working drawing of miniature lobby stage

Blind Bargain Sales

An unusual co-operative advertising idea for a page or double page spread. The appeal should be Blind Bargain Sales, with each contributing merchant to advertise his own Blind Bargain, a variety of goods at one price, with the declaration that all the merchandise is worth more. For instance: BLIND BARGAIN SHOE SALE—All Shoes to Go at Five Dollars, Regular Values from Six to Ten Dollars. The Blind Bargain Sales can be carried into window displays as well, Any Article in This Window One Dollar—Values Up To Five. An additional stimulant is the special coupon with every fifty cent purchase the coupon to be acceptable as part of admission to feature. Arrangements should be made to have the merchant refund every coupon presented at the theatre since his sale is being promoted thereby. Get advertising cards in the stores as well as cards in the windows for this

Shopping Bag Advertisers

Go to the largest local market and offer to split costs on printing a mutual advertisement on either side of the familiar brown market bags which are now in widespread use. You couldn't get more effective ballyhoos than thousands of women carrying your ad on streets, in public vehicles, etc.

Blind Bargain Auto Contest

Take down the license numbers of six or ten cars passing in front of your theatre each afternoon during picture's run. Publish them in following day's advertisement with note that persons recognizing their auto number may get two free passes to performance by calling for them in their car.

NOTE!

Here are a variety of promotion ideas suited to the need of every exhibitor.

Here are ideas for the small theatre and ideas for the larger houses.

Each one of them is practical in that it has proved its usefulness in some other form as a ticket-selling stimulant.

Each has the novelty that creates interest. They are all appropriate to the theme of the pictures, simple to execute and above all inexpressive.

"A Blind Bargain" will thrill and delight all audiences. It is up to you to tell your world about it!

Lobby Notice

Bring the public's attention forcibly to the dramtic punch of the film by a notice hung prominently in front of your house. This may also be used as a novel newspaper ad. Copy as follows: "NOTICE! Positively no one will be seated during the thrilling hand-to-hand battle between the surgeon and the wild ape man. This is one of the greatest and most exciting moments of screen acting and it is our desire that those already viewing the picture shall not be distracted during this thrilling episode. We shall be extremely grateful to our patrons for their kind co-operation in this matter. The Management."

Street Advertiser

On a float attractively decked out in colored crepe paper have the prettiest girl you can hire, with a band over her eyes and a pair of scales in her hand. Build up the four corners with the four cut-outs from the 24-sheet, The Devil, The Doctor, the Man, The Ape. Copy on banner to read "IS LOVE 'A BLIND BARGAIN'?—The most gripping film mystery of the year is at the Goldwyn Theatre."

Amateur Contest

Stage a Lon Chaney Contest for amateurs interested in character make-up. Offer two prizes, for the most original characterization and for the best disguise in the quickest time. Chaney's dual role makes this contest especially appropriate. Let the audience pick the winner by applause. Advertise the contest and prizes from a lobby frame.

Feminine Bill Posters

This ever successful street stunt is well suited as a novelty for "A Blind Bargain." Get several pretty girls to post the 24-sheet in prominent sections. To add mystery have them wear black domino masks. They should be dressed in colorful smocks or overalls with bright tam o'shanters.

Doctors' Preview

Considerable promotion should derive from word of mouth advertising owing to the unusual character of the story and from the problem of heredity it touches. Try to get a few doctors to attend a preview or the opening performance. Call it a Doctors' Preview for publicity purposes. To get regular patrons interested in the special performance announce in advance that certain stubs of the previous week's attractions bear lucky numbers admitting the holders free. List the selected numbers in the lobby.

Walking Ads

Men carrying signs reach those who don't see the newspaper ads. Send several men out with signs reading: "IS LOVE a BLIND bargain?" arranging the size of the words so that the question "IS LOVE BLIND?" stands out. Another method: Dress your ballyhoo in a white flowing garb, with blackened spectacles and a sign reading simply: "BLIND!" The second day have the sign read "a BLIND bargain." The third day your regular announcement.

Lobby Attractor

Many exhibitors will be able to locate a live monkey somewhere in town and the use of this animal in a cage in the lobby will prove diverting and interesting to the passersby. The tie-up is direct with the theme of the picture and it would be worth while to advertise in advance for any one in your city willing to hire out their pet. Over the cage should be a sign reading: "Do you believe that Man was once an Ape? Is it possible that Civilization will sink back again to the Ape World? A BLIND BARGAIN is the gripping story of a Mad Doctor and his amazing experiments. The Year's most thrilling mystery film."

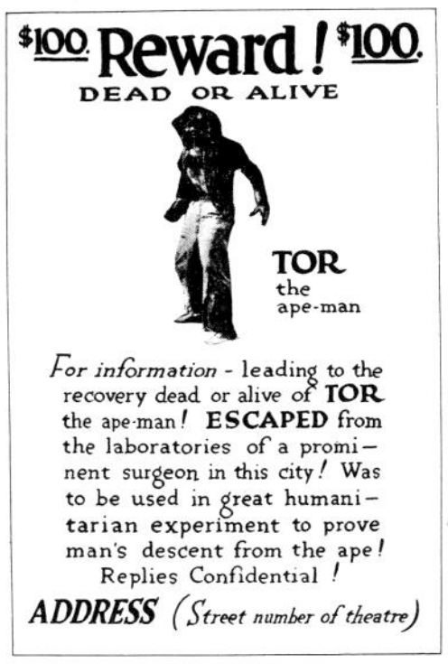

$100 Reward! $100
DEAD OR ALIVE
TOR the ape-man
For information - leading to the recovery dead or alive of TOR the ape-man! ESCAPED from the laboratories of a prominent surgeon in this city! Was to be used in great humanitarian experiment to prove man's descent from the ape! Replies Confidential!
ADDRESS (Street number of theatre)

The cards above and below are wonderful snipe attractors that will tease your town and create great advance interest in the mystery element of the picture.

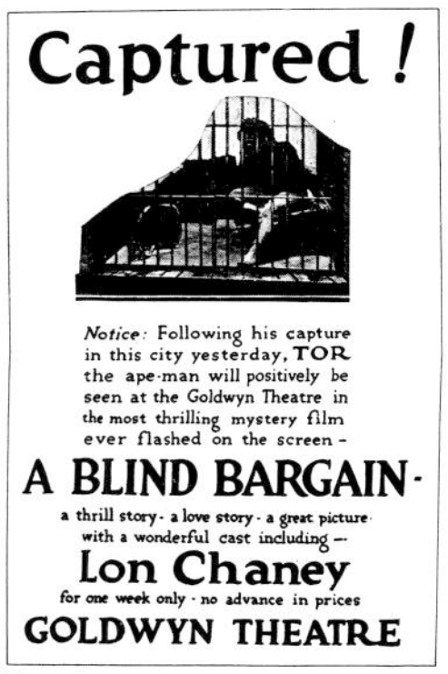

Captured!
Notice: Following his capture in this city yesterday, TOR the ape-man will positively be seen at the Goldwyn Theatre in the most thrilling mystery film ever flashed on the screen -
A BLIND BARGAIN
a thrill story - a love story - a great picture with a wonderful cast including -
Lon Chaney
for one week only - no advance in prices
GOLDWYN THEATRE

To make up the teaser snipe cards, order stills 60 and 61 in quantity and have your printer set up the type. Allow several days before posting the second card.

Traffic Tie-Up

Print cards for traffic stanchions with the following: "WATCH YOUR STEP! IS LOVE a BLIND bargain? — See the Year's Biggest Thriller at the Goldwyn Theatre." The words WATCH YOUR STEP! IS LOVE BLIND? should stand out.

Door-Knob Cards

Print a card about 4 inches square with perforation for a cord to hang on door-knobs. Copy: "WHAT LIES BEYOND THE DOOR? See the gripping mystery sensation A BLIND BARGAIN at the Goldwyn Theatre." You can get added value by pinning free passes to a scattered few hangers and putting a post-script in your newspaper ad as follows: "P. S.—Look at your door-knob tomorrow. FREE PASSES for the lucky ones."

Want Ads

Plant some of these want ads and personals and later call them to the attention of the editor by mailing the clippings in a blank envelope.

WANTED: Fifty strong, vigorous men as subjects for physical experiment. Only those in excellent physical condition need apply. Must be ready to take long chances. An interesting proposition for the right men. Address Dr. Lamb, 1432 Euclid Avenue.

WANTED: Physicians who possess information concerning the practise of grafting monkey glands on human subjects will learn something to their advantage by communicating with Dr. Lamb, 1432 Euclid Avenue.

PERSONAL: Angela. On account of "A Blind Bargain" entered into with Dr. Lamb will be unable to keep my appointment. Wish you would come to the Goldwyn Theatre ----(date)----, and then you will understand. Robert.

Window Tie-Ups

Go after windows in popular thoroughfares. They constitute an ever valuable source of advertising. Still number 67 is perfect for the center of a cigarette display. Still number 6 suggests a "Move to the Suburbs" appeal for real estate agencies. Still number 64 is excellent for dress shops and costumers. The one-sheet makes a stunning cut-out and can easily be placed in a window if backed with card-board and set on an easel. Cut-outs which ordinarily are not considered dressy enough to get into windows are immeasurably improved by being set on an easel.

Sunday Feature Idea

Sell your newspaper the idea of getting representative views of prominent physicians on the subject of evolution and heredity as it concerns "A Blind Bargain." It you have staged a Doctor's Preview, get each of the medical men to give his idea of the possibility of Dr. Lamb's great experiment in the picture concerning the grafting of monkey glands to men. There will be a difference of opinion among the medical men concerning the theory propounded in the photoplay, but they will be interested in its fiction possibilities, and will be glad to furnish a short paragraph of comment at your request. These paragraphs constitute interesting publicity and can be taken to the feature editor and run with some stills from the film under a streamer heading: "NEW HAVEN DOCTORS EXPRESS VIEWS ON ABSORBING HUMAN PROBLEM IN ANSWER TO MESSAGE OF GREAT PICTUREPLAY, 'A BLIND BARGAIN,' NOW SHOWING HERE." In asking doctors to contribute to this symposium you can suggest that they write of some notable human experimentation of which they have heard.

Open Letters to Local Doctors

An interesting and attention getting advertising campaign for this subject consists in addressing some straight open letter ads to prominent medical men in your city. Run one each day for several days prior to opening and you will arouse considerable interest in the forthcoming attraction. Supply the names of well known physicians and surgeons in your community. Set the copy in a simple ten point Roman and run a one point rule around it. The copy for successive days follows:

(1)

Doctor C. K. Johnstone:

You have long enjoyed the confidence and esteem of your fellow citizens of ----(town)---- As one of our greatest medical men you are cordially invited to attend the first showing on Sunday night of an absorbing story of a doctor's research into human origins. In this amazing photoplay, "A Blind Bargain," the question is propounded that since man is descended from the ape, is it not possible by modern science to turn man back again into his ape form. This theme is presented in one of the most fascinating and thrilling mystery dramas ever created for the screen and aside from its interesting medical aspects it represents the very best in motion picture entertainment. Trusting to see you with us on Sunday, I beg to remain,

Respectfully and sincerely,

Manager, Goldwyn Theatre

(2)

Dr. Robert H. Jones:

Beginning next Sunday we take great pleasure in presenting the most absorbing and mystifying story of human research ever flashed on the screen. This photoplay, "A Blind Bargain," treats in a daring and thrilling way one of the most baffling problems of man's heredity. As one of our leading physicians, we would consider it a privilege to have you in the audience on the opening night. You will be interested in Lon Chaney's performance as the great surgeon whose efforts to prove that man can, by proper treatment, be reverted to his aboriginal ape form, result in a powerful human drama. Hoping to have you as our guest at this great screen entertainment, I am,

Respectfully and sincerely,

Manager, Goldwyn Theatre.

(3)

Dr. Thomas Burns:

In your medical research you have recognized the astounding mysteries that exist between man and his aboriginal ancestor, the ape. An interesting phase of this age-old relation is graphically portrayed in "A BLIND BARGAIN," one of the most startling and entertaining photoplays ever conceived for the screen. The author asks why it is not possible for a man to be sent back along the paths of evolution to his ape form. This amazing belief actuates the life of a brilliant surgeon and furnishes a story that is ingenious, gripping and rich with entertainment qualities. We are expecting a representative group of -----(town)----- physicians at the opening performance Sunday night and we trust that you, too, will be our guest at the first showing of this great photodramatic achievement.

Respectfully and sincerely,

Manager, Goldwyn Theatre.

Accessories

Set of eight 11x14's

The Title Card

Strange things happen in the Mystery Mansion

No living soul knew Dr. Lamb's secret.

Called away mysteriously to face the unknown.

The world acclaimed him a brilliant surgeon.

No sacrifice could be too great for his mother.

What monstrous Fate lay beyond the door?

At last he learns what his bargain means

The Trailer Furnished by your exchange; also regular service trailer from National Screen Service, Inc., 126 West 46th St., N. Y. C. Western address, 732 So. Wabash Ave., Chicago, Ill.

*G*OLDWYN Press Books are prepared under the direction of HOWARD DIETZ, Director of Publicity and Advertising, and Silas F. Seadler, Assistant Advertising Manager. The publicity sections are prepared by the publicity staff of Goldwyn Pictures under the direction of Lynde Denig, Assistant Publicity Manager; Joseph A. Jackson, Studio Publicity Manager; Hal Burrows, Director of the Art Department.

Suddenly they heard the cry of a wild Ape

Two 22 x 28's

A mysterious stranger appeared at midnight

The Slide

Goldwyn presents
A BLIND BARGAIN
with LON CHANEY
by Barry Pain
directed by Wallace Worsley
a GOLDWYN PICTURE

The Devil   The Doctor   WHAT LIES BEYOND THE DOOR ?   The Man   The Ape

Thrills! Chills! Mystery! Suspense! Danger! Daring! Fights! Struggles! Love! Romance!

A mad scientist thought he had found the way—
—to make old men young!
—to double the span of life!
—to give humans eternal youth!
Why did he keep a horde of wild hairy Apes imprisoned in his strange mansion?
Here is a mystery sensation—unknown dangers, hidden thrills, the bravery of love—

DON'T MISS IT!
A BLIND BARGAIN
With *Lon Chaney* and a Great Cast

Posters They're crammed with mystery!

24 Sheet

Roto 1 Sheet

6 Sheet

One Sheet

```
ACCESSORIES AVAILABLE FOR "A BLIND BARGAIN"

LITHOGRAPHS        LOBBY CARDS              AD CUTS AND MATS      AD SLUGS
  24-sheet           Set of two 22 x 28s      S i x  1-col.         Two 1-col.
  6-sheet            Set of eight 11 x 14s    Two    3-col.         Two 2-col.
  3-sheet            Window Card              Two    4-col.         Two 3-col.
  1-sheet            Two-color Herald         One    6-col.
Rotogravure 1-sheet  Slide                    Three  2-col.
                     Trailer                  Five   1-col. portraits
```

3 Sheet

B & W	43	FADE OUT L S of mother in bedroom & nurse beside bed Mrs. Lamb enters
	44	S C U Doctor's library - Dr. bending over desk reading.
	45	INSERT: I HAVE ALREADY DEMONSTRATED IN PART THAT THE HUMAN SPECIES CAN BE SCIENTIFICALLY DEGRADED TO ITS ANCESTRAL TYPE THROUGH BLOOD TRANSFUSION. NOW I AM GOING TO DEMONSTRATE COMPLETELY WHAT I HAVE DEMONSTRATED IN PART.
	46	S C U Dr. reading
	47	L S of Hallway - Hunchback approaches in the foreground towards curtain
	48	M S Doctor putting book away
	49	S C U of Hunchback peeping through curtains
	50	M S Doctor as he exits towards curtains
	51	M S Hunchback as he looks thru curtains
	52	M S As he closes sliding doors behind curtains, locks them, and comes into foreground
	53	M S Hunchback as he crowds back as doors close beyond curtains
	54	M S Dr.
	55	M S Hunchback, as he parts curtains, and sees that doors have been closed and locked
	56	M S Doctor
	57	M S Hunchback as he takes key from pocket
	58	M S Doctor at desk - he turns, exits out to right
	59	S C U Back of doctor as he opens cabinet and presses key to trap door and bookcase swings out, ...
	60	C U of door crack open, hunchback looking in
	61	S C U as doctor exits through opening left by removal of bookcase - he draws bookcase back into place after him

B & W	83	S C U of hunchback closing door upon himself
	84	M S As bookcase revolves back, the doctor enters, closing trap-door after him, and exits
	85	M S Doctor's desk- doctor enters and examines blood test -IRIS OUT
GREEN	86	FADE IN - TITLE: ANGELA, THE GIRL OF ROBERT'S DREAMS. FADE OUT
	87	IRIS IN L S BOAT LANDING ... ANGELA COMES DOWN ON LANDING
	88	S C U Angela standing on landing
	89	L S Boat landing - Angela gets into boat and rows off
	90	L S looking across lake - canoe comes in
	91	TITLE: ..., WITH ALL THE MONEY HE WANTED, AS THE DOCTOR HAD PROMISED, ROBERT SOUGHT ANGELA
	92	L S Exterior of Angela's home - Robert going up walk to Angela's mother.
	93	S C U Angela's mother and Robert
	94	TITLE: ANGELA'S MOTHER GREETS ROBERT, BELIEVING HIS FALSE PROSPERITY TO BE GENUINE.
	95	S C U Angela's mother and Robert - as they converse
	96	L S As canoe approaches landing
	97	S C U Angela's mother and Robert - Robert exits
	98	L S As Robert comes down wharf - enters his machine drives off
	99	L S Angela pulling her canoe upon shore - exits out of scene.
	100	END PART THREE

Actual pages from the brittle cutting continuity describing the cut scenes. They were included in the European version.

N A	62	L S Stairway Doctor comes down stairs and turns on light at foot of stairs, lighting up an underground operating room
	63	M S Right hand side of operating room, Dr. goes up to door
B & W	64 M S	Hunchback as he crowds door open and comes in
	65	M S Looking toward bookcase and cabinet - hunch back in wheels round to spring trap door
N A	66	M S Doctor - opens door and looks into hallway beyond
	67	L S looking down long chamber toward the open door the doctor enters and lights the chamber up
	68	M S. of Dr. Lamb in front of cage holding ape
B & W	69	M S Hunchback feeling for spring
N A	70	M SM Dr. Lamb and ape
	71	L S looking down chamber as doctor goes from exhibit to exhibit, turning on lights as he goes. Hairy arms come out and try to grab doctor from cage - Dr. turns exits.
	72	M S Dr. Lamb closing doors of operating room
B & W	72x	M S hunchback feeling around in cabinet
N A	73	M S Dr. Lamb, as he experiments with blood test
B & W	74	M S Hunchback feeling in cabinet
B & W-	75	INSERT AS HAND COMES IN AND FINDS SPRING TO TRAP DOOR
	76	M S Hunchback as he finds spring to trap door and bookcase swings open and he enters the opening.
N A	77	M S Dr. experiments
	78	TITLE: THE TEST OF THE APE BLOOD
	79	M S ... Doctor experimenting
B & W	80	M S Hunchback behind bookcase - comes back into room closes trap door.
N A	81	M S Dr. finishes experiment - exits
	82	L S Of operating room - Doctor turns out lights and exits upstairs.

B-W.		PART FOUR
	2	C.U. DR. writing in diary - looks up
	3	INSERT: My subjects heretofore have been limited mentally or physically. My new subject is ideal. He is in the prime of youth, with genuine intellectual powers, and thus will offer a real test to my theory of degradation.
	4	Back to C.U. of Dr. lays down pen - blots diary and puts it away
Green	5	S.C.U. country road - automobile in - Robt. out of car and exits
	6	L.S. shore of lake - Robt. enters - gets in canoe and exits
	7	S.C.U. ext. Dr.'s house - Dr. comes thru door - goes to car (limousine)
B & W	8	Int. doorway - Mrs. Lamb and hunchback looks thru door -
Green	9	Dr. climbing in car
B&W	10	Int. Mrs. Lamb and hunchback peering thru door
Gr.	11	Ext. limousine drives out
B&W	12	Int. Mrs. Lamb turns and speaks title
	13	TITLE: "NOW IS OUR CHANCE TO FIND OUT".
	14	Back to scene - Mrs. Lamb and hunchback exits towards camera
	15	Reverse angle - Mrs. Lamb and hunchback - hunchback exits into library
	16	L.S. library - hunchback across to cabinet -
	17	S.C.U. hunchback at cabinet - opens trick door
	18	S.C.U. Mrs. Lamb watching in hallway
	19	S.C.U. hunchback goes thru doorway and closes bookcase
	20	S.C.U. Mrs. Lamb watching in the hall
BR	21	S.L.S. shore of lake - Robt. gets out of boat and exits
	22	L.S. top of hill by lake - Angela sees him - Robt comes up hill and calls to her
	23	C.U. Robt calling
	24	Back to L.S. Angela arises - runs to him and they embrace -

reen 25   C.U. Angela and Robt - they embracing - she speaks

26   TITLE   "IT'S BEEN SO LONG; BUT I KNEW YOU WOULD COME BACK."

27   Back to C.U.

B&W 28   S.C.U. bookcabinet - hunchback comes thru -

29   S.C.U. hallway - Mrs. Lamb watching and listening -

30   S.C.U. hunchback closes cabinet -

31   S.C.U. Mrs. Lamb watching - hunchback enters to her - writes on tablet

32   INSERT   EVERYTHING IS READY. IT WILL BE SOON NOW

33   Back to scene -

GREEN 34   S.C.U. canoe on lake - Robt kisses Angela - canoe exits

35   L.S. different angle - Robt and Angela in canoe -

36   TITLE   LOVE IS A CANOE--

37   Back to scene - Robt leans over - kisses Angela - canoe tips over

38-   TITLE --WHICH OFTENS TURNS OVER.
39   OUT
40   Back to scene - Angela and Robt struggling in water

B&W 41   S.C.U. Mrs. Lamb and hunchback - Mrs. Lamb speaks title

42   TITLE   "WE MUST STOP THIS - BUT HOW?"

43   Back to scene

GREEN 44   S.C.U. edge of lake - Robt carrying Angela to shore - kisses her - FADE OUT

NIGHT 45   FADE IN TITLE: THE HALL OF LOVE.
AMBER   Lap dissolve out and into
           FACING AS UNKNOWN DESTINY, ROBERT MADE
           THE ENGAGEMENT RECEPTION HIS LAST BURST
           OF GORGEOUS EXTRAVAGANCE.   FADE OUT

HANDSC 46   FADE IN LS ballroom - reception in progress - dancers appear in f.g.

N.A. 47   S.C.U. Robt, Angela, her mother and other woman watching -

HANDSC 48   L.S. reception room (or ballroom)

N.A. 75   S.C.U. corner of ballroom - Dr. enters - looks around and exits thru doorway

76   C.U. Robt and Angela - Angela speaks title

77   TITLE: " YOU HAVE MADE ME SO HAPPY, ROBERT."

78   Back to scene -

79   Reverse angle - Robt kisses Angela

80   SC.U. Doorway - Dr. enters - looks

81   C.U. Robt and Angela -

82   C.U. doctor - smiles

82 x   C.U. Robt and Angela - they look

83   C.U. Dr. starts toward camera

84   L.S. Dr. enters to Robt and Angela - speaks title

85   TITLE: "I HAVE BEEN PLAYING FATHER TO ROBERT. I AM GOING TO ADOPT ONE OF THE PRIVILEGES."

86   Back to scene - Dr. kisses Angela - Angela exits

87   C.U. Angela at doorway - turns - throws kiss and exits

88   S.C.U. Dr. and Robt - Dr. turns to him and speaks title

89   TITLE: "DO YOU THINK IT IS SAFE TO GO SO FAR?"

90   Back to scene - Robt speaks title -

91   TITLE   "I COULDN'T HELP IT! WE BELONG TO EACH OTHER. WON'T YOU EXTEND THE TIME?"

92   C.U. Dr. straightens up and speaks title

93   TITLE   "NOT AN HOUR, NOT A MINUTE! YOU BELONG TO ME AT SEVEN O'CLOCK TOMORROW MORNING."

94   Back to scene - Robt speaks title

95   TITLE   "VERY WELL! I WILL KEEP MY WORD."

96   Back to scene - Dr. exits

HANDSC 97   L.S. ballroom - dance in progress

N.A. 98   C.U. Robt - sits down IRIS OUT

99   END OF PART FOUR.

N.A. 49   S.C.U. four watching

HANDSC 50   L.S. ballroom - dancers finish

51   S.C.U. dancers march thru foam and disappear in water

N.A. 52   S.C.U. group of four

HANDSC 53   C.U. dome - heralds blow trumpets -

54   L.S. ballroom - crowd gathers

55   S.C.U. foot of dome - boat comes thru arch of dome -

N.A. 56   C.U. group watching

HANDSC 57   S.C.U. dome - boat comes to f.g.

58   C.U. little boy in boat - puts down paddle - opens lid of shell - little girl shoots it arrow

N. A. 59   C.U. Robt and Angela receive arrow

HANDSC 60   Flash of little girl with bow

N.A. 61   Robt and Angela - Robt removes engagement ring from arrow and places on her finger

62   S.C.U. group applauding

63   C.U. Robt and Angela

64   S.C.U. group applauding

HANDSC 65   L.S. ballroom - crowd applauding -

N.A. 66   S.C.U. group - Robt and Angela start toward camera

HANDSC 67   L.S. ballroom - dance starts -

N.A. 68   S.C.U. another corner of ballroom - Robt and Angela exits thru doorway

69   S.C.U. Angela's mother and two women - Dr. enters and speaks title

70   TITLE: "WHERE CAN I FIND ROBERT? I HAVE A LITTLE SURPRISE FOR HIM."

71   Back to scene - mother indicates - Dr. exits

HANDSC 72   L.S. ballroom - dance stops and starts again

N.A. 73   S.L.S. smoking room - Robt and Angela enter

74   S.C.U. Angela lights cigarette for Robt

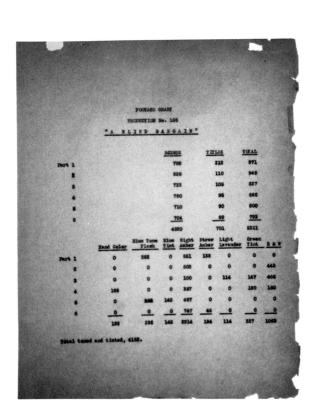

FOOTAGE CHART

PRODUCTION No. 165

"A BLIND BARGAIN"

	SCENES	TITLES	TOTAL
Part 1	759	212	971
2	835	110	945
3	722	105	827
4	790	95	885
5	710	90	800
6	704	89	793
	4520	701	5221

	Hand Color	Blue Tone Flesh	Blue Tint	Night Amber	Straw Amber	Light Lavender	Green Tint	B & W
Part 1	0	282	0	551	138	0	0	0
2	0	0	0	502	0	0	0	443
3	0	0	0	100	0	114	147	466
4	185	0	0	327	0	0	180	180
5	0	288	145	687	0	0	0	0
6	0	0	0	747	46	0	0	0
	185	282	145	2914	184	114	327	1089

Total toned and tinted, 4132.

Wallace Beery being madeup for his uncredited roll as the "beast man."

When Technicolor Holds The Mirror Up to Nature

Why You Will Find the Picture So Perfect That You Cannot Tell the Reflection From the Original

By Harriette Underhill

"Don't shoot till you see the whites of their eyes!" That is what Joseph Schenck said to Dr. Daniel Comstock only recently, and probably both of them were so excited that neither of them noticed that Mr. Schenck was emulating the commander who issued his now famous order at the time of the Bunker Hill disturbance. Dr. Comstock repeated it to us yesterday, without getting the significance of it, either, so we called his attention to it. It happened thus: Dr. Comstock is one of the inventors of the new Technicolor process which was used in the making of that exquisite new picture, "Toll of the Sea." Joseph Schenck is interested financially and otherwise, so when Dr. Comstock had some finished samples he begged for Mr. Schenck's honest opinion. "I have only one fault to find. The eyes aren't quite clear. Try a little more light and then don't shoot till you see the whites of their eyes." Of course, every one who knows anything about pictures knows that photographing a scene is called shooting. Anyway, Dr. Comstock took Mr. Schenck's advice, and the result is a picture in nature's own colors and without a flaw.

Colored pictures always have fascinated us. When we first began to review photoplays the Technicolor produced its first picture, called "The Gulf Between." The color in this early sample was as lovely as one could wish and far more satisfactory than any of the various processes which we have since seen. But there were features about it which made it impractical; so everybody set to work again to try to perfect it, and if one may judge from "Toll of the Sea," which was shown last week at the Rialto Theater, they have succeeded.

What we were most anxious to learn from Dr. Comstock was why this new Technicolor process has no fringes, flashes nor deep shadows. The actors on the screen appear to be real people walking about on the stage, not shadows on a screen. The face tints are absolutely natural and it is not necessary for the actors to put on any make-up, either. 'The exteriors are taken in the sunlight and the interiors are photographed under a strong arc light. Whatever is in front of the camera is photographed on the negative exactly as it appears, in color, tone and shape. Now, every color process is the result of throwing two colors on the screen, red and green, and letting the eye do the rest. One of the older processes had red and green screens through which the pictures were projected. These were in the form of shutters, and if at any time the film had suddenly stopped you would have seen reflected on the screen either a bright red or a bright green picture. Then there is the film which is made up of two celluloid strips pasted together—one green and one red. Still another process had a red film and a green one projected simultaneously on the screen by two different machines, and this is why most of the pictures done in natural colors are not clearly outlined—the pictures projected by this process are bound to be a little out of focus either in the foreground or the background.

Another common fault with colored pictures is the fact that it is almost impossible to lighten them. The shadows, being a combination of red and green, appear dark brown, and the pictures are about the color that nature appears when you view her through dark amber glasses.

"Now why," we asked of Dr. Comstock, "are the outlines in your pictures clear and perfect as in life?"

"That was the first thing I realized we must overcome, and it was difficult, but at the present time our camera takes simultaneously and at exactly the same angle two pictures—one of which will record red, yellow and orange and the other green, blue and violet. Then we print this negative and alternate the colors, so that there are two pictures on the finished film side by side exactly alike, but differing in sensitiveness. After that this film is passed through a dye and the different tones in the film will take some colors and reject others. When this film is projected on the screen you get the effect which you saw in 'Toll of the Sea.'"

It seems natural to suppose that since there are two pictures, instead of one, recording each pose that the film must be run off twice as fast as the ordinary film, though we forgot to ask about this. The second thing we asked of the inventor fas "How do you manage to keep your pictures so light and the tints so delicate? The colors are nature's own."

"And there is another thing with which we had to reckon. And Dr. Comstock replied: 'That is because we experimented until we found the right sort of film. It is what I call panchromatic film and if a shadow is grey it does not record it as black. It was a long and tiresome investigation this search for the film absolutely suited to the purpose, but we have found it —a trouble that the layman knows very little about. Did you know that celluloid changes its shape and size all the time as the weather changes? That was something that gave us a great deal of worry, but we have it so perfect now that if the film should shrink 20 per cent, which, of course, it will not do, we could still have the picture intact when it was projected. So that is all there is to it. Just be sure that you know how to shoot two pictures, a red, orange, yellow one and a green, violet, blue one, from exactly the same angle, that you have the correct sort of film and that you know how to correct the evils of shrinking and you may just go ahead and make pictures as beautiful as Technicolor. And Dr. Comstock says that it will be possible to have all pictures in the future made in these beautiful colors because the cost is not prohibitive. No one will be allowed to go ahead and use this process by himself, but Technicolor will photograph any picture for any company if the company so desires. At least that is the way we understand it, although at present the Metro has the rights to the one perfect sample which Technicolor has made."

"A Blind Bargain" Shows Advantages Of Screen Over Stage

One of the greatest two-fisted, knock-'em-down-and-drag-'em-out fights ever put on nightly behind the footlights was the one in which John Barrymore took a 50 per cent—at least—share when he was playing in "Kick In." There have been other rather juicy set-to's on the stage, but that one certainly is good enough for the present purpose.

The present purpose is to state unequivocally that fights on the spoken stage may be good now and then, but they don't hold a candle, as the saying goes, to the fights before the motion picture camera.

On the stage the actors not only have an opportunity but must fight every weekday night, not counting a couple of weekday afternoons; on the screen they only maul each other once, or at most, allowing for rehearsals, two or three times. Then they're through—in more ways than one. In a whole lot of screen fights the participants couldn't have put it on again to save their necks. Yet their one endeavor is multiplied sixty or a hundred times and keeps repeating itself through as many projecting machines the world over, for nobody can estimate how many years.

It's the same way with sets. They can't wreck a big set—really wreck it, that is—on the stage every night, not counting those aforesaid two matinee afternoons. But they can do it in the movies. And they sure do.

It's the same way with scenery. Great artists paint it for the stage. Super-fine lenses can the real thing for the movies.

It's the same way with crowds. On the stage they get a couple of dozen chaps at a dollar or so the evening to moan like lost souls. That makes a couple of thousand in a mob. Thirty or forty of these moaners make a million. On the screen they have the million. They've got the whole landscape in which to herd the million. They only have to herd 'em once. And the job is done. No moans are necessary.

Take fires. They have real ones in the movies. Train wrecks? What do a couple of passenger trains amount to in the expenses of putting on a big picture?

On the stage the hero is planning to rob a bank or do something equally exciting, but the heroine praying for him in London is invisible, unless she writes a letter, or a little bird walks on the stage and tells about it. In the movies such a situation is easy. You can see what's happening in London—and the real London at that—one minute, and what's transpiring in Oshkosh the next minute.

And did you ever hear of the same actor, playing two different parts, meeting himself and talking to himself with every appearance of reality on the speaking stage? Chances are you didn't. But it's being done, and one of the most artistic ways it's being done lately was by Lon Chaney, the "man of a thousand faces," in Goldwyn's "A Blind Bargain." "A Blind Bargain" is coming to the Capitol this Sunday, and that's what recalled the matter to our attention. Lon Chaney is an insane doctor in one character and a victim of the doctor's insanity in the other character. The two characters meet frequently, but—and they say it's because of the miracle called "double exposure" and the clever use of a metronome to get the timing right—the probabilities are that few spectators, if they hadn't been warned by their programs, would know that the two figures on the screen really were the same person.

"A Blind Bargain" teaches one of the big truths of this new age we're living in—if it doesn't teach anything else; and that is that the movies have some attributes that the stage never has had, never can have, and never will have. The movies have the world for a stage—old Dame Nature herself for a scene designer; the power of showing action in widely separated spots at the same time; the advantage of only having to have players go through the same violent scene once at its best and not on many consecutive occasions; the privilege of destroying sets after one use (witness the use of 200 barrels of soap, a gas tank and what not in that same "A Blind Bargain" for instance, to give the effect of a soap bubble ballet); and the advantage of permitting the same great player not only to play in two different rôles, but the power of deception that serves to hide the subterfuge, and make both characters seem as real as if they had been played by two different persons.

The movies may be a couple of laps behind the stage in some respects, but they might be said to be a nose ahead in others. If not, how about those histrionic fights?

"Broken Wing" on the Screen

B. P. Schulberg, president of Preferred Pictures, has secured the screen rights to "The Broken Wing," Paul Dickey's and Charles W. Goddard's comedy drama.

Agnes Ayres

In "A Daughter of Luxury," at the Rialto

Elsie Ferguson

In "Outcast," at the Rivoli Theater

Jacqueline Logan

In "A Blind Bargain," at the Capitol

"Covered Wagon" Is Paramount's Most Ambitious Effort

The making of Emerson Hough's "The Covered Wagon" undoubtedly is Paramount's most ambitious production undertaking, and in the filming of this epic of the West, adapted for the screen by Jack Cunningham, James Cruze has taken one of the most difficult directorial assignments in motion picture history.

Early last month Cruze left for Baker, Nev., accompanied by 100 technical assistants, the vanguard of an army of 3,000, who are to be in camp for nearly two months on an immense 200,000-acre ranch.

Later the same week Charles Ogle, Alan Hale, Ernest Torrence, Tully Marshall and Guy Oliver went direct to Antelope Island in the middle of the Great Salt Lake. There they were met by Director Cruze and are now engaged in staging a big buffalo hunt. On this island is the largest herd of American bison remaining in the United States, the group numbering nearly 500. This is the herd whose extermination by hunters was threatened a couple of years ago until a storm of protest from all parts of the country intervened.

Following the completion of the buffalo hunt scenes this company will rejoin the throng at Baker, where at the Baker ranch the other big episodes of the story of pioneer life are to be filmed. Some of the outstanding features will be an immense prairie fire, attacks by Indians upon a large village which is being completely built on the prairie, the breaking of horses and oxen for ranch use by a group of 100 cowboys and the trek of an immense wagon train across the plains.

To transport the throng of people and mass of material fifty railroad cars were required. In addition to these about one thousand Indians, squaws and papooses have been migrating overland to the Nevada location.

The Baker ranch now looks like the show grounds of a big circus, with its scores of motor trucks and prairie schooners, tons of supplies and equipment, hundreds of people of all types and thousands of animals—in fact, eliminating the modern motor trucks and electrical equipment, the scene of activity is quite comparable to those of the early days of the wagon trains during the great gold rush.

"Spider and the Rose" Goes on the Screen

Bennie Zeidman, the child producer, is at it again. Now he is going to do "The Spider and the Rose," and just because he has fourteen stars he is going to put them all in one picture. They are Alice Lake, Gaston Glass, Robert McKim, Noah Beery, Frank Campeau, Edwin Stevens, Joseph Dowling, Otis Harlan, Alec Francis, little Richard Headrick, Andrew Arbuckle, Harry Northrup and the inimitable Louise Fazenda.

"The Spider and the Rose" is a magazine story, written by Gerald C. Duffy. It is a romance of the old Spanish days in California, brimming with dramatic situation and action as well as atmospheric beauty. E. Richard Schayer adapted the story to the screen and Jack McDermott is directing the production. Glen MacWilliams is the cinematographer.

Cast Complete for Ballin's Picture of "Vanity Fair"

George Walsh has been added to the cast of "Vanity Fair," which Hugo Ballin is making for Goldwyn. This will be the first time George has played anything save a "stunt" role. Others in the cast are Mabel Ballin as Becky Sharp and Hobart Bosworth as Lord Steyne. Walsh will be seen as Rawdon Crowley.

Vaudeville

PALACE—Marion Harris, Four Mortons, the Doners, Gordon Dooley and Martha Morton, Clark and Bergman, Ted Lorraine and Jack Minto, assisted by Margaret Davies; Will Mahoney, William Halligan, in "Highlewbrow"; others.

RIVERSIDE—Raymond Hitchcock, Irving Fisher and Renee Robert and Giers-Dorf Symphonists, Bert Levy, "Around the Corner," others.

COLONIAL—Irene Franklin, Lewis and Dody, Joe Browning, Valerie Bergere, "Oklahoma" Bob Albright, Maurice Diamond, Joe Roberts, others.

EIGHTY-FIRST STREET—Bert and Betty Wheeler, William and Joe Mandel, Owen McGiveney, Dotson, in their own specialties and in "The Wager," an afterpiece. "Ebb Tide," film.

FORDHAM—First half: Miss Patricola, Tom Patricola, with Harrietta Towne, others. "Singed Wings," picture. Second half: Aunt Jemima and Band, others. "Ebb Tide."

HAMILTON—First half: Deagon and Mack, Pisano and Landauer, others. "Ebb Tide." Second half: Ona Munson and company, Mignon, others. "The Impossible Mrs. Bellew," picture.

MOSS'S BROADWAY—Cecile Weston, Miller and Mack, Allman and Harvey, Kennedy and Kramer, Arena Brothers, others. Reginald Denny, in "The Kentucky Derby," new picture.

LOEW'S AMERICAN—First half: "Creole Cocktail," others. Wallace Reid, in "Clarence." Second half: Cosmopolitan Dancers, others. "Trifling Women."

LOEW'S STATE—First half: "Four Queens and a Joker," others. "The Streets of New York," picture. Second half: Grace Cameron, Sonia Baraban, others. "Trifling Women."

CENTRAL—"Twentieth Century Revue," Shubert vaudeville unit. Four Marx Brothers, Olga Mishka and others.

PROCTOR'S FIFTH AVENUE—First half: Franklin Farnum and company, Corinne Tilton, Bostock's Riding School, others. Second half: California Ramblers, Henry and Moore, others.

PROCTOR'S TWENTY-THIRD STREET—First half: Aunt Sally and her Alabama Boys, others. Charles Ray in "The Tailor Made Man," picture. Second half: Gus King's Melody Land, others. "Ebb Tide," film.

PROCTOR'S FIFTY-EIGHTH STREET First half: Louis Seymour and company, Sandy Shaw, others. Hope Hampton in "The Light in the Dark," picture. Second half: Stella Mayhew, others. "Ebb Tide."

Picture Theaters

ASTOR—"The Town That Forgot God," Fox production. Sixth week.

CAMEO—"The Super-Sex," adapted from a story by Frank R. Adams. Robert Gordon, Charlotte Pierce, Tully Marshall and others in the cast.

CAPITOL—"A Blind Bargain," a Goldwyn picture, made from a story by Barry Pain. Lon Chaney, Jacqueline Logan and others in the cast. A single reel film explaining the Einstein theory; other films, orchestral, vocal, ballet and instrumental specialties.

CRITERION—Marion Davies in "When Knighthood Was in Flower," thirteenth week.

LYRIC—Douglas Fairbanks in "Robin Hood."

RIALTO—Agnes Ayres in "A Daughter of Luxury," adapted from "The Impostor," a play by Leonard Merrick and Michael Morton. Other films, orchestral, vocal, dance features.

RIVOLI—Elsie Ferguson in "Outcast," in which she appeared on the legitimate stage. David Powell, William David, Mary MacLaren, others, in the cast. Other films, instrumental, vocal, orchestral numbers.

SELWYN—D. W. Griffith will revive "The Birth of a Nation" for a week, beginning to-morrow.

STRAND—Maurice Tourneur's production of "Lorna Doone." Madge Bellamy plays the title role, and John Bowers, Frank Keenan, Donald Macdonald and others are in the cast. A Fokine ballet, other films, orchestral contributions, and a vocal and scenic prologue.

Three Successes in a Row Is Season's Score Thus Far for Arthur Hopkins

John Barrymore's triumph in and as "Hamlet" at the Sam H. Harris Theater was a triumph; also for Arthur Hopkins, the producer. Quite aside from the eulogistic greetings of his direction, "Hamlet" marked the third success which Mr. Hopkins had brought to Broadway in the course of the year. In two of the three cases, Robert Edmond Jones shared the honors with Mr. Hopkins.

"The Old Soak" was Mr. Hopkins's first production. It was one of the comedy hits of the season. Then came "Rose Bernd," with Ethel Barrymore, the performance being generally accepted as her best. Now comes "Hamlet," with brother John's interpretation of the melancholy Dane hailed as the finest of this generation.

Only last week "The Old Soak" celebrated its one hundredth birthday. "Al" continues to bootleg in a manner to make even William Jennings Bryan see the humor of prohibition, and the hired girl continues to tell the sad story of her parrot—"Nellie was a Lady!"

In a season which has been distinguished by much fine acting, it is doubtful if the performance of Harry Beresford as "The Old Soak" and Robert E. O'Connor as "Al" have been surpassed. Mr. Beresford took Mr. Marquis's character and lent it a genial reality which actually lives up to the conception of the author—a rare thing, as any author will admit. As for Mr. O'Connor, he is "Al," once the czar behind the bar—albeit a human, easygoing czar; but now reduced to the comparative ignominy of bootlegging. With the "Old Soak" he keeps alive the traditions of another day. Nothing daunts him—and particularly not the Eighteenth Amendment. His profession is chosen not for greed, be it understood, but because of "a friendly feeling for liquor." You may say what you want about him, but "Al" has a soul.

Buddy Messenger a Star

Julius Stern, president of Century Film Corporation, will shortly announce a series of small town boy stories featuring Buddy Messenger, the first of which will be called "Kid Gladiators." Among the supporting cast will be Marjorie Marcel and Joe Bonner.

Brooklyn Theaters

MONTAUK — Marjorie Rambeau in "The Goldfish."

MAJESTIC—Willie and Eugene Howard in "The Passing Show of 1922."

BUSHWICK — Eddie Foy and the younger Foys, "China Blue Plate," Santos and Hayes, Rita Gould, Gene Cass, Al Wohlman, William Ebs, Greene and Parker, others.

ORPHEUM—Fanny Brice, Yvette Rugel, Edna Aug, "The Weak Spot," Shaw and Lee, Weber and Ridnor, Jack Little, The Stanley Brothers, Four Tanarakis, others.

SHUBERT-CRESCENT — Fanny and Kitty Watson in "Stolen Sweets," Shubert vaudeville unit. Harry Steppe and Harry O'Neil, Berkes and Brazil, DeKoch Trio, Five Kings of Syncopation, others.

LOEW'S METROPOLITAN—First half: Mabel Blondell Revue, Tilyou and Rogers, others. Second half: Eddie Foyer, others. "Trifling Women" will be the feature film all week

STRAND — Constance Talmadge in "East Is West," from the play by Samuel Shipman and John B. Hymer. Other films, instrumental, vocal and orchestral numbers.

Outlying Houses

SHUBERT-RIVIERA—Joseph Schildkraut and Eva Le Gallienne will play a return engagement of a week in the Theater Guild's production of "Liliom," beginning to-morrow night.

BRONX OPERA HOUSE—Barney Bernard and Alexander Carr, en route to Chicago, will stop off here for a week in "Partners Again."

AMERICA'S FOREMOST THEATRES AND HITS, DIRECTION OF LEE AND J. J. SHUBERT

B.F. KEITH'S PALACE
B'WAY & 47th ST. Tel. BRYANT 4500

2.09	FOUR AMERICAN ACES — Bender & Armstrong	8.09
2.15	WILLIAM HALLIGAN in "HIGH LOW BROW" by J. Jay Kaufman	8.15
2.25	MARION HARRIS	8.25
3.00	WILL MAHONEY	9.00
3.14	CLARK & BERGMAN — HENRY	9.14
3.47	KITTY DONER	9.43
4.08	DOOLEY & MORTON	10.08
4.24	THE FOUR MORTONS	10.24
4.52	TED & LORAINE & MINTO	10.52

KEITH'S RIVERSIDE
B'WAY & 96th ST. 2 & 8 P.M. Week of Dec. 4
RAYMOND HITCHCOCK
BERT LEVY — RENEE ROBERT & GIERS-DORF SYMPHONISTS
IRVING FISHER

COLONIAL
B'WAY & 62d ST. Week of Dec. 4
IRENE FRANKLIN
JOE BROWNING — VALERIE BERGERE — BOB ALBRIGHT
LEWIS & DODY

81st STREET
B'WAY at 81st St.
J. A. WILLY WHEELER
"THE WAGER"
and Photodrama.

COLUMBIA
BROADWAY and 47th ST. BURLESQUE
ENTIRE CHANGE OF SHOW EVERY WEEK
TO-DAY—2 BIG SHOWS—2:15 & 8:15
Geo. STONE and PILLARD, ETTA, JOE HURTIG'S BIG SHOW
"A SMASHING WHITE WAY JOY"
TWICE DAILY. MODERATE PRICES.

CAMEO
TO-DAY AND ALL WEEK
"THE SUPER-SEX"
FRANK R. ADAMS PRODUCTION
CAMEO THEATRE 42d & B'way

F.F. PROCTOR'S
5th Ave. — 23d St. — 58th St. — 125th St.
CHARLES RAY in "A Tailor Made Man"
HOPE HAMPTON in "The Light in the Dark"

SHUBERT THEATRE TONIGHT
MONSTER BENEFIT
N.Y. AMERICAN XMAS FUND
30 STARS 30
POPULAR PRICES

NEWMAN
TRAVELTALKS
CARNEGIE HALL 57th ST & 7th AVENUE
TONIGHT AT 8:30
ACROSS AFRICA—CAPE TO CAIRO
CONGO to VICTORIA NYANZA
SENSATIONAL WILD ANIMAL MOTION PICTURES
PRICES 50c to $2.00
EXTRA WILD ANIMAL AND SAVAGE LIFE
MONDAY DEC. 11 at 3:30

CENTURY
MLLE. CECILE SOREL
Carnegie Hall, Tues. Ev., Dec. 12
ALDA

WINTER GARDEN
SUNDAY CONCERT TO-NIGHT

CENTURY ROOF
BALIEFF'S CHAUVE-SOURIS
FROM MOSCOW—PARIS—LONDON

The Moscow Art Theatre
Constantin Stanislavsky Director

CHAULIAPIN

4 FAREWELL MATINEES BY THE COMEDIE FRANCAISE COMPANY
CENTURY THEATRE

SHUBERT VAUDEVILLE
CENTRAL
MATINEE TODAY
4 MARX BROS.
ROYAL RUSSIAN BALLET

39th ST.
"Worth $1,000,000 as the Old Crow flies."

BOOTLEGGERS

JOHN GOLDEN XMAS PRESENTS
LAUGHS
MADGE KENNEDY
SPITE CORNER at LITTLE THEATRE
AND
7th HEAVEN AT THE BOOTH
THRILLS

R.U.R.
HAVE YOU SEEN THE ROBOTS?
FRAZEE Theat.

THE LUCKY ONE
A COMEDY
GARRICK Thea.

SIX CHARACTERS IN SEARCH OF AN AUTHOR
PRINCESS

DOUGLAS FAIRBANKS IN ROBIN HOOD
LYRIC THEATRE 42d St & B'way
MAT. TODAY at 3
The most wonderful motion picture I have ever seen.
TWICE DAILY 2:20 & 8:20

BROADHURST
SPRINGTIME of YOUTH

AMBASSADOR
THE LADY IN ERMINE

CASINO
SALLY, IRENE & MARY
With EDDIE DOWLING

SHUBERT-RIVIERA
LILIOM with JOSEPH SCHILDKRAUT and EVA LE GALLIENNE

A. A. MILNE'S
The Romantic Age
COMEDY

COMEDY
GRINGO by SOPHIE TREADWELL
RUBEN

RITZ
IT IS THE LAW
A New Melodrama by Elmer L. Rice

REPUBLIC
ABIE'S IRISH ROSE
"The play that can't die"

ASTOR THEATRE
WILLIAM FOX presents
THE TOWN THAT FORGOT GOD
Directed by Harry Millarde

BAYES
TOM'W NIGHT, 8:30
OUR NELL
A MUSICAL MELLODRAMMY

CENTURY
BLOSSOM TIME

BELMONT
THIN ICE By PERCIVAL KNIGHT

49th ST.
WHISPERING WIRES
SUPER MYSTERY PLAY

OPENING APOLLO THEATRE MONDAY, DEC. 18th
BEN-AMI in "JOHANNES KREISLER"

THE FOOL
CHANNING POLLOCK'S Powerful Play
TIMES SQ. THEATRE

MAXINE ELLIOTT'S
SAM H. HARRIS presents
JEANNE EAGELS in RAIN
By JOHN COLTON & CLEMENCE RANDOLPH
Based on W. SOMERSET MAUGHAM'S "MISS THOMPSON"

MOROSCO
Hopwood's Laughing Comedy
WHY MEN LEAVE HOME

APOLLO
D. W. GRIFFITH'S
ONE EXCITING NIGHT

BIJOU
To-morrow Night at 8:30
MILTON PRODUCTIONS Presents
LISTENING IN
An emotional comedy by CARLYLE MOORE
Author of "STOP THIEF" and "THE UNKNOWN PURPLE"

NATIONAL
TUESDAY EVE.
MAURICE S. REVNES presents
"FASHIONS FOR MEN"
By Ferenc Molnar Author of "Liliom"
With O. P. HEGGIE

WM. A. BRADY SUCCESSES
JOLSON'S 59th ST THEATRE
Century's Most Novel Sensation
THE WORLD WE LIVE IN (The Insect Play)
"Brilliant, amazing."
"Spectacular, dynamic."
"Always unusual."
"Beautiful, novel."
"Gorgeous, irresistible."
"Magnificently daring."
"Peerless, wonderful."

PLAYHOUSE
Corking Musical Comedy
UP SHE GOES
Laughs Galore
"Better than 'Irene.'"
"Gorgeously amusing."
"Tuneful, ingratiating."
"No dull moments."
"Pretty Girls."
"Fresh and pleasing."
"Buoyant with youth."

Greenwich Village Follies
Devised and Staged by John Murray Anderson
SHUBERT 44th St. West of Broadway

THE TALK OF THE TOWN—AL'S HERE!
THE OLD SOAK
By DON MARQUIS
PLYMOUTH THEATRE

LAST WEEK
ARTHUR HOPKINS presents
ETHEL BARRYMORE in "ROSE BERND" By Hauptmann
LONGACRE THEATRE

D. W. GRIFFITH'S
great classic of the screen
THE BIRTH OF A NATION
Opens TO-MORROW EVENING
For One Week Only
With special musical score as first presented
SELWYN THEATRE 42d St. W. of B'way
TWICE DAILY

MARK STRAND
A NATIONAL INSTITUTION
BROADWAY at 47th STREET
MANAGING DIRECTOR JOSEPH PLUNKETT
BEGINNING TODAY
MAURICE TOURNEUR'S STUPENDOUS PRODUCTION OF R. D. BLACKMORE'S FAMOUS STORY
"LORNA DOONE"
With FRANK KEENAN — MADGE BELLAMY — JOHN BOWERS
FOKINE BALLET
under personal direction of MICHEL FOKINE
Clyde Cook in "Lazy Bones"
STRAND SYMPHONY ORCHESTRA — CARL EDOUARDE

CAPITOL
B'WAY at 51st ST.
WORLD'S LARGEST AND FOREMOST MOTION PICTURE PALACE
MANAGING DIRECTOR EDWARD BOWES
GOLDWYN presents
"A BLIND BARGAIN"
WITH LON CHANEY
By BARRY PAIN
Directed by WALLACE WORSLEY
"Impressions of Ethelbert Nevin"
CAPITOL GRAND ORCHESTRA — ERNO RAPEE
DEMENTIA AMERICANA
"REVERSIBILITY AND RELATIVITY"
Presentations by ROTHAFEL

RIVOLI
BROADWAY
"My Greatest Picture"—Elsie Ferguson
ADOLPH ZUKOR presents
ELSIE FERGUSON—OUTCAST
RIVOLI CONCERT ORCHESTRA

COMING—THE EINSTEIN THEORY OF RELATIVITY

RIALTO
BROADWAY and 42nd St.
ADOLPH ZUKOR presents
AGNES AYRES in 'A Daughter Of Luxury'
from "The Imposter," the play by Leonard Merrick and Michael Morton
RIESENFELD'S CLASSICAL JAZZ—FAMOUS RIALTO ORCHESTRA

WAGNERIAN OPERA FESTIVAL
MANHATTAN OPERA HOUSE
"Der Ring des Nibelungen"

N.Y. HIPPODROME
NEXT SUN. AFT., DEC. 10th
McCORMACK

GRACE CRISTIE
LYRIC DRAMA-DANCE
With MARTHA BAIRD — MILDRED DILLINGS

Better Times at the HIPPODROME

SCHLEGEL
MÜNZ
LONG
LEVIN
RUBINSTEIN
THIBAUD
INDERMAUR

A BLIND BARGAIN opened at Goldwyn's Capital theater in New York City on December 3, 1922. It would be released nationally on December 10th and Worldwide one year later. The total studio costs were $84,719.26. Now the "Lost Lon Chaney film" A BLIND BARGAIN, is reconstructed in stills and special recreational techniques—as close to the original cutting continuity as possible.

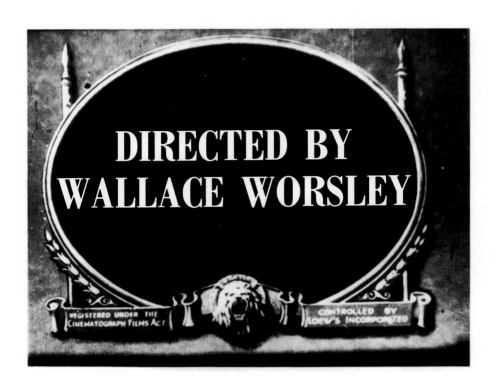

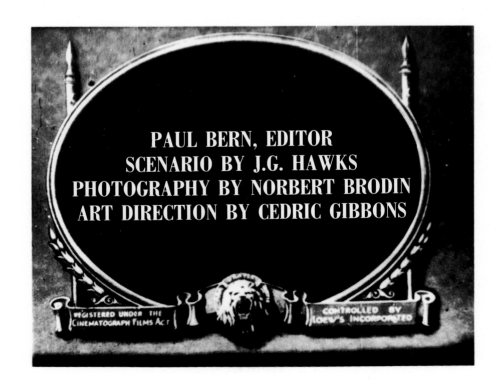

"Science does know its debt to imagination," declared Emerson. This is the story of a scientist whose vivid imagination led him in strange paths and practices.

GOLDWYN PICTURES

Dr. Anthony Lamb, surgeon and scientist . . . .Lon Chaney

Most recent researches of the scientific world.

If were were to judge the span of human life by that of some of the lower animals, we would find that man should live at least one hundred and fifty years.

The claim has also been made if it were possible

A strange loping creature enters the scene. It turns and hobbles to the doorway on the left, the Doctor's study.

A victim of
the scientist's
earlier researches.
. . . Lon Chaney

The ape-like hunchback watches the Doctor from behind a set curtains.

117

The noted surgeon mused over his discovery, taking no notice of
the hunchback. He sets down a volume on the theories of
Darwin and takes out his diary and begins to write:

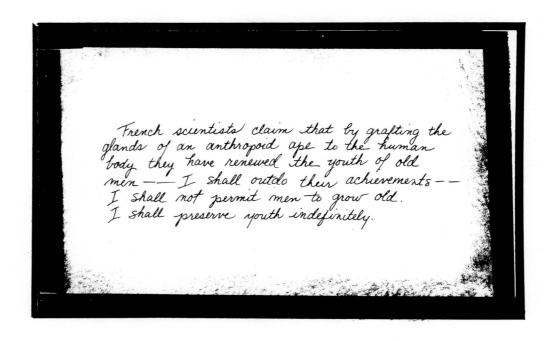

French scientists claim that by grafting the
glands of an anthropoid ape to the human
body they have renewed the youth of old
men —— I shall outdo their achievements ––
I shall not permit men to grow old.
I shall preserve youth indefinitely.

In another part of the
city former sergeant
Robert Sandell, A.E.F.
faces a new test of courage.
Robert Sandell. . . Raymond McKee
Mrs. Sandell, his mother. . .
Virginia True Boardman

Robert Sandell sits at a battered table, his head bowed upon his
arms anticipating the worse from the doctor. He looks up as the
Doctor finishes his examination.

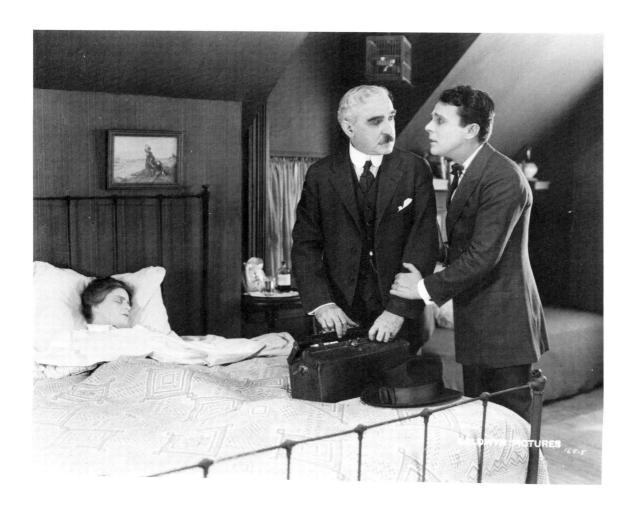

Doctor:

Her condition is very serious
She should be operated on
at once by the best
specialist you can secure.

Doctor:

That is the
only hope I
can give you.

With a sympathetic clasp of the hand the Doctor leaves him and his dying mother.

GOLDWYN PICTURES

Alone, he became conscious again of the crumpled piece of
paper he holds so tightly, the telegram which has so completely
shattered his dreams of being a writer.

Mr. Robert Bandell,
451 Cedar St.

Dear Sir:

Our readers have found your
reminiscences of the Army of Occupation
interesting. We regret, however, that
we have for the present discontinued
the publication of war stories.

Sincerely,

THE EDITORS.

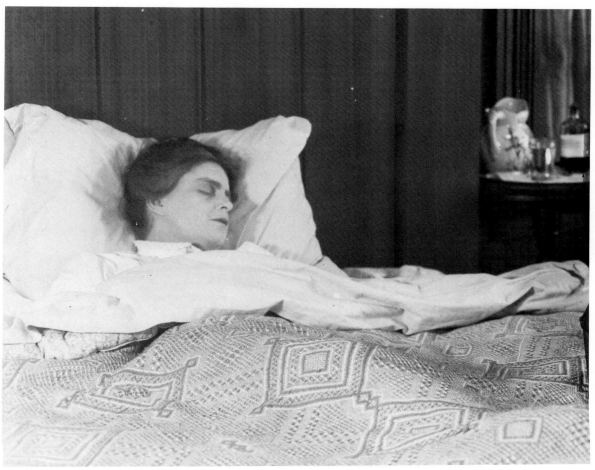

Dr. Lamb walks briskly through a park on his way home from a consultation with his colleague. Robert, having almost given up on his folly, sits on a bench in despair. At that moment he sees the Doctor. To him the surgeon is opporunity; his dire need of money forces him to action.

Weakened by anxiety and the lack of food made Robert no match for the Doctor's powerful grasp. A twist of the hand at the assailants throat and he falls to the ground in a crumpled heap. Dr. Lamb studies the pale, worried face. His kean eye detects no criminal tendency. He hesitates a second, then a shrewd look comes over his face. He lifts up the limp form and hails a passing taxi.

His big house on the
outskirts of the city
has been the scene of
many secret experiments.

The taxi pulls up in front of Dr. Lamb's home. From within, the little hunchback opens the door.

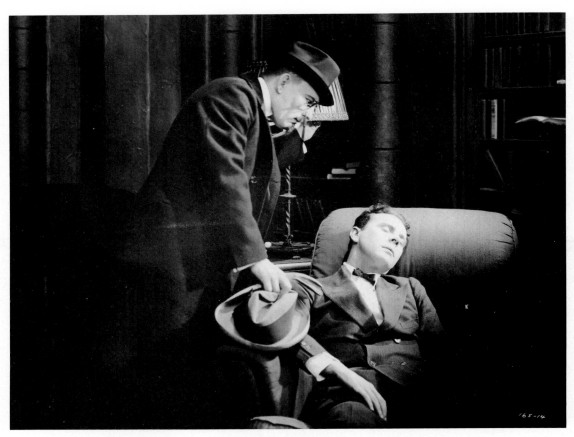

Again, from behind the curtains the hunchback furtively watches the surgeon's movements. A shudder runs through his bent body as he realizes what is occurring.

After depositing Robert in the chair the doctor goes to his medicine cabinet and takes out a needle, some glass slides and a bottle of alcohol. He returns to Robert and draws some blood.

The tests are positive. He calms and revives Robert by wiping his brow with a cold washcloth.

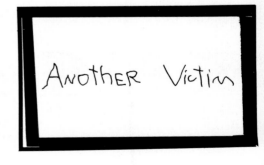

Another Victim

On the floor above Mrs. Lamb enters the scene and moves to the top of the stairway. She sees the Hunchback below listening at the curtain. He turns to her and signals for her to be quiet. She comes down the stairs and listens also. Unable to contain herself she starts into the room. The Hunchback pleads with her and writes on his pad.

Doctor:

You are not a
thief. Why did
you attack me.

Robert:

I was desperate.
I had to have money.

Doctor:

Suppose you tell
me about it.

GOLDWYN PICTURES

Robert:

We were a
prosperous family—

Robert:

—When I left
college my mother
encouraged me to
be a writer.

Robert:

I was engaged
to marry a girl
living next door
to us.
Angela Marshall. . .
Jacqueline Logan

After my father's death,
things went from bad
to worse—we
lost our home.

Some postponed
weddings may be
unlucky but I
know ours
won't be.

Robert:

I'm going to
work night and
day and I'm
coming back to
you—A success.

Fade out:

End of Reel One.

130

During the recital the eagerness in Dr. Lamb's eyes has grown in intensity, until his face seems a mere background for the two bright sparks shining beneath his straight eyebrows.

Fade in:

Robert: Doctor:

Then the war came—I was in Germany—when I got home I found my mother seriously ill—

How much sacrifice would you be willing to make for your mother?

Wait

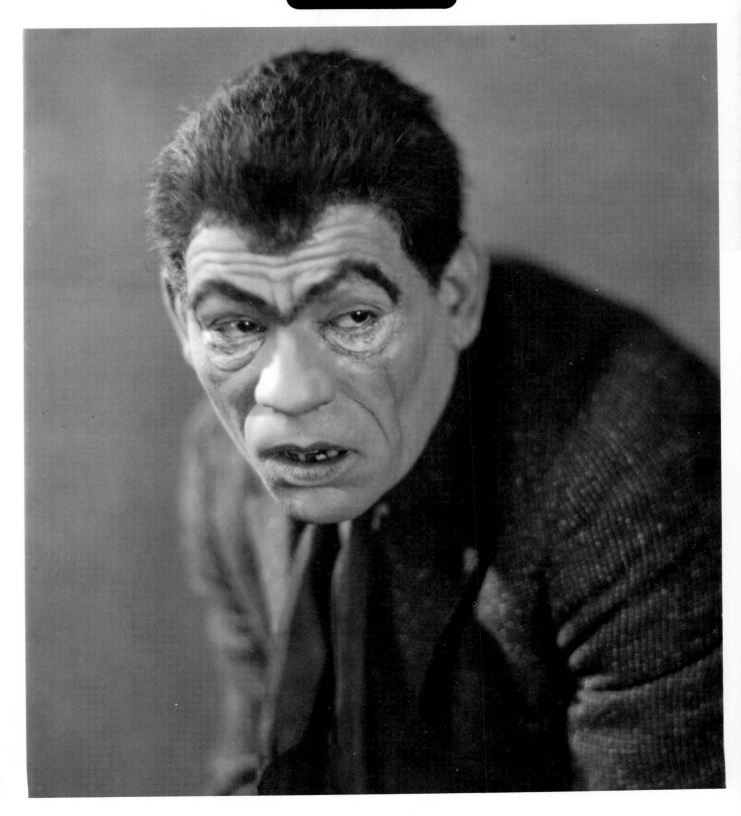

The terror of
the hunchback was
not for himself!

Doctor, there isn't anything I wouldn't do for her.

The doctor mixes Robert a seditive, which he drinks and falls asleep immediately. Mrs. Lamb, despite the protests of the hunchback, enters the study.

Mrs. Lamb:

Remember
the others!

Doctor:

I shall not
fail this time.
See that a room
is prepared for him.

Dr. Lamb orders his wife to leave. He then instructs the hunchback to carry Robert to his room and goes to the phone.

Send my ambulance
at once for
Mrs. Margaret Sandell.
451 Cedar Street.

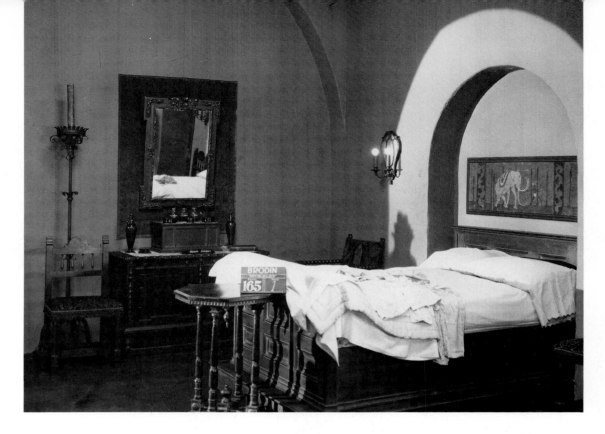

As the doctor gets involved in his blood test below, Mrs. Lamb enters Robert's room.

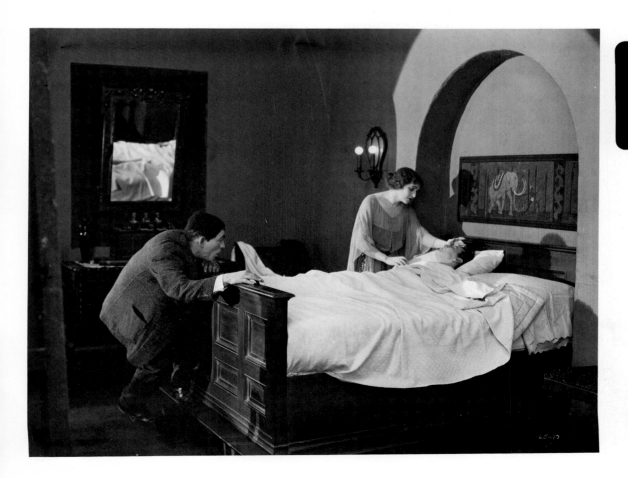

You poor boy.
I wish I
could help you.

Fade out:

Fade in:

LATE MORNING.

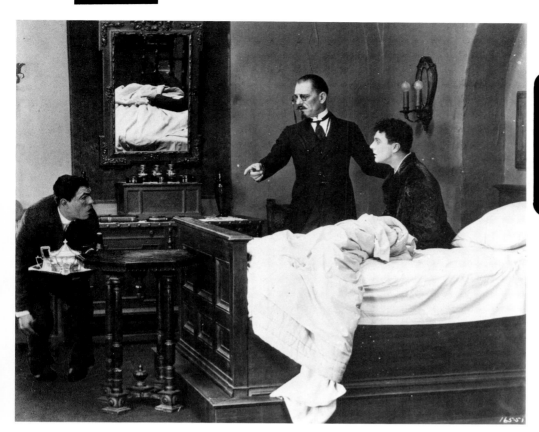

I must go to my mother!
I have left her alone.

The doctor reassures Robert by taking him to the next door. Robert sees his mother in the bed attended by a nurse.

Robert:

I don't know how
to thank you, Doctor.
But—why have you
done all this
for me?

Doctor:

I had your mother
brought here. I
wanted to make a
thorough examination.

Your mother is dying!

Doctor, save her!
You must save
my mother's life!

I'll save your mother—
IF—

—if, when she has recovered
you will submit yourself
to a surgical experiment
in which I am interested.

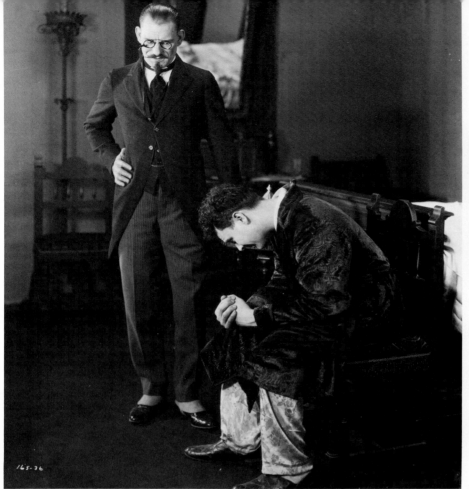

Doctor:

If I fail—well, it may mean
your life for your mother's.
That is the chance you take.
But I shall NOT fail!

Robert:

If you can save
my mother I'll go
through with
anything!

Robert opens his mouth to express that he is ready to agree when his attention is arrested for a brief instant by the face of the hunchback, grimacing from behind the folds of the portiere that covered the door. The eyes held a warning, a plea, his head shakes back and forth in a vigorous movement of disapproval. But the life of Robert's mother was at stake, so the warning passes as if unnoticed.

Dr. Lamb takes a Bible from the shelf and brings it to Robert. The Bargain is made! Robert is then allowed to see his mother. The little hunchback registers his compassion and hopelessness as he broods in the corner.

Everything is going to be
all right, Mother.
Dr. Lamb is going
to make you well.

How can you
ever pay him?

I have found
a way!

End of Reel Two.

Within a week, at
the college of surgery,
Dr. Lamb performed his
part of the bargain.

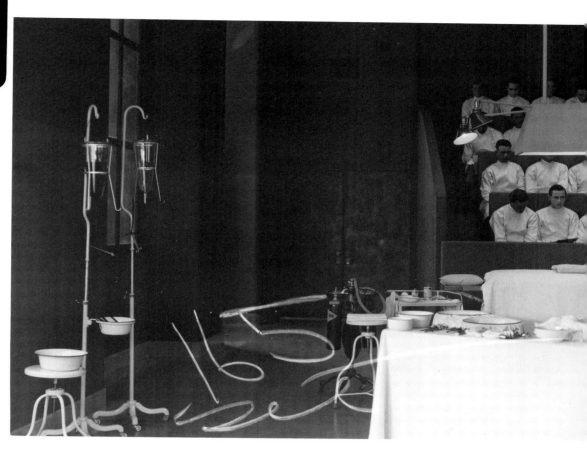

Robert waits outside the operating theatre.

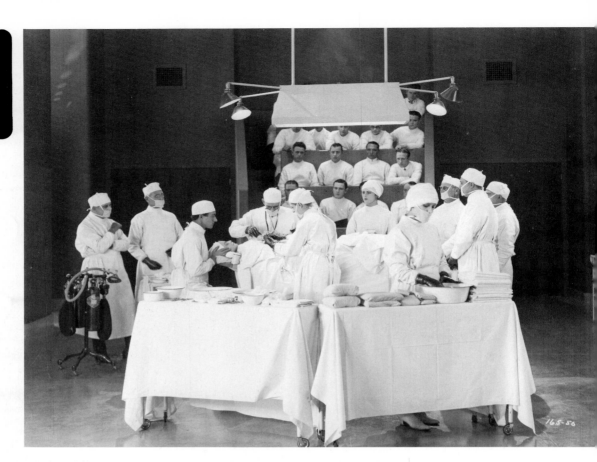

Lamb is a marvel! The most difficult operation of it's kind I ever saw!

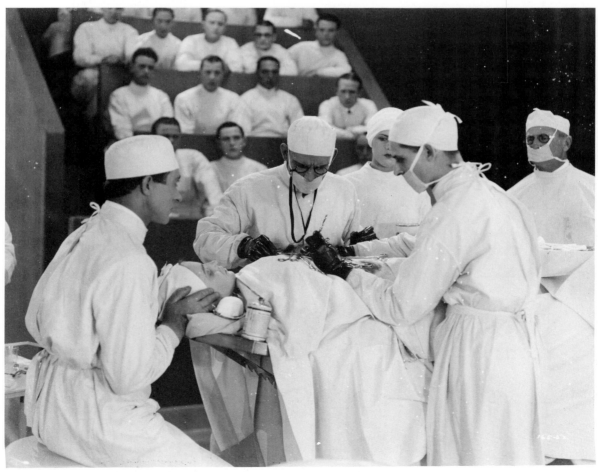

144

Robert looks into the study and sees the doctor bent over a notebook writing. He quietly enters unnoticed by the doctor. His unexpected presence startles the doctor, who jumps up and orders him out of the room. He quickly regains his composure.

Robert begins to express doubts, maybe another means of fulfilling the bargain, but the doctor sends him on his way.

This will tide you over. Accept it as a loan if you prefer. Go and see that girl you told me of.

I will come for you when I am ready.

Holding the mother as
a hostage, Lamb felt
that the son would
not foreswear his oath.

Your mother is out of danger.
I want you to go away
for a few days and clear
your mind of worry. You must
be in the best possible
condition for our experiment.

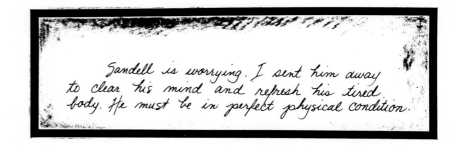

Sandell is worrying. I sent him away to clear his mind and refresh his tired body. He must be in perfect physical condition.

The doctor again writes in his diary as Robert goes to his mother's room to say goodbye.

Iris out

Knowing that his mother was on the road to recovery, and certain his luck was about change, Robert hurried to tell Angela the good news.

Cut to:

L.S. looking over a peaceful lake. Robert gets out of a boat and exits. Looking out from a bluff over the lake he sees Angela reading. He calls to her.

It's been a long time but I knew you would come.

Cut to:

> *Until now I have been handicapped. My subjects have been inferior. Sandell is a perfect specimen of youth in its prime. Through him I will prove to the world that I can transfer to the human species the strength and virility of the strongest animal. I shall double the years of man. There is no logical reason why they should die at the comparatively early age of*

CUT TO: Dr. Lamb is writing in his diary.
The Doctor blots the book as:
CUT TO: L.S. looking out over the lake as Angela and Robert are happily floating in a canoe. Fade out;

Fade in: Mrs. Lamb and the hunchback as she speaks title:

Mrs. Lamb:

Meanwhile, Mrs. Lamb and the hunchback, who are bound together by a unique tie, a common terror of the surgeon. sought ways of preventing this new sacrifice of the madness of the scientist. Together they go to the study where the hunchback finds the button to open the door of the hidden laboratory. They enter and go down the steps. Here they find all the details of the horror to come. He writes on his pad.

Cut to:

End of Reel Three.

**At a fashionable
Charity Ball**

Robert and Angela are now engaged. Dancing girls float around the ballroom in a sea of bubbles. (These scenes were hand colored.)

Cut To:

EVERYTHING IS READY IT WILL BE SOON NOW

We must stop this—but how?

153

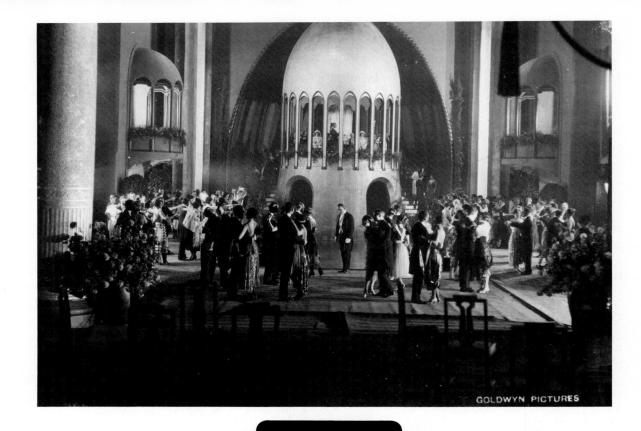

Have you seen
Robert Sandell?

GOLDWYN PICTURES

Doctor:

Pardon the intrusion, but I also have an interest in Robert. I should like to speak with him alone.

Removing his glasses Dr. Lamb gazes at the young woman with a smirk.

Scene cut from final print.

With an uneasy backwards glance at her fiance, the girl withdrew from the smoking room. When she was beyond hearing:

Doctor: I advise you not to make too many plans, Sandell. You had better fulfill one obligation before you assume another.

Robert: I fully intend to keep my promise to you.

Doctor: Very well. The time is at hand. I want to return to my house immediately.

Robert: Very well. I am ready.

A foreboding of
danger filled
Angela with dread.

Robert finds Angela waiting for him outside wearing her cloak.

There is something
I should know, Robert.
You are hiding the truth
from me. What hold has
that man on you?

Don't worry dearest. It is only
a business appointment I have
with Dr. Lamb. Everything
is going to be all right.

Not knowing that the doctor is about to reenter the room the hunchback begins to open the secret door. Dr. Lamb sees the hunchback.

Dr. Lamb sees the hunchback.

I will have no more
of your interference.
Do you understand?

Deceiving his mother with a gay description of the charity ball.

Robert bids his mother good night and goes to his room.

Cut to: Dr. Lamb writing in his Diary.

I shall operate in the morning. Everything is in readiness. The world will yet proclaim me the greatest modern scientist. And yet, what I shall accomplish was known to the

After Dr. Lamb had retired to his room.

162

Robert is interrupted by the cautious entrance of the hunchback bearing in his hand a note from Mrs. Lamb.

Go with him.
Mrs. Lamb

Led by a vague fear, a curiosity that seemed in some way apart from his own future the young man followed his strange guide. The course leads him down to the physician's study, through a secret door in the wall, to a dimly lit passageway and then down a long flight of steps into a subterranean laboratory.

End of Reel Four.

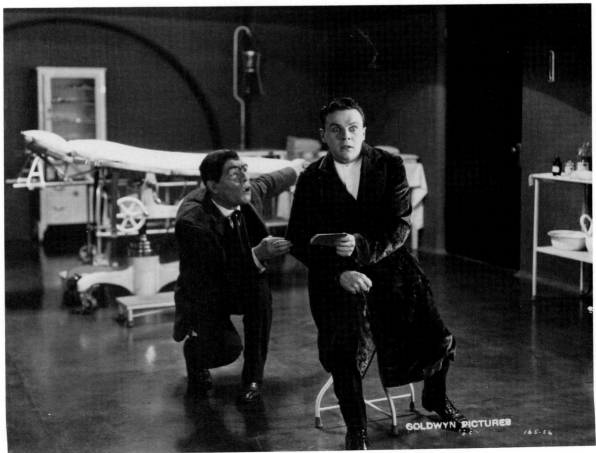

Robert's fear gets the better of him and he sits for a second. The hunchback crooked his bony finger for Robert to follow again as he opened a huge iron door. When he switches on the light there is snarling and growling from the passageway beyond, as the occupants of the rows of cages, half men, half apes, become aware of the visitor's presence.

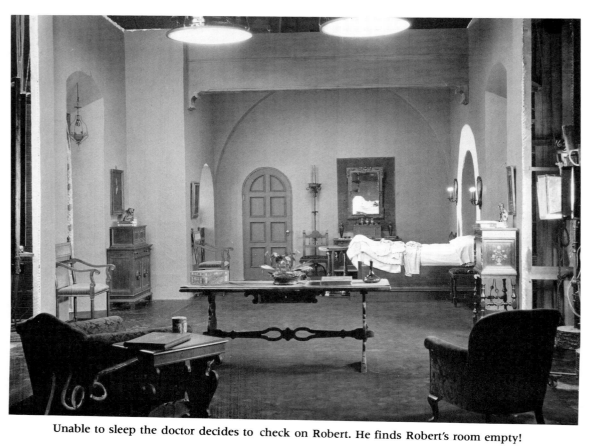

Unable to sleep the doctor decides to check on Robert. He finds Robert's room empty!

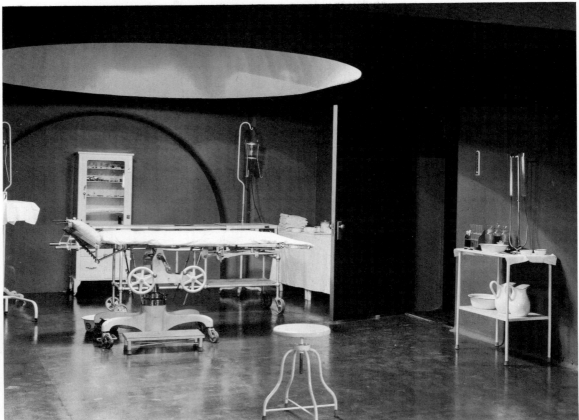

When the doctor sees the entrance to the cage corridor, he continues there and finds Robert and the hunchback. Robert goes from cage to cage until he realizes his fate. At that moment the doctor makes his presence known.

166

At last Robert realized
the horror awaiting him.

"This is what he would make of you," the hunchback's eyes warns the young man, who has turned away in misery from the wretched sights, realizing at last the grim nature of his bargain. The next second a strong arm flings the hunchback up against the cages and grasps Robert tightly about the shoulders.

You fiend! You would
have me like him!

The doctor ignore's Robert's comments and begins to give him a tour of the experiments.

167

Doctor:

The hunchback was my first experiment. If he had been as perfect a subject as you I would have triumphed.

Doctor:

The other I took one hour from death. A wasted maniac and gave him the virility of a powerful animal.

Doctor:

With them I
have failed. With you
I shall succeed.

Doctor:

You will have the
strength of twenty men.
You will have 150 years
yet to live. Your bodily
appearance will not
change as theirs has.

Doctor:

You should be proud to assist in this magnificent contribution to science.

Robert tries to humor the madman by saying "Tomorrow I shall be ready."

Not tomorrow! Now! I shall operate immediately.

Robert:

I was willing to risk my life in payment for my mother's. But to be like them would be worse than death.

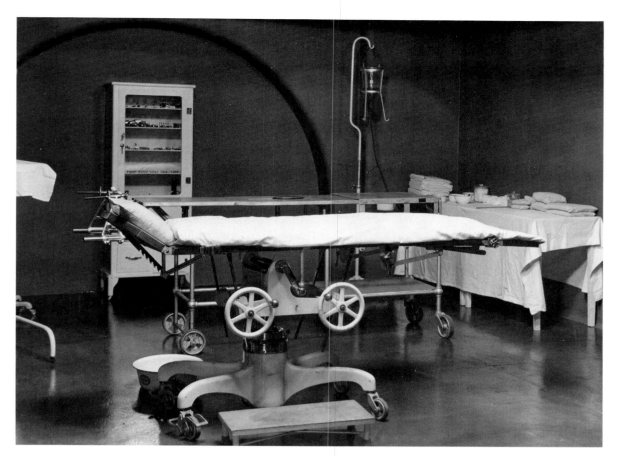

Dr. Lamb seizes Robert in a grasp that is like bands of iron. The little hunchback cowers in the shadows. Back and forth the two men fight. Down the passageway, then into the operating room. It was a matter of seconds before the unconscious victim is strapped to the table. The Doctor takes a gun from a drawer and hurries back to the cages to procure the ape gland that is to be transferred to Robert's body.

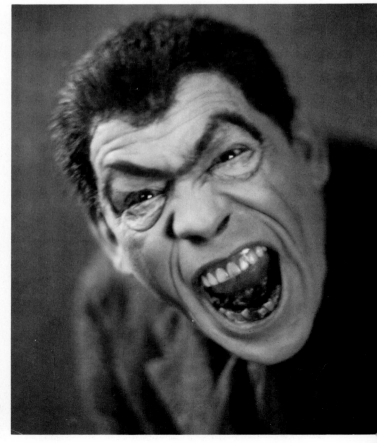

He encounters the huncback and waves him away: excepting him to obey as usual. But the little hunchback takes a stand, unleashing all the hatred he has stored for the insane doctor.

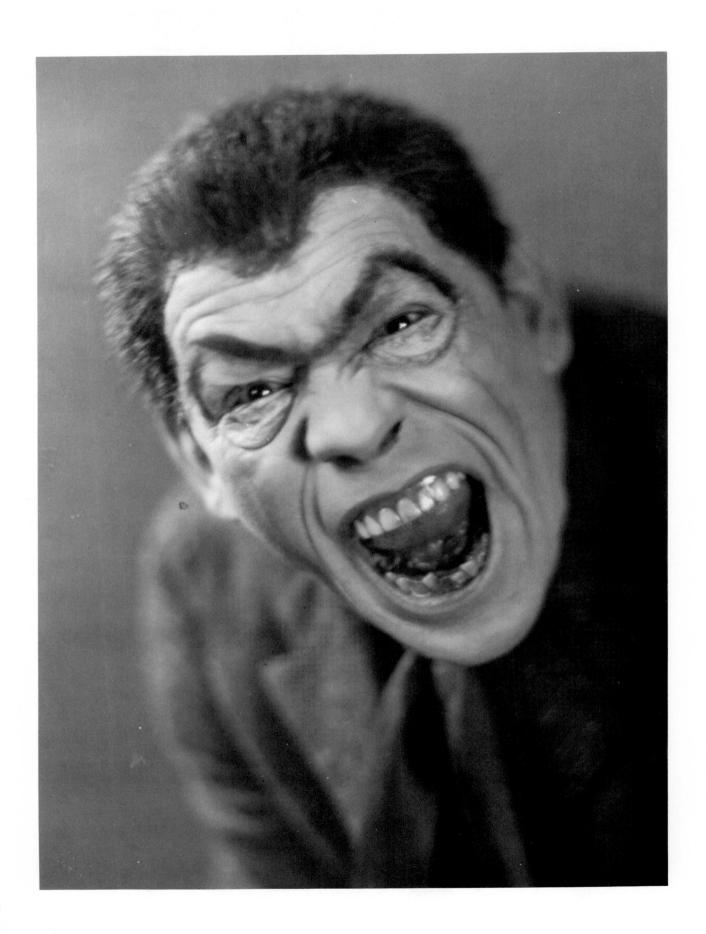

The little hunchback snarls at the doctor who draws his revolver. Without warning the apeman springs for the lever which releases the crazed beast man.

The cry of a wild ape rings out bringing Mrs. Lamb and the nurse to the operating room where they begin to revive Robert.

The doctor tries to escape but the beast man lunges at him. The doctor fires four shoots point blank into the chest of the beast-man. The beast-man falters for a second but regains his strength. With a crazed animal fury it leaps on the doctor and with one movement snaps his back bone in two. As the maniac crumbles the body of the doctor to the floor the bullets finally do their work and it falls on the body of Dr. Lamb—dead!

Robert's lips form the word, "Dead?" and the hunchback nods in assent.

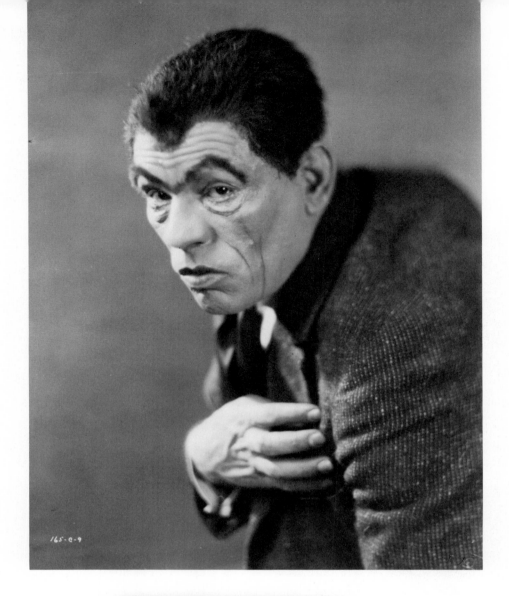

Mrs. Lamb:

He was a great
man. Even in his
madness. But in
his search for
knowledge he
forgot his God.

Fade out:

BURTON PUBLISHING CO
PHILADELPHIA

Mr. Robert Sandell.
15 Fairview Ave.

My dear Mr. Sandell;

  Encloses find check for the
serial rights to your novel " A Sacrifice to Science". We are all very
enthusiastic about the story which we
have larned is an account of your
actual experiences. We look forward
with pleasure to seeing more of your
works.

    Very truly yours,

     R K ADAMS
     Editor.

Fade out:

Fade in:

End of Reel Five.

A BLIND BARGAIN

Goldwyn production, starring Lon Chaney and directed by Wallace Worsley. Harry Pain is the author, with the scenario having been adapted from a story of his. At the Capitol, New York, Dec. 3.

Dr. Lamb	Lon Chaney
The Hunchback	
Robert	Raymond McKee
Angela	Jacqueline Logan
Mrs. Lamb	Fontaine LaRue
Mrs. Sandell	Virginia True Boardman
Bessie	Aggie Herring
Angela's mother	Virginia Madison

Another addition to the "horror" situation so prevalent in fiction, theatre and on the screen for the past year. The script is shy of originality in plot and in telling, seemingly having borrowed numerous instances from at least one novel, as well as a stage production which has only been out of New York about three weeks. Somewhat fantastic, it takes a bit of stretching of the imagination to swallow this story, and beyond the work of the star himself there is nothing to raise this film above the average feature.

It deals with a prominent surgeon who is a fanatic on prolonging the life of man, and to this end carries on secretive experiments with human subjects. A hidden operating room, paneled passages and iron barred cells, where the subjects of previous failures are kept, are all included in the screening. The main topic is of a young former A. E. F. sergeant, made destitute by the war, offering his services to the surgeon without knowing what he is getting into in compensation for an operation which will save his mother's life. One of the results of Dr. Lamb's experiments, a hunchback, who has reverted back to the half ape stage of development, is kept at the house as an assistant. The wife and this half animal constantly attempt to frustrate the doctor's plans.

The ex-soldier is pulled away from a charity ball by the surgeon and taken to the house for the fulfilment of his bargain. Morning is to see the operation performed, but

the hunchback reveals to the youngster the predicament he is in, though being discovered in the act, and the mad physician decides to go through with it immediately. It leads to a struggle, with the youngster being overpowered and strapped to the table, after which the doc goes into the alleyway between the cells to get the hunchback. The degenerated human pushes a spring which releases a crazed physical giant, another specimen that failed, who attacks the surgeon and kills him by brute force.

The latter scene is the kick, revealed in flashes of the struggle and by the facial expressions of the hunchback. Love interest has been interspersed through an affair between the former "doughboy" and a girl with the concluding footage, showing the mother entirely recovered, the boy and girl married and a publishing company accepting the story of the actual experience.

Chaney, doubling as the doctor and the hunchback, gives a creditable performance and allows for some double photography that is by no means unworthy of mention. Always at his best in a grotesque make-up, Chaney predominates in the character of the man-ape, using the ungainly lope of the supposed animal as a means of locomotion throughout the interpretation of the character. Other than that the cast is just ordinary and lends no noticeable support. The production runs almost entirely to interiors, with the scene of the charity ball being the most lavish so far as settings are concerned. Colored photography is used to enhance the scene, though it is questionable if it helped materially the picture as a whole.

The Sunday night audience at the Capitol, generally demonstrative if the feature is to their liking, accepted the "Bargain" calmly, minus an applause finish. *Skig.*

Lon Chaney and Einstein.

A BLIND BARGAIN, adapted from a story by Harry Pain, directed by Wallace Worsley, with Lon Chaney, Raymond McKee, Jacqueline Logan and others; "Reversibility and Relativity," more or less about the Einstein theory; "The Split Outfit," one of Robert C. Bruce's "Wilderness Tales"; "Kitten on the Keys," a novelty musical number with Thalia Zanou and Alexander Oumansky, accompanied by the orchestra. At the Capitol.

Lon Chaney, having demonstrated in "The Miracle Man," and other pictures his ability to impersonate a variety of characters, has been made one of the favorite trick actors of the screen and is seldom allowed to appear as a plausible human being in a creditable photoplay. In "A Blind Bargain," at the Capitol this week, he is further exhibited at his stunts. He appears straight and slick, as a half-mad doctor determined to experiment on human beings until he does something or other to them, and also as a muted hunchback, the victim of one of the doctor's experiments. Exactly what it is the doctor wants to do and why his resourceful wife never thinks of putting him in an asylum are questions avoided by the rambling story, for, if considered, there wouldn't be any story and the chance to show Mr. Chaney in contrasted rôles would be last—until some one turned up with a real plot and conceivable action. It is interesting at times, though, to watch Mr. Chaney, and some of Director Worsley's pictures are interesting, too.

"Reversibility and Relativity," a one-reel film announced as a combination of science and comedy produced under the direction of Professor Delmar Watson, goes just far enough to suggest that the Einstein Theory might be explained in part on the screen and also that it might be used as the starting point for bright and original comedy, but it goes no further. After you have seen it you don't know any more about the celebrated Theory than you did before, and the comedy introduced bears no discernible relation to anything in particular, being simply a more or less ingenious piece of nonsense accomplished by camera tricks. It looks as though some one had started out to explain Einstein in pictures and then, realizing the hopelessness of his task, had turned to random fooling.

Also at the Capitol is another of the Bruce "Wilderness Tales," namely, "The Split Outfit," which includes Mr. Bruce's familiar, but still impressive, mountain scenery, and the slight, but human, story of two prospectors who have gotten on each others nerves after too much of each other in the wilderness.

D 4, 1922, 20:2

NEXT ATTRACTION:

GRETA GARBO
IN
THE DIVINE WOMAN
(MGM, 1928)

APPENDIX I

GOLDWYN PRODUCTIONS

NO.	RELEASE TITLE	STAR	DIRECTOR	DATE RELEASED
1	FIELD OF HONOR	Mae Bush, Geo. Cooper		1918
2	FIGHTING ODDS	Maxine Elliot		1918
3	SUNSHINE ALLEY	Mae Marsh		1918
4	ETERNAL MAGDALENE	M. Marsh, M. Elliot		1918
5	POLLY OF THE CIRCUS	Mae Marsh		1918
6	BABY MINE	Madge Kennedy		1918
7	SPREADING DAWN	Jane Cowl		1918
8	THE CINDERALLA MAN	Mae Marsh		1918
9	NEARLY MARRIED	Madge Kennedy		1918
10	JOAN OF PLATTSBURGH	Mabel Normand		1918
11	THAIS	Mary Gordon		1918
12	BELOVED TRAITOR	Mae Marsh		1918
13	OH, MARY BE CAREFUL!	Madge Kennedy		1918
14	SPLENDID SINNER	Mary Gordon		1918
15	DODGING A MILLION	Mable Normand		1918
16	OUR LITTLE WIFE	Madge Kennedy		1918
17	THE FLOOR BELOW	Mable Normand		1918
18	FACE IN THE DARK	Mae Marsh		1918
19	DANGER GAME	Made Kennedy		1918
20	GLORIOUS ADVENTURE	Mae Marsh		1918
21	FAIR PRETENDER	Made Kennedy		1918
22	THE VENUS MODEL	Mable Normand		1918
23	ALL WOMAN	Mae Marsh		1918
24	THE SERVICE STAR	Madge Kennedy		1918
25	MONEY MAD	Mae Marsh		1918
26	JUST FOR TONIGHT	Tom Moore		1918
27	BACK TO THE WOODS	Mable Normand		1918
28	FRIEND HUSBAND	Madge Kennedy		1918
29	HIDDEN FIRES	Mae Marsh		1918
30	YOUTH (KINGDOM OF)	Madge Kennedy		1918
31	PICK'S BAD GIRL	Mable Normand		1918
32	A PERFECT LADY	Madge Kennedy		1918
33	THE BONDAGE OF BARBARA	Mae Marsh		1918
34	A PERFECT 36	Mae Marsh		1918
35	THIRTY A WEEK	Tom Moore		1918
36	THE RACING STRAIN	Mae Marsh		1918
37	DAY DREAMS	M. Kennedy, John Bowers	Badger	1918
38	GO WEST YOUNG MAN	Tom Moore	Beaumont	1918
39	DAUGHTER OF MINE	M. Kennedy, J. Bowers	Badger	1919
40	SIS HOPKINS	M. Normand	Badger	1919
41	WOMAN OF THE INDEX	P. Frederick	Henley	1919
42	A MAN AND HIS MONEY	Tom Moore	Beaumont	1919
43	SPOTLIGHT SADIE	Mae Marsh	Trimble & Saintly	1919
44	ONE WEEK OF LIFE	P. Frederick	Henley	1919
45	THE PEST	Mable Normand	Cabanne	1919
46	ONE OF THE FINEST	Tom Moore, Seena Owen	Beaumont	1919
47	LEAVE IT TO SUSAN	M. Kennedy, Wallace McDonald	Badger	1919
48	**PEACE OF ROARING RIVER**	P. Frederick	Henley	1919
49	THE CITY OF COMRADES	Tom Moore	Beaumont	1919
50	WHEN DOCTORS DISAGREE	Mable Normand	Schertzinger	1919
51	STRICTLY CONFIDENTIAL	J. Bowers, M. Kennedy	Badger	1919
52	LORD AND LADY ALGY	Tom Moore	Beaumont	1919
53	THE FEAR WOMEN	P. Frederick, Milton Sills	Barry	1919
54	**THROUGH WRONG DOOR**	M. Kennedy, J. Bowers	**Badger**	1919
55	UPSTAIRS	Mable Normand	Shertzinger	1919
56	BONDS OF LOVE	P. Frederick	Barker	1919

57	HEARTEASE	Tom Moore	Beaumont	1919
58	ALMOST A HUSBAND	Will Rogers	Badger	1919
59	JINX	Mable Normand	Schertzinger	1919
60	THE GAYLORD QUEX	Tom Moore	Beaumont	1919
61	THE LOVES OF LETTY	P. Frederick	Lloyd	1919
62	WATER, EVERYWHERE	Will Rogers	Badger	1919
63	THE PALISER CASE	P. Frederick, Alec Francis	Parke	1919
64	THE CUP OF FURY	A.E. Hughes	Beaumont	1919
65	PINTO	Mable Normand	Schertzinger	1919
66	TOBY'S BOW	Tom Moore	Beaumont	1919
67	STREET CALLED STRAIGHT	I. Rich, M. Sills	Worsley	1919
68	OUT OF THE STORM	Barbara Castleton, J. Bowers	Parke	1919
69	TURN OF THE WHEEL	Geraldine Farrar	Barker	1919
70	JUBILO	Will Rogers	Badger	1919
71	THE HELL CAT	Geraldine Farrar	Barker	1919
72	SHADOWS	Geraldine Farrar	Barker	1919
73	THE STRONGER VOW	Geraldine Farrar	Barker	1919
74	THE WORLD & ITS WOMAN	Geraldine Farrar	Lloyd	1919
75	FLAME OF THE DESERT	Geraldine Farrar	Barker	1919
76	THE WOMAN & THE PUPPET	Geraldine Farrar	Lloyd	1919
77	LAUGHING BILL HYDE	Will Rogers		1919
78	TOO FAT TO FIGHT	Frank McIntyre		1919
79	THE BRAND	Kay Laurell	Barker	1919
80	THE CRIMSON GARDENIA	Owen Moore	Barker	1919
81	THE GIRL FROM OUTSIDE	C. Horton, C. Landis	Barker	1919
82	THE SILVER HORDE	C. Landis, M. Stedman	Lloyd	1919
83	LITTLE SHEPHERD	J. Pickford, P. Starke	Worsley	1919
84	GOING SOME	H. Ferguson, K. Harlen	Beaumont	1919
85	DANGEROUS DAYS	W. Lawson Butt, P. Starke	Barker	1919
86	DUDS	Tom Moore	Mills	1919
87	THE BLOOMING ANGEL	M. Kennedy, Pat O'Maley	Schertzinger	1919
88	THE WOMAN IN ROOM 13	P. Frederick	Lloyd	1919
89	STRANGE BOARDER	Will Rogers, Irene Rich	Badger	1919
90	EARTH BOUND		Hunter	1919
91	PARTNERS OF THE NIGHT		Scardon	1920
92	EDGAR & TEACHER'S PET	L. Rickson, J. Jones	Hopper	1920
93	THE SLIM PRINCESS	M. Normand	Schertzinger	1920
94	DOLLARS AND SENSE	M. Kennedy	Beaumont	1920
95	ROADS OF DESTINY	P. Frederick, J. Bowers	Lloyd	1920
96	JES' CALL ME JIM	Will Rogers, Irene Rich	Badger	1920
97	THE GREAT ACCIDENT	Tom Moore	Beaumont	1920
98	THE PENALTY	Lon Chaney, Ethel Terry	Worsley	1920
99	DOUBLE DYED DECEIVER	Jack Pickford	Green	1920
100	BRANDING IRON	B. Castleton, J. Kirkwood	Barker	1920
101	HELP YOURSELF	Madge Kennedy	Ballin	1920
102	EDGAR'S HAMLET	L. Rickson, J. Jones	Hopper	1920
103	SCRATCH MY BACK	Helen Chadwick	Olcott	1920
104	NORTH WIND'S MALICE		Harbaugh	1920
105	EDGAR'S JONAH DAY	L. Rickson, J. Jones	Hopper	1920
106	MILESTONES	Lewis Stone	Scardon	1920
107	MADAME X	P. Frederick	Lloyd	1920
108	EDGAR TAKES THE CAKE	L. Rickson, J. Jones	Litson	1920
109	IT'S A GREAT LIFE	C. Landis, C. Horton	Hopper	1920
110	CUPID THE COWPUNCHER	H. Chadwick, Wil Rogers	Badger	1920
111	WHAT HAPPENED TO ROSA	M. Normand, H. Thompson	Schertzinger	1920
112	TRUTH	M. Kennedy, T. Carrigan	Wyncham	1920
113	OFFICER 666	Tom Moore	Beaumont	1920
114	EDGAR AND GOLIATH	L. Rickson, J. Jones	Hopper	1920
115	MAN WHO HAD EVERYTHING	J. Pickford, P. Bonner	Green	1920
116	GIRL WITH A JAZZ HEART	M. Kennedy	Wyndham	1920
117	GODLESS MEN	H. Chadwick, John Bowers	Barker	1920
118	THE GREAT LOVER	J. Davidson, C. Windsor	Lloyd	1920
119	STOP, THIEF	T. Moore, Irene Rich	Beaumont	1920
120	HONEST HUTCH	Will Rogers	Badger	1920
121	HEAD OVER HEELS	M. Normand, A. Menjou	Schertzinger	1920

122	THE HIGHEST BIDDER	Madge Kennedy	Worsley	1920
123	JUST OUT OF COLLEGE	J. Pickford, I. Rich	Green	1920
124	HOLD YOUR HORSES	T. Moore, M. Kennedy	Hopper	1920
125	A VOICE IN THE DARK	A. Hale, I. Rich	Lloyd	1920
126	EDGAR CAMPS OUT	L. Rickson, J. Jones	Hopper	1920
127	GUILE OF WOMAN	Will Rogers	Badger	1920
128	BUNDY PULLS THE STRINGS	Leatrice Joy	Barker	1920
129	EDGAR THE EXPLORER	L. Rickson, J. Jones	Litson	1920
130	THE CONCERT	L. Stone, M. Steadman	Schertzinger	1920
131	GET RICH QUICK, EDGAR	L. Rickson, J. Jones	Litson	1920
132	BOYS WILL BE BOYS	W. Rogers, I. Rich	Badger	1920
133	MR. BARNES OF NEW YORK	Tom Moore	Schertzinger	1920
134	EDGAR'S LITTLE SAW	L. Rickson, J. Jones	Litson	1920
135	A TALE OF TWO WORLDS	L. Joy, W. Beery	Lloyd	1920
136	SNOW BLIND	P. Starke, C. Landis	Barker	1920
137	DON'T NEGLECT YOUR WIFE	Lewis Stone	Worsley	1920
138	DANGEROUS CURVE AHEAD	R. Dix, H. Chadwick	Hopper	1920
139	AN UNWILLING HERO	Will Rogers	Badger	1920
140	EDGAR'S COUNTRY COUSIN	J. Jones, L. Rickson	Litson	1920
141	EDGAR'S FEAST DAY	J. Jones, L. Rickson	Litson	1920
142	EDGAR THE DETECTIVE	J. Jones, L. Rickson	Bern	1920
143	THE NIGHT ROSE	L. Joy, Lon Chaney	Worsley	1920
144	MADE IN HEAVEN	H. Chadwick, T. Moore	Hopper	1920
145	THE INVISIBLE POWER	I. Rich, H. Peters	Lloyd	1920
146	ALL'S FAIR IN LOVE	M. Collins, R. Dix	Hopper	1920
147	THE OLD NEST	C. Landis, H. Chadwick	Barker	1920
148	DOUBLING FOR ROMEO	Will Rogers	Badger	1920
149	BEATING THE GAME	T. Moore, H. Daley	Schertzinger	1920
150	THE GRIM COMEDIAN		Lloyd	1920
151	THE ACE OF HEARTS	L. Joy, J. Bowers, L. Chaney	Worsley	1920
152	THE GLORIOUS FOOL	R. Dix, H. Chadwick	Hopper	1920
153	POVERTY OF RICHES	J. Bowers, L. Joy, R. Dix	Barker	1920
154	A POOR RELATION	W. Rogers, S. Breamer	Badger	1920
155	THE MAN FROM LOST RIVER	H. Peters, A. Forrest	Lloyd	1920
156	FROM THE GROUND UP	T. Moore, H. Chadwick	Hopper	1921
157	MAN WITH TWO MOTHERS	C. Landis, M. Alden	Bern	1921
158	GRAND LARCENY	Elliot Dexter, C. Windsor	Worsley	1921
159	THE WALL FLOWER	R. Dix, C. Moore	Hopper	1921
160	THE SIN FLOOD	R. Dix, H. Chadwick	Lloyd	1921
161	BACK AGAINST THE WALL	R. Hatton, V. Valli	Lee	1921
162	YELLOW MEN AND GOLD	H. Chadwick, R. Dix	Willat	1921
163	HUNGRY HEARTS	H. Ferguson, B. Washburn	Hopper	1921
164	WATCH YOUR STEP	Cullen Landis	Beaudine	1921
165	A BLIND BARGAIN	Lon Chaney, R. McKee	Worsley	1921
166	WHIMS OF THE GODS		Lee	1921
167	COME ON OVER	C. Moore, R. Graves	Green	1921
168	REMEMBRANCE	Patsy Ruth Miller	Hughes	1921
169	UNDER THEIR SKIN	C. Windsor, Mae Bush	Hopper	1921
170	THE DUST FLOWER	H. Chadwick	Lee	1922
171	LOOK YOUR BEST	C. Moore, A. Moreno	Hughes	1922
172	THE CHRISTIAN	R. Dix, M. Bush, G. Hughes	Tourneur	1922
173	LOST AND FOUND	H. Peters, P. Starke	Walsh	1922
174	BROKEN CHAINS	C. Moore, C. Windsor	Hollabar	1922
175	GIMME	H. Chadwick, G. Glass	Hughes	1922
176	THE STRANGER'S BANQUET	H. Bosworth, C. Windsor	Neilan	1922
177	THE ETERNAL THREE	H. Bosworth, A.B. Francis	Neilan	1923
178	SOULS FOR SALE	E. Boardman, Mae Bush	Hughes	1923
179	GREED	Zasu Pitts	Von Stroheim	1923
180	TRUE AS STEEL	E. Boardman, A. Pringle	Hughes	1923
181	RED LIGHTS	Marie Provost	Badger	1923
182	THREE WISE FOOLS	Eleanor Boardman	Vidor	1923
183	SIX DAYS	Frank Mayo, C. Griffith	Brabin	1923
184	IN THE PALACE OF THE KING		Flynn	1923
185	NAME THE MAN	Conrad Nagel, Mae Bush	Seastrom	1923

THE FILMS OF LON CHANEY

1913 -
POOR JAKE'S DEMISE
THE SEA URCHIN
RED MARGARET
MOONSHINER
THE TRAP
BACK TO LIFE
ALMOST AN ACTRESS
BLOODHOUNDS OF THE NORTH
1914-
THE LIE
THE HONOR OF THE MOUNTED
BY THE SUN'S RAYS
THE ADVENTURES OF FRANCOIS VILLON
A MINER'S ROMANCE
VIRTUE ITS OWN REWARD
THE SMALL TOWN GIRL
HER LIFE'S STORY
THE LION, THE LAMB, THE MAN
A RANCH ROMANCE
HER GRAVE MISTAKE
THE TRAGEDY OF WHISPERING CREEK
DISCORD AND HARMONY
THE EMBEZZLER
THE LAMB, THE WOMAN, THE WOLF
THE FORBIDDEN ROOM
RICHELIEU
THE PIPES OF PAN
LIGHTS AND SHADOWS
A NIGHT OF THRILLS
HER BOUNTY
THE OLD COBBLER
REMEMBER MARY MAGDALEN
THE MENACE TO CARLOTTA
HER ESCAPE
THE END OF THE FEUD
THE UNLAWFUL TRADE
1915 -
STAR OF THE SEA
MAID OF THE MIST
THREADS OF FATE
THE STRONGER MIND
THE MEASURE OF A MAN
SUCH IS LIFE
BOUND ON THE WHEEL
QUITS: THE SIN OF OLGA BRANDT
THE GRIND
WHEN THE GODS PLAYED A BADGER GAME
WHERE THE FOREST ENDS
ALL FOR PEGGY
THE DESERT BREED
THE STOOL PIGEON
OUTSIDE THE GATES
FOR CASH
THE OYSTER DREDGER
THE VIOLIN MAKER
THE TRUST
MOUNTAIN JUSTICE
THE CHIMNEY'S SECRET
THE GIRL OF THE NIGHT
AN IDYLL OF THE HILLS
STEADY COMPANY
THE PINE'S REVENGE
ALAS AND ALACK
THE FASCINATION OF THE FLEUR DE LIS
LON OF LONE MOUNTAIN
A MOTHER'S ATONEMENT
THE MILLIONAIRE PAUPERS
FATHER AND THE BOYS

STRONGER THAN DEATH
UNDER THE SHADOW
1916 -
THE GRIP OF JEALOUSY
TANGLED HEARTS
DOLLY'S SCOOP
THE GILDED SPIDER
BOBBIE OF THE BALLET
GRASP OF GREED
THE MARK OF CAIN
IF MY COUNTRY SHOULD CALL
FELIX ON THE JOB
PLACE BEYOND THE WINDS
THE PRICE OF SILENCE
THE PIPER'S PRICE
1917 -
HELL MORGAN'S GIRL
THE MASK OF LOVE
A DOLL'S HOUSE
THE GIRL IN THE CHECKERED COAT
FIRES OF REBELLION
THE FLASHLIGHT
PAY ME-VEGEANCE OF THE WEST
THE EMPTY GUN
THE RESCUE
ANYTHING ONCE
TRIUMPH
BONDAGE
THE SCARLET CAR
1918 -
THE GRAND PASSION
BROADWAY LOVE
THE KAISER—THE BEAST OF BERLIN
FAST COMPANY
A BROADWAY SCANDAL
RIDDLE GAWNE
THAT DEVIL, BATEESE
THE TALK OF THE TOWN
DANGER—GO SLOW
THE FALSE FACES
1919 -
THE WICKED DARLING
A MAN'S COUNTRY
PAID IN ADVANCE
THE MIRACLE MAN
WHEN BEARCAT WENT DRY
VICTORY
1920 -
DAREDEVIL JACK
TREASURE ISLAND
THE GIFT SUPREME
NOMADS OF THE NORTH
THE PENALTY
1921 -
OUTSIDE THE LAW
FOR THOSE WE LOVE
BITS OF LIFE
THE ACE OF HEARTS
THE NIGHT ROSE-VOICES OF THE CITY
1922 -
THE TRAP
FLESH AND BLOOD
THE LIGHT IN THE DARK
SHADOWS
OLIVER TWIST
QUINCY ADAMS SAWYER
A BLIND BARGAIN
1923 -
ALL THE BROTHERS WERE VALIANT
WHILE PARIS SLEEPS
THE SHOCK

THE HUNCHBACK OF NOTRE DAME
1924 -
THE NEXT CORNER
HE WHO GETS SLAPPED
1925 -
THE MONSTER
THE UNHOLY THREE
THE PHANTOM OF THE OPERA
THE TOWER OF LIES
1926 -
THE BLACK BIRD
THE ROAD TO MANDALAY
TELL IT TO THE MARINES
1927 -
MR WU
THE UNKNOWN
MOCKERY
LONDON AFTER MIDNIGHT
1928 -
THE BIG CITY
LAUGH, CLOWN, LAUGH
WHILE THE CITY SLEEPS
WEST OF ZANZIBAR
1929 -
WHERE EAST IS EAST
THUNDER
1930 -
THE UNHOLY THREE

THE FILMS OF WALLACE WORSLEY
(A complete listing of films from 1916 to 1920 is not available at this time.)

1921 -
THE ACE OF HEARTS
BEAUTIFUL LIAR
DON'T NEGLECT YOUR WIFE
THE HIGHEST BIDDER
THE NIGHT ROSE (VOICES OF THE CITY)
1922 -
ENTER MADAME
GRAND LARCENY
RAGS TO RICHES
WHEN HUSBANDS DECEIVE
A BLIND BARGAIN
1923 -
THE HUNCHBACK OF NOTRE DAME
IS DIVORCE A FAILURE
A MAN'S MAN
NOBODY'S MONEY
1924 -
THE MAN WHO FIGHTS ALONE
1926 -
SHADOW OF THE LAW
1928 -
THE POWER OF SILENCE

THE FILMS OF RAYMOND McKEE
(The years were so obscure I have just listed the titles)

PICTURES
UNBELIEVERS
DOWN TO THE SEA IN SHIPS
VARIOUS SENNETT FAMILY COMEDIES
FAMILY PICNIC
FROZEN RIVERS
LOOK OUT BELOW

HUNTING THE HUNTER
JACK WHITE TALKING COMEDIES
DRUMMING IT IN
A BLIND BARGAIN
SOCIAL
TROUBLE FOR TWO
JESSE WEIL SHORTS
WROTE EPISODES OF BERTIE AND HONEY ON THE ROAD FOR RADIO

JACQUELINE LOGAN

ZIEGFIELD FOLLIES GIRL
1921 - PERFECT CRIME
WHITE AND UNMARRIED
SALOMI JANE
EBB TIDE
BURNING SAND
1922 - THE LIGHT THAT FAILED
A BLIND BARGAIN
PEACOCK FEATHERS

1923-1929

10 FEATURES FOR FOX followed by

FOOTLOOSE WIDOWS
KING OF KINGS
THE COP
POWER
LEOPARD LADY
MIDNIGHT MADNESS
STOCKS AND BLONDS
NOTHING TO WEAR
RIVER WOMAN
LOOK OUT GIRL
STOCK MAD
SHIP OF THE NIGHT
SHOW OF SHOWS
FAKER
GENERAL CRACK

THE SCRIPTS OF J. G. HAWKS

1921 -
BUNTLY PULLS THE STRINGS
GODLESS MEN
RICH GIRL POOR GIRL
SNOW BLIND
1922 -
A BLIND BARGAIN
DANGEROUS AGE
GLORIOUS FOOL
SIN FLOOD
THE STORM
1923 -
ETERNAL STRUGGLE
HEARTS AFLAME
THE WANTERS
WILD BILL HICOCK
1924 -
INEZ FROM HOLLYWOOD
THE SEA HAWK
SILENT WATCHER
SINGER JIM MCKEE
WOMAN WHO GIVE

1925 -
HER HUSBAND'S SECRET
ONE YEAR TO LIVE
PERCY
THE PRICE OF PLEASURE
THE SPLENDID ROAD
THE WINDS OF CHANCE
1926 -
BREED OF THE SEA
THE COMBAT
1927 -
CLANCY'S KOSHER WEDDING
THE COWARD
MOLDERS OF MEN
SHANGHAIED
SONARA KID
1928 -
FREEDOM OF THE PRESS
THE MICHIGAN KID
1929 -
THE CHARLATAN
THE DRAKE CASE
THE LAST WARNING
MAN, WOMAN, & WIFE
MELODY LANE
SILKS AND SADDLES

THE CLOWN
THE BUSHLEAGUER
ONE ROUND LOGAN
A RENO DIVORCE
BRASS KNUCKLES
1928 -
BEWARE OF BACHELORS
5 & 10 CENT ANNIE
LION AND THE MOUSE
LITTLE SNOB
PAY AS YOU GO
TURN BACK THE HOURS
1929 -
HER PRIVATE AFFAIR
PARIS BOUND
RICH PEOPLE
THIS THING CALLED LOVE
1930 -
DIVORCEE
HOLIDAY
LET US BE GAY
1933 -
MADE ON BROADWAY
BROADWAY TO HOLLYWOOD
DELUGE
COUNCIL AT LAW

THE FILMS OF PHOTOGRAPHER NORBERT BRODIN (E)

1921 -
TALE OF TWO WORLDS
THE MAN FROM LOST RIVER
THE GRIM COMEDIAN
THE INVISIBLE POWER
1922 -
A BLIND BARGAIN
GRAND LARCENY
REMEMBRANCE
SIN FLOOD
1923 -
BRASS
DULCY
LOOK YOUR BEST
PLEASURE MAN
VOICES FROM THE MINARET
1924 -
BLACK OXEN
FOOLISH VIRGINS
THE SEA HAWK
SILENT WATCHER
THE SPLENDID ROAD
1925 -
HER HUSBAND'S SECRET
WINDS OF CHANCE
WHAT FOOLS MEN
1926 -
WISE GUYS
SPLENDID ROAD
PARIS AT MIDNIGHT
EAGLE OF THE SEA
1927 -
RICH MAN'S SONS
POOR GIRLS
ROMANTIC AGE

APPENDIX II

The following is a list of titles for which no materials survive. Thousands of films made from the 1890's through 1950 no longer exist in any form. These listed are particularly significant because they feature the work of legendary performers or directors.

Lillian Gish in ANGELS OF CONTENTION (1914)

Lon Chaney in LONDON AFTER MIDNIGHT (1927)

John Barrymore in THE MAN FROM BLANKLEYS (1930)

Gloria Swanson in MADAME SANS-GENE (1925)

Laurel and Hardy in THE ROGUE SONG (1930)

W.C. Fields in THAT ROYLE GIRL, directed by D.W. Griffith (1925)

Emil Jannings in THE PATRIOT, directed by Ernst Lubitsh (1928)

Theda Bara in CLEOPATRA (1917)

THE MATINEE IDOL, directed by Frank Capra (1928)

THE HONEYMOON (Part Two of THE WEDDING MARCH), directed by Erich von Stroheim

Rudolph Valentino in THE YOUNG RAJAH (1922)

THE FOUR DEVILS, directed by Josef von Sternberg (1928)

Greta Garbo in THE DIVINE WOMAN (1928)

If you have knowledge of the existence of these films, please contact:

MAGICIMAGE FILM BOOKS
P.O. Box 128
Brigantine Island, N.J. 08203
(609) 266-6500

NATIONAL CENTER FOR FILM AND VIDEO PRESERVATION
The American Film Institute
The John F. Kennedy Center for the Performing Arts
Washington, D.C. 20566
(202) 828-4000

Forrest J Ackerman and Phillip J. Riley (in background) at the Ackerman Archives, (1976).

MAGICIMAGE FILMBOOKS has been founded to aid in the preservation of America's Motion Picture Heritage. Founded through the inspiration of Forrest J Ackerman, realized through the support of Herbert S. Nusbaum of MGM-UA and in association with PerfecType, inc., we pledge to provide the best possible academic documentation of the many lost silent classics as well as bringing to you invaluable books of the actors, directors and technicians of the early days of the 20th Century's greatest art form—The MOTION PICTURE.

Each volume will contain the rarest most sought after material so that future generations will benefit from the exhaustive research of our authors.